RELIGION

AND THE

HUMANIZING OF MAN.

edited by
JAMES M. ROBINSON

Plenary Addresses
International Congress of Learned Societies
in the Field of Religion.
1 - 5 September 1972
Century Plaza Hotel, Los Angeles, California

COUNCIL ON THE STUDY OF RELIGION

1972

BL
21
.I65
1972

CONTENTS

PREFACE

The International Congress of Learned Societies in the Field of Religion, at which the papers in this volume were first presented, was originally proposed by the Society of Biblical Literature, which appointed a Congress Committee in 1968. The project was adopted by the emerging Council on the Study of Religion in 1969 and has become the first public event sponsored by that body, a symbol of the kind of cooperation of learned societies in the field of religion which the CSR is designed to promote. The Congress has brought together into a unified program the regular annual meetings of many of these societies, which are usually held at divergent times and places, thus providing a maximum opportunity for visitation at the programs of societies other than one's own, for discussions across departmental and methodological lines, and for experimentation in coordinating meetings, which is essential for the future development of the CSR itself. The Congress includes meetings of the member societies of the CSR, namely the American Academy of Religion, the American Society of Christian Ethics, the American Society of Church History, the Catholic Biblical Association of America, the Catholic Theological Society of America, the College Theology Society, the Society of Biblical Literature, and the Society for the Scientific Study of Religion. In addition, there are meetings of the American Catholic Historical Association, the American Schools of Oriental Research, the American Society for Reformation Research, the Foundation for Reformation Research, the International Organization for Masoretic Studies, the International Organization for Septuagint and Cognate Studies, the Late Medieval Seminar, and the Society for Asian Comparative Philosophy. Three Europe-based societies, the Society for New Testament Studies, the Society for Old Testament Studies, and the Societas Ethica, are participating, and delegates have been sent from the New Testament Society of South Africa, the Northeast Asia Association of Theological Schools, the Japan Society of Christian Studies, and the Society for Old Testament Studies in Japan. The Congress thus provides a first opportunity for the executive officers and delegated representatives of these many societies to meet together.

RELIGION AND THE HUMANIZING OF MAN was chosen as the theme of the Congress in order to bring into focus an essential dimension of the academic study of religion: the role it has played, could play, and should play in the humanizing of man. The present century opened with an aura of optimism in which the Western world conceived of itself as at least adequately humanized —

i

"civilized." The tragedy of the century has been that the promise offered by higher education and technology has not been inevitably realized, to put it mildly, where it counts most — in leading humans to be humane to their fellow humans. If anything, a humane society has been established at most for our animal pets! In fact ours is an age of inhumanity to our fellow humans. Yet the urgency of humanizing humans presses upon us.

English usage has associated with the variant spellings of the same term "human" or "humane" the two conflicting dimensions of man. Humans are not necessarily humane. "To err is *human*" — all too human. Yet one could hardly be too *humane*. The dialectic terminology points to the basic human dilemma.

It is with this basic human dilemma that religion is concerned. We should not delude ourselves with the assumption that religion has consistently been on the side of humaneness. From the conquest of Canaan to the strife in Northern Ireland, religion has also been used in efforts to justify inhumanity toward those outside the fold. And even the ideal for humanity within the fold appears upon reflection not to be in all cases really humane. Yet in a very fundamental sense religion does seek to be a humanizing force — its appeal to God is in effect a recognition of the human dilemma and a pointer toward its solution. It is in the interest both of religion and of humanity that this fact be brought into focus.

The study of religion has rightly been part of the humanities. Student protests that the universities have become engrossed in technical specialization rather than in the student as human being have in part been met by the increasing prominence given to religious studies in the secular context of the state university. The academic study of religion has moved out of the pre-scientific category of indoctrination, via the objectivity of critical reflection, to a significant role in the liberal arts, whose objective is to liberate humans to full humanity.

The General Sessions of the Congress address themselves explicitly to this encompassing horizon of Religion and the Humanizing of Man. Distinguished spokesmen for different disciplines, methods, confessions, and dimensions of the issue approach it each in his or her own way. Far from providing comprehensive coverage or attaining a consensus, their addresses like flares light up whole areas in need of further study and attest the pluralism of avenues and objectives characteristic of the study of religion today. When brought together in one volume, they clearly do not "solve" the problem, which, after all, is the human dilemma itself. It is our hope that as the focal center of the Congress they will leave an indelible imprint on the academic study of religion. The responsibility of religion in the humanizing of man is an important issue that must be faced through all the approaches, methods, disciplines, and confessions involved in the academic study of religion.

Eleven addresses at the general sessions of the Congress are brought together in this volume. Three additional addresses were added late in the planning and hence could not be included here if the volume were to be ready for the Congress itself: James M. Lawson's address, "The Humanizing of Man and Religion in Black America," Leslie A. Fiedler's address, "Can Salvation Come Out of Galilee?" and N. Scott Momaday's address "The Man Made of Words." These, as well as additional copies of this volume, will be available through the Executive Office of the Council on the Study of Religion.

Acknowledgement should be made to the Officers of the Council on the Study of Religion and to the constituent societies for their cooperation in coordinating the programs of the societies into this International Congress of Learned Societies in the Field of Religion. In particular, appreciation should be expressed to the members of the Congress Committee, consisting primarily of the permanent executive officers of those societies: G.W. Anderson (SOTS), Robert S. Barbour (SNTS), Harry M. Buck (AAR), Francis J. Buckley, S.J. (CTS), William D'Antonio (SSSR), Robert W. Funk (SBL), Edwin S. Gaustad (ASCH), Paul L. Garber (SBL), Hans J. Hillerbrand (ASRR), Joseph Jensen, O.S.B. (CBA), Samuel Z. Klausner (SSSR), George W. MacRae, S.J. (CBA), Paul S. Minear (SBL), Phillip D. Morris (CTSA), Harry M. Orlinsky (SBL), Carl J. Peter (CTSA), James J. Smylie (ASCH), Douglas Sturm (ASCE), Sallie TeSelle (AAR), Claude Welch (CSR), James Wieland (CTS), and Robert B. Wright (AAR). We are especially indebted to Robert W. Funk and Robert B. Wright, who carried through the detailed arrangements for the coordination of the society programs and for the meeting itself. And finally, appreciation must also be expressed to the staff of the Institute for Antiquity and Christianity, which has functioned as Congress office. David Schindler and Edgar W. Smith, Jr., Research Associates, carried through the copy editing of this volume, with the able secretarial assistance of Sandra L. Miller. Thanks are especially due to George W. MacRae, S.J., who corrected proofs with his accustomed skill and dispatch. In order for the volume to be available at the Congress itself, the addresses, prepared with oral presentation in view, are published with only a minimum of editorial standardization.

James M. Robinson
Congress Committee Chairman

TECHNOLOGY AND RESPONSIBILITY:

REFLECTIONS ON THE NEW TASKS OF ETHICS

Hans Jonas

All previous ethics — whether in the form of issuing direct enjoinders to do and not to do certain things, or in the form of defining principles for such enjoinders, or in the form of establishing the ground of obligation for obeying such principles — had these interconnected tacit premises in common: that the human condition, determined by the nature of man and the nature of things, was given once for all; that the human good on that basis was readily determinable; and that the range of human action and therefore responsibility was narrowly circumscribed. It will be the burden of my talk to show that these premises no longer hold, and to reflect on the meaning of this fact for our moral condition. More specifically it will be my contention that with certain developments of our powers the *nature of human action* has changed, and since ethics is concerned with action, it should follow that the changed nature of human action calls for a change in ethics as well: this not merely in the sense that new objects of action have added to the case material on which received rules of conduct are to be applied, but in the more radical sense that the qualitatively novel nature of certain of our actions has opened up a whole new dimension of ethical relevance for which there is no precedent in the standards and canons of traditional ethics.

I.

The novel powers I have in mind are, of course, those of modern *technology*. My first point accordingly is to ask how this technology affects the nature of our acting, in what ways it makes acting under its dominion *different* from what it has been through the ages. Since throughout those ages man was never without technology, the

1

question involves the human difference of *modern* from previous technology.

Let us start with an ancient voice on man's powers and deeds which in an archetypal sense itself strikes, as it were, a technological note — the famous Chorus from Sophocles' *Antigone* (11.335-370):

> Many the wonders but nothing more wondrous than man.
> This thing crosses the sea in the winter's storm,
> making his path through the roaring waves.
> And she, the greatest of gods, the Earth —
> deathless she is, and unwearied — he wears her away
> as the ploughs go up and down from year to year
> and his mules turn up the soil.
>
> The tribes of the lighthearted birds he ensnares, and the races
> of all the wild beasts and the salty brood of the sea, with
> the twisted mesh of his nets, he leads captive, this clever man.
> He controls with craft the beasts of the open air,
> who roam the hills. The horse with his shaggy mane
> he holds and harnesses, yoked about the neck,
> and the strong bull of the mountain.
>
> Speech and thought like the wind
> and the feelings that make the town,
> he has taught himself, and shelter against the cold,
> refuge from rain. Ever resourceful is he.
> He faces no future helpless. Only against death
> shall he call for aid in vain. But from baffling maladies
> has he contrived escape.
>
> Clever beyond all dreams
> the inventive craft that he has
> which may drive him one time or another to well or ill.
> When he honors the laws of the land and the gods' sworn right
> high indeed is his city; but stateless the man
> who dares to do what is shameful.

This awestruck homage to man's powers tells of his violent and violating irruption into the cosmic order, the self-assertive invasion of nature's various domains by his restless cleverness, but also of his building — through the self-taught powers of speech and thought and social sentiment — the home for his very humanity, the artifact of the city. The raping of nature and the civilizing of himself go hand in hand. Both are in defiance of the elements, the one by venturing into them and overpowering their creatures, the other by

2

securing an enclave against them in the shelter of the city and its laws. Man is the maker of his life *qua* human, bending circumstances to his will and needs, and except against death he is never helpless.

Yet there is a subdued and even anxious quality about this appraisal of the marvel that is man, and nobody can mistake it for immodest bragging. With all his boundless resourcefulness, man is still small by the measure of the elements: precisely this makes his sallies into them so daring and allows those elements to tolerate his forwardness. Making free with the denizens of land and sea and air, he yet leaves the encompassing nature of those elements unchanged, and their generative powers undiminished. Them he cannot harm by carving out his little dominion from theirs. They last, while his schemes have their shortlived way. Much as he harries Earth, the greatest of gods, year after year with his plough — she is ageless and unwearied; her enduring patience he must and can trust, and to her cycle he must conform. And just as ageless is the sea. With all his netting of the salty brood, the spawning ocean is inexhaustible. Nor is it hurt by the plying of ships, nor sullied by what is jettisoned into its deeps. And how many illnesses he contrives to cure, mortality does not blow to his cunning.

All this holds because man's inroads into nature, as seen by himself, were essentially superficial, and powerless to upset its appointed balance. Nor is there a hint, in the *Antigone* chorus or anywhere else, that this is only a beginning and that greater things of artifice and power are yet to come — that man is embarked on an endless course of conquest. He had gone thus far in reducing necessity, had learned by his wits to wrest that much from it for the humanity of his life, and reflecting on it he was awed by his own audacity. The room thus made was filled by the city of men — meant to enclose, and not to expand — and thereby a new balance was struck within the larger balance of the whole. All the well or ill to which man's inventive craft may drive him one time or another is inside the human enclave and does not touch the nature of things.

The immunity of the whole, untroubled in its depth by the importunities of man, that is, the essential immutability of Nature as the cosmic order, was indeed the backdrop to all of mortal man's enterprises, including his intrusion into that order itself. Man's life was played out between the abiding and the changing: the abiding was nature, the changing his own works. The greatest of these works was the city, and on it he could confer some measure of abidingness by the laws he made for it and undertook to honor. But no long-range certainty pertained to this contrived abidingness. As a precarious artifact, it can lapse or go astray. Not even within its artificial space, with all the freedom it gives to man's determination of self, can the arbitrary ever supersede the basic terms of his being. The very inconstancy of human fortunes assures the constancy of the human condition. Chance and luck and folly, the great equalizers in human affairs, act like an entropy of sorts and make all definite designs in the long run revert to the perennial norm. Cities rise and fall, rules come and go, families prosper and decline; no change is there to stay, and in the end, with all the temporary deflections balancing each other out, the state of man is as it always was. So here too, in his very own artifact, man's control is small and his abiding nature prevails.

Still, in this citadel of his own making, clearly set off from the rest of things and entrusted to him, was the whole and sole domain of man's responsible action. Nature was not an object of human responsibility — she taking care of herself and, with some coaxing and worrying, also of man: not ethics, only cleverness applied to her. But in the city, where men deal with men, cleverness must be wedded to morality, for this is the soul of its being. In this intrahuman frame dwells all traditional ethics and matches the nature of action delimited by this frame.

II.

Let us extract from the preceding those characteristics of human action which are relevant for a comparison with the state of things today.
1. All dealing with the non-human world, i.e. the whole realm of *techne* (with the exception of medicine), was ethically neutral — in respect both of the object and the subject of such action: in respect of the object, because it impinged but little on the self-sustaining nature of things and thus raised no question of permanent injury to the integrity of its object, the natural order as a whole; and in respect of the agent subject because *techne* as an activity conceived itself as a determinate tribute to necessity and not as an indefinite, self-validating advance to mankind's major goal, claiming in its pursuit man's ultimate effort and concern. The real vocation of man lay elsewhere. In brief, action on non-human things did not constitute a sphere of authentic ethical significance.
2. Ethical significance belonged to the direct dealing of man with man, including the dealing with himself: all traditional ethics is *anthropocentric*.
3. For action in this domain, the entity "man" and his basic condition were considered constant in essence and not itself an object of reshaping *techne*.
4. The good and evil about which action had to care lay close to the

act, either in the praxis itself or in its immediate reach, and were not a matter for remote planning. This proximity of ends pertained to time as well as space. The effective range of action was small,t the time span of foresight, goal-setting, and accountability was short, control of circumstances limited. Proper conduct had its immediate criteria and almost immediate consummation. The long run of consequences beyond was left to chance, fate, or providence. Ethics accordingly was of the here and now, of occasions as they arise between men, of the recurrent, typical situations of private and public life. The good man was he who met these contingencies with virtue and wisdom, cultivating these powers in himself, and for the rest resigning himself to the unknown.

All enjoinders and maxims of traditional ethics, materially different as they may be, show this confinement to the immediate setting of the action. "Love thy neighbor as thyself"; "Instruct your child in the way of truth"; "Strive for excellence by developing and actualizing the best potentialities of your being *qua* man" ; "Subordinate your individual good to the common good"; "Never treat your fellow man as a means only but always also as an end in himself." And so on. Note that in all these maxims the agent and the "other" of his action are sharers of a common present. It is those alive now and in some commerce with me that have a claim on my conduct as it affects them by deed or omission. The ethical universe is composed of contemporaries, and its horizon to the future is confined by the foreseeable span of their lives. It is similar with its horizon of place, in whose confinement the agent and the other meet as neighbor, friend, or foe, as superior and subordinate, weaker and stronger, and in all the other roles in which humans interact with one another. To this proximate range of action all morality was geared.

III.

It follows that the *knowledge* that is required, besides the moral will, to assure the morality of action, fitted these limited terms: it was not the knowledge of the scientist or the expert, but knowledge of a kind readily available to all men of good will. Kant went so far as to say that "human reason can, in matters of morality, be easily brought to a high degree of accuracy and precision even in the most ordinary intelligence";[1] that "there is no need of science and philosophy for knowing what man has to do in order to be honest and good, and indeed to be wise and virtuous . . . [Ordinary intelligence] can have as good hope of hitting the mark as any philosopher can promise himself";[2] and again: "I need no far-reaching ingenuity to find out what I have to do in order to possess a good will. Inexperienced in the ways of the world, unable to anticipate all the chances that happen in its course," I can yet know how to act in accordance with the moral law.[3]

Not every thinker in ethics, it is true, went so far in discounting the cognitive side of moral action. But even when it received much greater emphasis, as in Aristotle, where the discernment of the situation and what is fitting for it makes considerable demands on experience and judgment, such knowledge has nothing to do with the science of things. It implies, of course, a general conception of the human good as such, a conception predicated on the presumed invariables of man's nature and condition, which may or may not find expression in a theory of its own. But its translation into practice requires a knowledge of the here and now, and this is entirely non-theoretical. This "knowledge" proper to virtue (of the "where, when, to whom, and how") stays with the immediate issue, in whose defined context the action as the agent's own takes its course and within which it terminates. The good or bad of the action is wholly decided within that short-term context. Its moral quality shines forth from it, visible to its witnesses. No one was held responsible for the unintended later effects of his well-intentioned, well-considered, and well-performed act. The short arm of human power did not call for a long arm of predictive knowledge; the shortness of the one is as little culpable as the other. Precisely because the human good, known in its generality, is the same for all time, its realization or violation takes place at each time, and its complete locus is always the present.

IV.

All this has decisively changed. Modern technology has introduced actions of such novel scale, objects, and consequences that the framework of former ethics can no longer contain them. The *Antigone* chorus on the *deinotes*, the wondrous power, of man would have to read differently now; and its admonition to the individual to honor the laws of the land would no longer be enough. To be sure, the old prescriptions of the "neighbor" ethics — of justice, charity, honesty, and so on — still hold in their intimate immediacy for the nearest, day by day sphere of human interaction. But this sphere is overshadowed by a growing realm of collective action where doer, deed, and effect are no longer the same as they were in the proximate sphere, and which by the enormity of its powers forces upon ethics a new dimension of responsibility never dreamt of before.

6

Take, for instance, as the first major change in the inherited picture, the critical *vulnerability* of nature to man's technological intervention — unsuspected before it began to show itself in damage already done. This discovery, whose shock led to the concept and nascent science of ecology, alters the very concept of ourselves as a causal agency in the larger scheme of things. It brings to light, through the effects, that the nature of human action has *de facto* changed, and that an object of an entirely new order, no less than the whole biosphere of the planet, has been added to what we must be responsible for because of our power over it. And of what surpassing importance an object, dwarfing all previous objects of active man! Nature as a human responsibility is surely a *novum* to be pondered in ethical theory. What kind of obligation is operative in it? Is it more than a utilitarian concern? Insofar as the ulterior referent that makes it a *moral* concern is the fate of *man* as affected by the condition of nature, it still retains the anthropocentric focus of all classical ethics. Even so, the difference is great. The containment of nearness and contemporaneity is gone, swept away by the spatial spread and time-span of the cause-effect trains which technological practice sets afoot, even when undertaken for proximate ends. Their irreversibility conjoined to their aggregate magnitude injects another novel factor into the moral equation. To this take their cumulative character: their effects add themselves to one another, and the situation for later acting and being becomes increasingly different from what it was for the initial agent. The cumulative self-propagation of the technological change of the world thus constantly overtakes the conditions of its contributing acts and moves through none but unprecedented situations, for which the lessons of experience are powerless. And not even content with changing its beginning to the point of unrecognizability, the cumulation as such may consume the basis of the whole series, the very condition of itself. All this would have to be co-intended in the will of the single action if this is to be a morally responsible one. Ignorance no longer provides it with an alibi.

Knowledge, under these circumstances, becomes a prime duty beyond anything claimed for it heretofore, and the knowledge must be commensurate with the causal scale of our action. The fact that it cannot really be thus commensurate, i.e. that the predictive knowledge falls behind the technical knowledge which nourishes our power to act, assumes itself ethical importance. Recognition of ignorance becomes the obverse of the duty to know and thus part of the ethics which must govern the ever more necessary self-policing of our outsized might. No previous ethics had to consider the global condition of human life and the far-off future, even existence, of the race. Their now being an issue demands, in brief, a new conception of duties and rights, for which previous ethics and metaphysics provide not even the principles, let alone a ready doctrine.

And what if the new kind of human action would mean that more than the interest of man alone is to be considered — that our duty extends further and the anthropocentric confinement of former ethics no longer holds? It is at least not senseless anymore to ask whether the condition of extra-human nature, the biosphere as a whole and in its parts, now subject to our power, has become a human trust and has something of a moral claim on us not only for our ulterior sake but for its own and in its own right. If this were the case it would require quite some rethinking in basic principles of ethics. It would mean to seek not only the human good, but also the good of things extra-human, that is, to extend the recognition of "ends in themselves" beyond the sphere of man and make the human good include the care for them. For such a role of stewardship no previous ethics has prepared us — and the dominant, scientific view of *nature* even less. Indeed, the latter emphatically denies us all conceptual means to think of nature as something to be honored, having reduced it to the indifference of necessity and accident, and divested it of any dignity of ends. But still, a silent plea for sparing its integrity seems to issue from the threatened plenitude of the living world. Should we heed it, should we grant its claim as sanctioned by the nature of things, or dismiss it as a mere sentiment on our part, which we may indulge as far as we wish and can afford to do? If the former, it would (if taken seriously in its theoretical implication) push the necessary rethinking beyond the doctrine of action, i.e. ethics, into the doctrine of being, i.e. metaphysics, in which all ethics must ultimately be grounded. On this speculative subject I will say no more than that we should keep ourselves open to the thought that natural science may not tell the whole story about nature.

V.

Returning to strictly intrahuman considerations, there is another ethical aspect to the growth of *techne* as a pursuit beyond the pragmatically limited terms of former times. Then, so we found, *techne* was a measured tribute to necessity, not the road to mankind's chosen goal — a means with a finite measure of adequacy to well-defined proximate ends. Now, *techne* in the form of modern technology has turned into an infinite forward-thrust of the race, its most significant enterprise — in whose permanent, self-transcending advance to ever greater things the vocation of man tends to be seen, and whose success of maximal control over things

8

and himself appears as the consummation of his destiny. Thus the triumph of *homo faber* over his external object means also his triumph in the internal constitution of *homo sapiens*, of whom he used to be a subsidiary part. In other words, technology, apart from its objective works, assumes ethical significance by the central place it now occupies in human purpose. Its cumulative creation, the expanding artificial environment, continuously reinforces the particular powers that created it, by compelling their unceasing inventive employment in its management and further advance, and by rewarding them with additional success, which only adds to the relentless claim. This positive feedback of functional necessity and reward — in whose dynamics, pride of achievement must not be forgotten — assures the growing ascendancy of one side of man's nature over all the others, and inevitably at their expense. If nothing succeeds like success, nothing also entraps like success. Outshining in prestige and starving in resources whatever else belongs to the fullness of man, the expansion of his power is accompanied by a contraction of his self-conception and being. In the image he entertains of himself — the potent self-formula which determines his actual being as much as it reflects it — man now is evermore the maker of what he has made and the doer of what he can do — and most of all the preparer of what he will be able to do next. But not you or I: it is the aggregate, not the individual doer or deed that matters here; and the indefinite future, rather than the contemporary context of the action, constitutes the relevant horizon of responsibility. This requires imperatives of a new sort. If the realm of making has invaded the space of essential action, then morality must invade the realm of making, from which it had formerly stayed aloof, and must do so in the form of public policy. With issues of such inclusiveness and such lengths of anticipation public policy had never to deal before. In fact, the changed nature of human action changes the very nature of politics.

For the boundary between "city" and "nature" has been obliterated: the city of men, once an enclave in the non-human world, spreads over the whole of terrestrial nature and usurps its place. The difference between the artificial and the natural has vanished, the natural is swallowed up in the sphere of the artificial, and at the same time the total artifact, the works of man working on and through himself, generates a "nature" of its own, i.e. a necessity with which human freedom has to cope in an entirely new sense. Once it could be said, *Fiat justitia, pereat mundus*, "Let justice be done, and may the world perish" — where "world," of course, meant the renewable enclave in the imperishable whole. Not even rhetorically can the like be said anymore when the perishing of the whole through the doings of man — just or unjust — has become a real possibility. Issues never legislated on come into the purview of the laws which the total city must give itself so that there will be a world for the generations of man to come.

For the boundary between "city" and "nature" has been obliterated: the city of men, once an enclave in the non-human world, spreads over the whole of terrestrial nature and usurps its place. The difference between the artificial and the natural has vanished, the natural is swallowed up in the sphere of the artificial, and at the same time the total artifact, the works of man working on an through himself, generates a "nature" of its own, i.e. a necessity with which human freedom has to cope in an entirely new sense. Once it could be said, *Fiat justitia, pereat mundus*, "Let justice be done, and may the world perish" — where "world," of course, meant the renewable enclave in the imperishable whole. Not even rhetorically can the like be said anymore when the perishing of the whole through the doings of man — just or unjust — has become a real possibility. Issues never legislated on come into the purview of the laws which the total city must give itself so that there will be a world for the generations of man to come.

That there *ought* to be through all future time such a world fit for human habitation, and that it ought in all future to be inhabited by a mankind worthy of the human name, will be readily affirmed as a general axiom or a persuasive desirability of speculative imagination (as persuasive and as undemonstrable as the proposition that there being a world at all is "better" than there being none): but as a moral proposition, namely, a practical *obligation* toward the posterity of a distant future, and a principle of decision in present action, it is quite different from the imperatives of the previous ethics of contemporaneity; and it has entered the moral scene only with our novel powers and range of prescience.

The *presence of man in the world* had been a first and unquestionable given, from which all idea of obligation in human conduct started out. Now it has itself become an *object* of obligation — the obligation, namely to ensure the very premise of all obligation, i.e., the *foothold* for a moral universe in the physical world. The difference this makes for ethics may be illustrated in one example.

VI.

Kant's categorical imperative said: "Act so that you *can* will that the maxim of your action be made the principle of a universal law." The "can" here invoked is that of reason and its consistency with itself: *given* the existence of a community of human agents (acting

10

rational beings), the action must be such that it can without self-contradiction be imagined as a general practice of that community. Mark that the basic reflection of morals here is not itself a moral but a logical one: The "I *can* will" or "I *cannot* will" expresses logical compatibility or incompatibility, not moral approbation or revulsion. But there is no self-contradiction in the thought that humanity would once come to an end, therefore also none in the thought that the happiness of present and proximate generations be bought with the unhappiness or even nonexistence of later ones — as little as, after all, in the inverse thought that the existence or happiness of later generations be bought with the unhappiness or even partial extinction of present ones. The sacrifice of the future for the present is *logically* no more open to attack than the sacrifice of the present for the future. The difference is only that in the one case the series goes on, and in the other it does not. But that it *ought to go on*, regardless of the distribution of happiness or unhappiness, even with a persistent preponderance of unhappiness over happiness, nay, even of morality over immorality[4] — this cannot be derived from the rule of self-consistency *within* the series, long or short as it happens to be: it is a commandment of a very different kind, lying outside and "prior" to the series as a whole, and its ultimate grounding can only be metaphysical.

An imperative responding to the new type of human action and addressed to the new type of agency that operates it might run thus: "Act so that the effects of your action are compossible with the permanence of genuine human life"; or expressed negatively: "Act so that the effects of your action are not destructive of the future possibility of such life"; or simply: "Do not compromise the conditions for an indefinite continuation of humanity on earth"; or briefer still: "In your present choices, include the future wholeness of Man among the objects of your will."

It is immediately obvious that no rational contradiction is involved in the violation of this kind of imperative. I can will the present good with sacrifice of the future good. It is also evident that the new imperative addresses itself to public policy rather than private conduct, which is not in the causal dimension to which that imperative applies. Kant's categorical imperative was addressed to the individual, and its criterion was instantaneous. It enjoined each of us to consider what would happen *if* the *maxim* of my present action were made, or at this moment already were, the principle of a universal legislation: the self-consistency or inconsistency of such a *hypothetical* universalization is made the test for my *private* choice. But it was no part of the reasoning that there is any probability of my private choice *in fact* becoming universal law, or that it might contribute to its becoming that. The universalization is a thought

11

experiment by the private agent to test the immanent morality of his action. Indeed, real consequences are not considered at all, and the principle is one not of objective responsibility but of the subjective quality of my self-determination. The new imperative invokes a different consistency: not that of the act with itself, but that of its eventual *effects* with the continuance of human agency in times to come. And the "universalization" it contemplates is by no means hypothetical, i.e. a purely logical transference from the individual "me" to an imaginary, causally unrelated "all" ("*if* everybody acted like that"); on the contrary, the actions subject to the new imperative — actions of the collective whole — have their universal reference in their actual scope of efficacy: they "totalize" themselves in the progress of their momentum and thus are bound to terminate in shaping the universal dispensation of things. This adds a *time* horizon to the moral calculus which is entirely absent from the instantaneous logical operation of the Kantian imperative: whereas the latter extrapolates into an ever-present order of abstract compatibility, our imperative extrapolates into a predictable real *future* as the open-ended dimension of our responsibility.

VII.

Similar comparisons could be made with all the other historical forms of the ethics of contemporaneity and immediacy. The new order of human action requires a commensurate ethics of foresight and responsibility, which is as new as are the issues with which it has to deal. We have seen that these are the issues posed by the works of *homo faber* in the age of technology. But among those novel works we haven't mentioned yet the potentially most ominous class. We have considered *techné* only as applied to the nonhuman realm. But man himself has been added to the objects of technology. *Homo faber* is turning upon himself and gets ready to make over the maker of all the rest. This consummation of power, which may well portend the overpowering of man, this final imposition of art on nature, calls upon the utter resources of ethical thought, which never before has been faced with choosable alternatives to what were considered the definite terms of the human condition.

1. Take, for instance, the most basic of these "givens," man's mortality. Who ever before had to make up his mind on its desirable and *eligible* measure? There was nothing to choose about the upper limit, the "threescore years and ten, or by reason of strength fourscore." Its inexorable rule was the subject of lament, submission, or vain (not to say foolish) wish-dreams about possible exceptions — strangely enough, almost never of affirmation. The intellectual imagination of a G.B. Shaw and a Jonathan Swift speculated on the

privilege of not having to die, or the curse of not being able to die. (Swift with the latter was the more perspicacious of the two.) Myth and legend toyed with such themes against the acknowledged background of the unalterable, which made the earnest man rather pray "teach us to number our days that we may get a heart of wisdom" (Psalm 90). Nothing of this was in the realm of doing and effective decison. The question was only how to relate to the stubborn fact.

But lately, the dark cloud of inevitability seems to lift. A practical hope is held out by certain advances in cell biology to prolong, perhaps indefinitely extend the span of life by counteracting biochemical processes of aging. Death no longer appears as a necessity belonging to the nature of life, but as an avoidable, at least in principle tractable and long-delayable, organic malfunction. A perennial yearning of mortal man seems to come nearer fulfillment. And for the first time we have to ask the question in earnest: "How desirable is this? How desirable for the individual, and how for the species?" These questions involve the very meaning of our finitude, the attitude toward death, and the general biological significance of the balance of death and procreation. Even prior to such ultimate questions are the more pragmatic ones of who should be eligible for the boon: persons of particular quality and merit, of social eminence, those that can pay for it, everybody? The last would seem the only just course. But it would have to be paid for at the opposite end, at the source. For clearly, on a population-wide scale, the price of extended age must be a proportional slowing of replacement, i.e. a diminished access of new life. The result would be a decreasing proportion of youth in an increasingly aged population. How good or bad would that be for the general condition of man? Would the species gain or lose? And how *right* would it be to preempt the place of youth? Having to die is bound up with having been born: mortality is but the other side of the perpetual spring of "natality" (to use Hannah Arendt's term). This had always been ordained; now its meaning has to be pondered in the sphere of decision. To take the extreme (not that it will ever be obtained): if we abolish death, we must abolish procreation as well, for the latter is life's answer to the former, and so we would have a world of old age with no youth, and of known individuals with no surprises of such that had never been before. But this perhaps is precisely the wisdom in the harsh dispensation of our mortality: that it grants us the eternally renewed promise of the freshness, immediacy and eagerness of youth, together with the supply of otherness as such. There is no substitute for this in the greater accumulation of prolonged experience: it can never recapture the unique privilege of seeing the world for the first time and with new eyes, never relive the wonder which, according to

Plato, is the beginning of philosophy, never the curiosity of the child, which rarely enough lives on as thirst for knowledge in the adult, until it wanes there too. This ever-renewed beginning, which is only to be had at the price of ever-repeated ending, may well be mankind's hope, its safeguard against lapsing into boredom and routine, its chance of retaining the spontaneity of life. Also, the role of the *memento mori* in the individual's life must be considered, and what its attenuation to indefiniteness may do to it. Perhaps a non-negotiable limit to our expected time is necessary for each of us as the incentive to number our days and make them count.

So it could be that what by intent is a philanthropic gift of science to man, the partial granting of his oldest wish — to escape the curse of mortality — turns out to the detriment of man. I am not indulging in prediction and, in spite of my noticeable bias, not even in valuation. My point is that already the promised gift raises questions that had never to be asked before in terms of practical choice, and that no principle of former ethics, which took the human constants for granted, is competent to deal with them. And yet they have to be dealt with ethically and by principle and not merely by the pressure of interests.

2. It is similar with all the other, quasi-utopian powers about to be made available by the advances of biomedical science as they are translated into technology. Of these, *behavior control* is much nearer to practical readiness than the still hypothetical prospect I have just been discussing, and the ethical questions it raises are less profound but have a more direct bearing on the moral conception of man. Here again, the new kind of interventions exceeds the old ethical categories. They have not equipped us to rule, for example, on mental control by chemical means or by direct electrical action on the brain via implanted electrodes — undertaken, let us assume, for defensible and even laudable ends. The mixture of beneficial and dangerous potentials is obvious, but the lines are not easy to draw. Relief of mental patients from distressing and disabling symptoms seems unequivocally beneficial. But from the relief of the *patient*, a goal entirely in the tradition of the medical art, there is an easy passage to the relief of *society* from the inconvenience of difficult individual behavior among its members: that is, the passage from medical to social application; and this opens up an indefinite field with grave potentials. The troublesome problems of rule and unruliness in modern mass society make the extension of such control methods to non-medical categories extremely tempting for social management. Numerous questions of human rights and

dignity arise. The difficult question of preempting versus enabling care insists on concrete answers. Shall we induce learning attitudes in school children by the mass administration of drugs, circumventing the appeal to autonomous motivation? Shall we overcome aggression by electronic pacification of brain areas? Shall we generate sensations of happiness or pleasure or at least contentment through independent stimulation (or tranquilizing) of the appropriate centers — independent, i.e. of the objects of happiness, pleasure, or content, and their attainment in personal living and achieving? Candidacies could be multiplied. Business firms might become interested in some of these techniques for performance increase among their employees.

Independently of the question of compulsion or consent, and independently also of the question of undesirable side-effects, each time we thus bypass the human way of dealing with human problems, short-circuiting it by an impersonal mechanism, we have taken away something from the dignity of personal selfhood and advanced a further step on the road from responsible subjects to programmed behavior systems. Social functionalism, important as it is, is only one side of the question. Decisive is the question of what kind of individuals the society is composed of, to make its existence valuable as a whole. Somewhere along the line of increasing social manageability at the price of individual autonomy, the question of the worthwhileness of the whole human enterprise must pose itself. Answering it involves the image of man we entertain. We must think it anew in light of the things we can do to it now and could never do before.

3.   This holds even more with respect to the last object of a technology applied on man himself — the genetic control of future men. This is too wide a subject for cursory treatment. Here I merely point to this most ambitious dream of *homo faber*, summed up in the phrase that man will take his own evolution in hand, with the aim of not just preserving the integrity of the species but of modifying it by improvements of his own design. Whether we have the right to it, whether we are qualified for that creative role, is the most serious question that can be posed to man finding himself suddenly in possession of such fateful powers. Who will be the image-makers, by what standards, and on the basis of what knowledge? Also the question of the moral right to experiment on future human beings must be asked. These and similar questions, which demand an answer before we embark on a journey into the unknown, show most

vividly how far our powers to act are pushing us beyond the terms of all former ethics.

VIII.

The ethically relevant common feature in all the examples adduced is what I like to call the inherently "utopian" drift of our actions under the conditions of modern technology, whether it works on non-human or on human nature, and whether the "utopia" at the end of the road be planned or unplanned. By the kind and size of its snowballing effects, technological power propels us into goals of a type that was formerly the preserve of Utopias. To put it differently, technological power has turned what used and ought to be tentative, perhaps enlightening plays of speculative reason into competing blueprints for projects, and in choosing between them we have to choose between extremes of remote effects. The one thing we can really know of them is their extremism as such — that they concern the total condition of nature on our globe and the very kind of creatures that shall, or shall not, populate it. In consequence of the inevitably "utopian" scale of modern technology, the salutary gap between everyday and ultimate issues, between occasions for common prudence and occasions for illuminated wisdom, is steadily closing. Living now constantly in the shadow of unwanted, built-in, automatic utopianism, we are constantly confronted with issues whose positive choice requires supreme wisdom — an impossible situation for man in general, because he does not possess that wisdom, and in particular for contemporary man, who denies the very existence of its object — viz., objective value and truth. We need wisdom most when we believe in it least.

If the new nature of our acting then calls for a new ethics of long-range responsibility, coextensive with the range of our power, it calls in the name of that very responsibility also for a new kind of humility — a humility not like former humility, i.e. because of the littleness — but because of the excessive magnitude of our power, which is the excess of our power to act over our power to foresee and our power to evaluate and to judge. In the face of the quasi-eschatological potentials of our technological processes, ignorance of the ultimate implications becomes itself a reason for responsible restraint, as the second best to the possession of wisdom itself.

One other aspect of the required new ethics of responsibility for and to a distant future is worth mentioning: the insufficiency of representative government to meet the new demands on its normal principles and by its normal mechanics. For according to these, only *present* interests make themselves heard and felt and enforce their consideràtion. It is to them that public agencies are accountable, and this is the way in which concretely the respecting of rights comes about (as distinct from their abstract acknowledgment). But the "Future" is not represented, it is not a force that can throw its own weight into the scales. The non-existent has no lobby, and the unborn are powerless. Thus accountability to them has no political reality behind it yet in present decision-making, and when they can make their complaint, then we, the culprits, are no longer there.

This raises to an ultimate pitch the old question of the power of the wise, or the force of ideas not allied to self-interest, in the body politic. What *force* shall represent the future in the present? However, before *this* question can become earnest in practical terms, the new ethics must find its theory, on which do's and don'ts can be based. That is, before the question of what *force*, comes the question of what *insight* or value-knowledge shall represent the future in the present.

IX.

And here it is where I get stuck, and where we all get stuck. For the very same movement which put us in possession of the powers that have not to be regulated by norms — the movement of modern knowledge called science — has by a necessary complementarity eroded the foundations from which norms could be derived; it has destroyed the very idea of norm as such. Not, fortunately, the feeling for norm and even for particular norms. But this feeling becomes uncertain of itself when contradicted by alleged knowledge or at least denied all sanction by it. Anyway and always does it have a difficult enough time against the loud clamors of greed and fear. Now it must in addition blush before the frown of superior knowledge, as unfounded and incapable of foundation. First, Nature had been "neutralized" with respect to value, the Man himself. Now we shiver in the nakedness of a nihilism in which near-omnipotence is paired with near-emptiness, greatest capacity with knowing least what for. With the apocalyptic pregnancy of our actions, that very knowledge we lack has become more urgently needed than at any other stage in the adventure of mankind. Alas, urgency is no promise of success. On the contrary, it must be avowed that to seek for wisdom today requires a good measure of unwisdom. The very nature of the age which cries out for an ethical theory makes it suspicously look like a fool's errand. Yet we have no choice in the matter.

It is a question whether without restoring the category of the sacred, the category most thoroughly destroyed by the scientific

17

enlightenment, we can have an ethics able to cope with the extreme powers which we possess today and constantly increase and are almost compelled to use. Regarding those consequences imminent enough still to hit ourselves, fear can do the job — so often the best substitute for genuine virtue or wisdom. But this means fails us towards the more distant prospects, which here matter the most, especially as the beginnings seem mostly innocent in their smallness. Only awe of the sacred with its unqualified veto is independent of the computations of mundane fear and the solace of uncertainty about distant consequences. But religion as a soul-determining force is no longer there to be summoned to the aid of ethics. The latter must stand on its worldy feet, that is, on reason and its fitness for philosophy. And while of faith it can be said that it either is there or is not, of ethics it holds that it must be there.

It must be there because men act, and ethics is for the ordering of actions and for regulating the power to act. It must be there all the more, then, the greater the powers of acting that are to be regulated; and with their size, the ordering principle must also fit their kind. Thus, novel powers to act require new ethical rules and perhaps even a novel ethics.

"Thou shalt not kill" was said because man has the power to kill and often the occasion and even inclination for it — in short, because killing is actually done. It is only under the *pressure* of real habits of action, and generally of the fact that always action already takes place, without *this* having to be commanded first, that ethics as the ruling of such acting under the standard of the good or the permitted enters the stage. Such a *pressure* emanates from the novel technological powers of man, whose exercise is given with their existence. *If* they really are as novel in kind as here contended, and if by the kind of their potential consequences they really have abolished the moral neutrality which the technical commerce with matter hitherto enjoyed, then their pressure bids to seek for new prescriptions in ethics which are competent to assume their guidance, but which first of all can hold their own theoretically against that very pressure. To the demonstration of those premises was this paper devoted. If they are accepted, then we all who make thinking our business have a task to last us for our time. We must do it in time, for since we act anyway we shall have some ethic or other in any case, and without a supreme effort to determine the right one, we may be left with a wrong one by default.

18

NOTES

1   Kant, *Groundwork of the Metaphysics of Morals*, Preface.

2   *Ibid.*, Ch. 1.

3   *Ibid.*

4   On this last point, the biblical God changed his mind to an all-encompassing "yes" after the Flood.

CHRISTIAN HUMANISM

Walter Kasper

I. A THEOLOGY FOR MAN

It is already trite to say that theology finds itself today in a state of transition and upheaval. This upheaval is so fast, indeed so hectic, that the state of theology seems chaotic to many both inside and outside of theological circles. They no longer see the forest for the trees. Therefore they either lose nerve in face of their own courage or run aimlessly and breathlessly after whatever happens to be the latest theological rage. The question arises therefore what would be the focus and the goal of a theology which seeks to renew itself. What should be the guiding concern of such a theology?

I would like to propose the following thesis: a renewed theology, which is deserving of the name, is a theology for man. Obviously a theology for angels or for sparrows never existed. But there existed and still exists a "theology in itself." Such a "theology in itself" is continually occupied with the question, who is God "in himself" or who is Christ "in himself" without asking what all of this means for us. Such a "theology in itself" can be very scientific and learned; but it moves within an academic ghetto; such a theology can also be accurate and correct, so accurate in fact, that it is no longer true, for truth is concrete; such a theology moves, moreover, in an ecclesiastical ghetto. It forgets that man does not exist for the Sabbath, but that the Sabbath exists for man. The world without God, with which we are confronted, is a reaction against a God apart from the world and apart from man.[1]

A "theology for man" is nevertheless not simply anthropology and sociology. If man were the ultimate value for man and if politics were to become religion, then this would constitute a new form of mythology which would not free man but rather enclose him. A "theology for man" is therefore first of all theology. But wherever there is talk about God there is, at least in tendency and by implication, talk not only about man but also about reality as a whole. A "theology for man" therefore cannot be a theology which has been narrowed down and reduced to anthropology. Man is not an abstract being who sits comfortably apart from the world; the word man always implies the world of man as well. "Theology for man" is therefore not only transcendental and personal theology, but also "theology of the world," "theology of history," and "political theology."

If understood in this way, a "theology for man" is not an absolutely new bill of fare. Such a theology would have to be the basic goal of any theology which is oriented toward the Bible. The canon of the biblical writings was drawn up in the second century in opposition to Marcion, who separated the God of Creation from the God of Redemption. In that the early Church set up the Bible as canon, it wanted to say the following: the Christian message is a message of redemption, that is, of liberation *for* the world and not a message of redemption and liberation *from* the world. The unity of creation and redemption is therefore the basic principle of interpretation in biblical theology. But even from a systematic viewpoint man and his world are constitutively situated in the Gospel. The Word of God comes forth as human word; it reaches its goal where it is humanly heard, understood, and accepted; God meets us as a man and through men.

The world which is always the world of man becomes such at its point of contact with the Gospel *(locus theologicus)*[2]. This statement says more than that the world is the goal of the Gospel or that the world is the object of missionary activity. The world of man is not only the destination but also the source of theological statements. This does not need to be misunderstood in a liberalistic or modernistic way. The Gospel is not merely a symbolic codification of common human experience. That would not be theology but rather mythology and ideology. The Word of God nevertheless never encounters us as a naked reality; it has its own *Sitz im Leben*; it has human form. What then is man?

II. WHAT IS MAN?

Theology cannot answer the question "What is man?" without taking seriously all those things which the present-day sciences of man have to say about him. In order to be able to speak about man in such a complicated and disturbed situation as our own, good common sense — as important as it normally is — is not sufficient.

Information about man is for us today no longer as available as it previously was in a commonly accepted philosophy. If a "theology of man" does not want to proceed in a manner characteristic of a dilettante — and the danger of dilettantism is presently a great one in theology — then it must be interdisciplinary theology.[3] Interdisciplinary is a fashionable word. But as soon as one earnestly agrees to it, the real difficulty of theology first comes to light. However, at no other time are the anguishing problems of contemporary theology so clear, as when one asks: "What is man?"

Never before in history has man known so much about himself. Never before has the amount of information about himself made him so insecure. Bit by bit the self-understanding which has been handed down to man is being demythologized. If man saw himself previously as the center, the crown, and the lord of creation, he now finds himself, since he began at the start of the modern age to penetrate searchingly into the cosmos — in the words of Pascal — alone in an isolated corner of the universe.[4] The grade of difference between man and animal, to which man attributed his exceptional position, has slowly but surely been abolished by modern biology. Since Darwin the boundaries have become fluid. Man has had to realize that from a biological point of view he makes up only a small corner of the animal world.[5] Finally, with the depth psychology of Sigmund Freud the disillusionment with, and the destruction of, the former concept of man have been completed. The long-lasting, painful, and furious protest against this demythologizing of man is only too understandable. Today this protest has for the most part become silent. Even the churches, which indeed over the centuries have condemned almost every fundamental break-through of man, are leaving the matter open. They have no other choice. Modern science has plainly won the victory. And so the protest has been silenced; only the universal perplexity has remained: "What then is man?"

We have acquired an amazing amount of knowledge with which to approach this question. Yet the more answers there are to this question, the less man seems to know with which answer he should identify himself. The greater the number of possible answers becomes, the more man comes up against himself as if he were in a hall of a thousand mirrors and images, and finds that he has no clear image of himself.[6] Or do we know more today than before about the meaning of human existence, the meaning of love, of suffering, of death? "Raising the question is embarrassing since the answer is so painfully clear. While we have created wonderful things we have failed to make of ourselves beings for whom this tremendous effort would seem worthwhile. Ours is not a life of brotherliness, happiness, contentment but of spiritual chaos and bewilderment dangerously close to a state of madness."[7] The more we know about

22

man, the more we ask whether we also know that which is really worth knowing. The more we are able to manipulate our human existence, the more we ask what we are permitted to do and what we ought to do.

Here the topical interest of a theology which understands itself as a theology for man become evident in an almost unexpected manner. And this is so even if much, even if most of the traditional theological statements about man need correction. Religion and theology have a purpose as long as they continually confront man with the question: What is man?

It is precisely this question which really makes man human.[8] Man is bound up in his environment in so many ways; in so many ways he is manipulated and determined. Nevertheless he distinguishes himself from other living beings in that he recognizes his plight and suffers because of it. In the very consciousness of his misery man's greatness is still evident. His greatness is that in the midst of his misery he can still question himself.[9] Thus it belongs to the very human existence of man that he asks himself about himself. If man were at some point no longer to ask this question, he would finally know what is wrong with him, for there would be nothing wrong with him any more; then he would cease to be. Man would then have retrogressed back to a resourceful animal.[10]

This danger cannot be denied in our civilization which is becoming more and more one-dimensional.[11] Where everything is reduced to questions of technical feasibility, and where the question concerning man's meaning is put in brackets because it is uncomfortable and even dangerous, there religion and theology become new objects of pressing importance. That naturally means at the same time that religion and theology will only be actual as long as they have the courage to be a thorn in the flesh, as long as they ask questions and stand in question in order to create room once again for human hope. But if on the contrary religion and theology only say what all other disciplines are saying, and for the most part are saying better, then their salt has lost its savor. If this is the case, then theology would have to keep silent, since it has nothing more to say. But whenever theology does speak, then it has the task of exercising the other disciplines in the discipline of humanity. Indeed what is man? What is the Christian understanding of man?

III. THE MYSTERY OF MAN

The most famous and almost classical statement on man is that he is an *animal rationale*.[12] This definition of ancient philosophy is practically common property of the entire philosophical and theological tradition. The problematic of this definition has already been frequently pointed out. It connotes from the very start a certain dualism in man and does not do justice to his unity. Even more essentially problematic, however, is the fact that this definition generally defines man without ever asking whether it is as a general principle possible to give a definition of man. The classical definition presupposes from the very start a definable, uniform, and fixed nature of man.[13] This presupposition ranges from Stoic and neo-Scholastic teaching on natural law and the encyclical "Humanae Vitae" to popular Marxism and popular Freudianism. It shows up again in the conservative and socio-romantic attempt to return to the wholesomeness of nature, as well as in the often cynical reference to the so-called objective pressures which come from economic and political realities. All of these positions rest on a fatalism which shrinks back from responsibility. Man is here continually being subjected to the almost fatal necessity of the powers of nature. His freedom is seen as an insight into necessity; his spirit is becoming merely a subtle detector of nature and acts either as its superstructure, its sublimation, or its substitute. But modern anthropology defines man in terms of his openness to the world.[14] Whereas all other living beings instinctively fit into their surroundings and thus are definable, man is "the X, who can maintain himself in unlimited measure open to the world."[15] He is the "unsettled animal."[16] "The animal is a bent-over slave"; man on the other hand is "the first freed being of creation."[17] This thesis of man's openness to the world is certainly being modified by the latest findings of the behavioral sciences,[18] but is not being basically refuted. There are, as we now know, "innate forms of experience" and pre-programmed ways of behavior in man which stem from the history of his race. Still these factors are obviously ambivalent. Aggressive as well as altruistic behavior is present in man. This means that man's behavior cannot be deduced from a clearly definable nature of man.[19] Even cultural anthropology[20] points out the astounding degree of historical variability and plasticity of the phenomenon man. "Plundering, incest, infanticide, and patricide all have their place in the category of virtuous behavior"; "the only certain thing is that, using pure reason as a measure, there is nothing which is right; everything fluctuates with time."[21] Even the question "What is man?" is an historically conditioned question. But if the knowledge of the nature of man is an historical process, then even the active self-realization of man is a happening in process.[22]

It is therefore valid to distinguish between that "which nature makes out of man" and that "which he as a free agent makes or can

24

and should make out of himself,"[23] between the humanness of man (*hominitas*) which he is given by nature and the humanity of man (*humanitas*) which he must develop historically.[24] What human human-existence ultimately means remains an open question which defies any conclusive definition. The human in human-existence is that *per definitionem* it is not definable.

There is hardly a critique of any definition of man which is sharper than the theological statement that man is the image of God.[25] For if man is not permitted to make an image of God, then the statement, "man is an image of God," means that to make an image of man is not possible or permissible. If God is the hidden One, then man is also out of reach of the very grasp of man. If God is for man an ever greater mystery, so is man. A mystery is different from a puzzle. A puzzle can be solved; a mystery cannot. "The 'solved puzzle' of man would then be the final dissolution of human existence."[26]

To speak of man as the image of God is a proposition of an eminently critical theology.[27] Such a proposition is in any case more critical than its modern inversion that it is not man who represents God's image, but rather God who represents the image of man, the projection of his anxieties, the wish-fulfillment of his longings, and the mirror and sanction of his relation to the world as its Lord. We could think that we had thus conclusively laid bare the mystery of man; in reality we have done nothing more than destroy his freedom. The result of such demythologizing is a new myth and a current deification of man. An idolized, an ideal, or a total man is not more human, but less human. If politics were to replace religion, then politics would not make man free, but restrict him and become totalitarian.

It is precisely the theological proposition about man which is a contribution to man's humanization. For it has a critically-liberating power over against all other attempts to grab hold of man and define him. A "theology for man" therefore will have to be critical theology. It will not offer cheap answers or a questionable model. Theology knows, in a strict sense, not more but rather less about man than the other sciences. Theology will have to grasp the tradition of negative theology and will have to be a negative anthropology.[28] For it defines man as the being of absolute mystery.[29] Such a definition has a critically-liberating power over against all self-deceit and self-infatuation; a critically-liberating power above all in the face of all totalitarian attempts to fit man into a system. Theology is a defender of man's freedom.

IV. CONCRETE HOPE

To define man's being as freedom[30] is the second great attempt of Western tradition to find a clue to the being of man. We encounter this attempt above all in the modern age. The way had been prepared by the biblical tradition and, to no small degree, by the liberating anthropological turning point in the theology of Thomas Aquinas.[31] The modern Enlightenment and the French Revolution bring the force of the new picture of man to an erupting point, and not without the embittered opposition of the churches and theologians. Not man's proper place in a metaphysical scheme, not obedience towards the authority established by God, but rather emancipation and liberation now become a way of defining man. Not a return to the "always-the-same" of nature, but an opening up to the "new" of the future is to characterize him. Man discovers that he occupies an eccentric position and a utopian stance over against the world and himself.[32] Whenever man understands himself as freedom, he can no longer allow his being finally to be defined in an absolute way; he can only define his human existence as always critical and experimental.[33] Man is now understood as "the one who can say no," "life's ascetic," the "eternal protestor against every mere reality," the "eternal Faust," "the *bestia cupidissima rerum novarum,* never content with the surrounding realities, always eager to break through the barriers of his here-and-now-this-is-the-way-it-is existence, always striving to transcend the reality around him — including his own given understanding of himself at any moment."[34]

This dynamic and historic understanding of man has not come into existence without the pervasive influence of the Christian tradition. At the beginning of the Christian history of salvation there stands the call to the exodus and the liberation from the bondage of Egypt, as well as the promise of a future that was to surpass all that had come before it.[35] Eschatology also dynamizes and mobilizes by its very nature the Christian understanding of man. Man is called to a continual re-thinking; he does not simply exist, he is becoming; he is freedom given over to itself, which first achieves its finality through history. Thus man is an experiment which has been handed over to itself, which can succeed, but which can also fail.

This emphatic stress on man's freedom can easily turn into its opposite. For if reality is seen in such a one-sided manner as history continually transcending itself, then the negative consequences for ethics are immense. Albert Camus has warned of this consequence. In effect then there is no longer anything which in itself would be good or evil; there is only that which is before its time or beyond its

26

time. Everything is allowed if it only lies in the progressive direction which is presupposed as right; indeed it can even be allowed and commanded to suppress freedom in the present for the sake of freedom in the future, or to sacrifice the present generation for the generation of the future[36]. Therefore it is precisely a conception so closely linked to the freedom of man which stands in danger of turning into a cynical totalitarianism. One can go still one step further in this critique and say: If the utopian stance of man in the world and his radical rootlessness were to be thought to its conclusion, then the present reality is the absolutely "perverted" and the radically "evil." The existing world is then of the devil and must be radically overthrown. We are left as a result with a new form of gnosticism.[37] Thus the nihilistic feature of Western thought which was exposed by Martin Heidegger comes to light once again.[38]

At this point Christian eschatology brings two points of view into play which are essential for anthropology: Christian hope is hope in the world and it is hope for the world. It is hope in the world. In this way it is different from fanaticism.[39] It is sober. It takes into consideration the boundaries which are placed on all human existence: birth and death. For whenever these boundaries are disregarded, whenever death in particular is being suppressed, whenever there is talk about a kind of supersociety of abundance with little work, much automation, the eradication of all sickness, the complete equality of the sexes, the resolution of all conflicts, then there could result at the end a repulsive boredom. When the pain which comes from the yearning for transcendence dies down, there is then no longer any history, but only a higher form of Fellah or prehistoric society.[40] Because hope is in the world, Christian hope is hope for the world. It is not a romantic flight into a utopian future, not a "great refusal,"[41] but the power to engage oneself in the present against all hope. Since hope believes in the God for whom all is possible, it also takes into account the still latent possibilities of other men. "In love the hope of the earth is near."[42] Hope therefore does not only criticize, but, in its critique and in its suffering under present unjust conditions, hope helps create Utopia and real possibilities for a happier human existence. "Therefore it is in creating, reconciling and hopeful love that the deepest possibilities for human beings are found in an inhuman world."[43] Christian hope finds God in the concrete and yet knows that God transcends all that is concrete. Because hope knows of this absolute future which transcends every concrete future, it is never permitted to identify itself once and for all with a concrete humanism. Nor can hope allow itself to sanction that vision of man which has historically developed in our Western culture. Hope must recognize that there can and increasingly must be a plurality of humanisms. "Christianity

27

therefore is not the drawing up of a concrete humanism, but rather the suppression of any humanism as absolute. It must view the acceptance of any particular humanism's experience as continually questionable."[44] We experience this questionability more today than ever before. Therefore more decisively than ever before we must ask: What is it that remains amid all the necessary upheaval? And so, once more: What is man?

V. ECCE HOMO!

In general one can say that the discovery of the personal dignity of each man is the specifically Christian contribution to anthropology. Not man as nature or even man as freedom, but rather man as person characterizes the Christian understanding of man. The notion of person attempts to forge a synthesis between the two notions of man as nature and man as freedom.[45] According to the classical definition which has been customary since Boethius, a person is the unchangeably unique and therefore direct manner in which a spiritual nature exists.[46] The human person is defined as a spiritual nature and therefore as freedom, but this freedom is not utopian but rather has its concrete locus; it stands in itself. In the person the infinity which is freedom finds its home. This is the reason why the person possesses infinite value, why an absolutely inviolable dignity belongs to him which is independent of the usefulness which the person has for the advancement of society, for a party, a state, or even for the Church. By reason of his personhood man is an end in himself and may never become a means to an end.[47]

This message of the personal dignity of every man is, according to the Pastoral Constiution of Vatican II, the decisive contribution of Christianity to the humanization of the world.[48] This statement is of great importance. Nevertheless the question is whether once again the official teaching office of the Church did not come out with it too late. According to all the evidence, it seems that even the notion of person has not been spared from the epochal upheaval which we experience today. Romano Guardini had already spoken of the "end of the modern era" and described the development as an end of the modern ideal of person.[49] In reality man's person is becoming more and more unclear; it is disappearing more and more behind the function and the role which it must play in the great and anonymous clockwork of our society. The notion of person is being asked to renounce any distinct shape or form. But is it enough if personhood, in the face of this threat by an ever more perfect and advancing system — as Romano Guardini says — were to retreat to its nuclear essence and thus just rescue what is most important to it? Would not such an understanding of person which is so sublime, so purely interior, and so narrowly limited to the private sphere be totally abstract? Indeed in the face of a concrete lack of freedom would not such an understanding be candidly cynical? This danger cannot be overcome simply by understanding the person as relation or as I-Thou encounter. All I-Thou encounters exist in the realm of general relationships to things, to common tasks, and to common interests.

If the stress on the personal dignity of each man is not to be a romantic escape, then such a stress needs a concrete humanism as its base.[50] To live human existence in a human way means that man needs, as the concrete presupposition to such a life, the necessary components such as food, clothing, housing, work, room to move, education and freedom. The minimum definition of such concrete humanity can be different from place to place. But the following is essentially true: the personal dignity of man demands for its concrete realization that it be publicly recognizable.[51] Person is a publicly-juridical, a political concept. And with this statement we have almost unexpectedly arrived at the biblical understanding of man and at the biblical command to love our neighbor. For what is love except an unconditional recognition of the other? Through such recognition love creates justice for the other. Love and justice are not therefore, as one often assumes, opposites. Love is rather the unconditional decision for justice for all.

Love thus borrows that in the classical concept of person which is continually valid. But love also transforms that concept as well. To speak by way of illustration: the classical notion of person came about through the baptism of the pagan understanding of man; but in order to become fully Christian, the notion of person must still undergo a second painful baptism — that of radical re-thinking. The stress on the independence, on the "in-itself and for-itself-existence" of man is an expression of an almost egoistic desire to assert the self. The "will to power," which Martin Heidegger pointed out as the basic impulse of the history of Western philosophy, is apparent here.[52] The catastrophies of our century and the still greater dangers of the future which the will to power conjures up, frankly force us to go to the root of the problem and radically to re-think our understanding of the person.

How can a Christian theology in light of the situation behave other than to reflect on its origin and its center, on Jesus Christ. *Ecce Homo!* Behold a picture of man! The vision of man, as we encounter it in Jesus of Nazareth,[53] is nevertheless not an ideal personality, but rather its opposite: the rejected and abused, the suffering and the crucified man, who knows that he stands united with all abused and weak men. But he overcomes the misery of miseries not with violence so as only to create new violence. He takes the lost and destitute condition of man upon himself. He allows himself to be abused without abusing others, he allows himself to be struck without striking back, he allows all force and violence to die in him. The renunciation of force and violence therefore means hope for those who are so powerless and hopeless that they can no longer revolt any more. His power is the powerlessness of self-renouncing love. Thus he converts lordship into service, power into love. This is the really Christian revolution and the most radical liberation which man can conceive. Christian love concerns a liberation from that which dominates the entire world — i.e., from the will to power, and it concerns as well a revolution, which reaches to the very depths of man's understanding of reality. The highest ideal is now no longer the person who possesses himself and who exists in and for himself, but rather existence "for the many," for the others.[54] The ultimate is no longer self-sufficient substance, but that which in Aristotelian-Thomistic philosophy was considered the weakest, namely relation. The fulfillment of man's humanity no longer consists in his being by himself, but rather in his being for others, not in having oneself at one's own disposal, but sacrificing his will to power.[55]

There is still much to be done in order to translate this fundamental realization into the language of philosophy. There is still more to be done in order to translate it into practice in society, in the churches, and in individuals. The closer the contact becomes between men, all the stronger the will to power becomes, and with it the danger that men will mutually attempt to subjugate each other. But the other possibility increases as well that men will come together and work together in a united fashion. Today the power of man is already so great that the use of the will to power can obliterate all of mankind. Only the growth of love among men can hinder this destruction. Therefore it is critically important that the death of Jesus on the cross stand at the center of Christian faith, and that Christianity is and remains Christianity only to the extent that it has its center in the cross. Certainly whoever reflects on how much this past and present center of Christianity is being ridiculed, not so much in theory as in practice, will not be surprised that Christianity is in difficult straits.[56] Christianity's chance for survival lies in recognizing the Crucified one as the beginning and the foundation of a new reconciled humanity. Thus the vision of man which we encounter in Jesus of Nazareth could be a guide to preserve man's humanity in its most threatened hour. Only love can effect the ideal of human human-existence in a human world — that it not remain a mere dream, but become an effective hope in an inhuman world.

NOTES

1   Cf. Y. Congar, "Christus in der Heilsgeschichte und in unseren dogmatischen Traktaten," *Concilium* II (1966), 10.

2   Cf. W. Kasper, "Die Welt als Ort des Evangeliums," *Glaube und Geschichte*, 1970, pp. 209-223.

3   Cf. *Die Theologie in der interdisziplinären Forschung*, ed. J. B. Metz and T. Rendtorff, 1971; W. Kasper, "Die Theologie im interdisziplinären Gespräch — Gesichtspunkte und Fragen," *Evangelische Theologie* XXXII (1972), 292-300.

4   B. Pascal, *Pensées*, 72.

5   M. Scheler, *Man's Place in Nature*, tr. H. Meyerhoff, 1961, p. 6.

6   J. Moltmann, *Mensch: Christliche Anthropologie in den Konflikten der Gegenwart* (Themen der Theologie 11), 1971, p. 12.

7   E. Fromm, *Psychoanalysis and Religion*, 1950, p. l.

8   Cf. H. Plessner, *Zwischen Philosophie und Gesellschaft: Ausgewählte Abhandlungen und Vortrage*, 1953, p. 280; K. Lowith, "Natur und Humanität des Menschen," *Gesammelte Abhandlungen zur Kritik der geschichtlichen Existenz*, 1960, p. 199; F. J. J. Buytendijk, *Mensch und Tier: Ein Betrag zur vergleichenden Psychologie*, 1958, p. 113; H. D. Bastian, *Theologie der Frage: Ideen zur Grundlegung einer theologischen Didaktik und zur Kommunikation der Kirche in der Gegenwart*, 1969, pp. 131ff.

9   B. Pascal, *Pensées*, 397, 410, 416.

10   K. Rahner, "Meditation über das Wort 'Gott,'" *Wer ist das eigentlich — Gott?*, ed. H. J. Schultz, 1969, p. 18.

11   H. Marcuse, *One Dimensional Man, Studies in the Ideology of Advanced Industrial Society*, 1964.

12   The definition of man as *Zōon logikon (animal rationale)* is found in Sextus Empiricus, *Pyrrhonic Elements* II, 26; Stobaeus, *Eclogae* II, 132. On the problem of this definition, cf. M. Heidegger, *Brief über den Humanismus: Platons Lehre von der Wahrheit*, 2nd ed., 1954, pp. 64ff.; J. Möller, *Zum Thema Menschsein: Aspekte einer philosophischen Anthropologie*, 1967, pp. 7ff.; K. H. Volkmann-Schluck, "Gedanken zu Platons Politikos: Die Geschichtliche Herkunft der überlieferten Wesenbestimmung des Menschen," *Die Frage nach dem Menschen: Aufriss einer philosophischen Anthropologie* (Festschrift für M. Müller), ed. H. Rombach, 1966, pp. 311-325.

13   For the conception of nature, cf. J. B. Metz, "Natur," *Lexikon für Theologie und Kirche*, 2nd ed., VII, 805-808; *Das Naturrecht im Disput*, ed. F. Böckle, 1966; *Naturgesetz und christliche Ethik: Zur wissenschaftlichen Diskussion nach Humanae vitae*, 1970.

14 M. Scheler, *Man's Place in Nature*, pp. 37ff.; A. Gehlen, *Der Mensch: Seine Natur und seine Stellung in der Welt*, 8th ed., 1966, pp 31ff.; A. Portmann, *Zoologie und das neue Bild vom Menschen*, 1956, pp. 64f.; W. Pannenberg, *Was ist der Mensch? Die Anthropologie der Gegenwart im Lichte der Theologie*, 2nd ed., 1964, pp. 5-13.

15 M. Scheler, *Man's Place in Nature*, p. 39.

16 F. Nietzsche, *Jenseits von Gut und Böse*, ed. Schlechta, II, 623.

17 J. G. Herder, *Über den Ursprung der Sprache* (1770, reprint 1959), pp. 18ff.

18 I. Eibl-Eibesfeld, *Grundriss der vergleichenden Verhaltensforschung. Ethologie*, 1967; *idem*, *Liebe und Hass: Zur Naturgeschichte elementarer Verhaltensweisen*, 1970; K. Lorenz, *On Aggression*, tr. M. Wilson, 1966; W. Wickler, *Antworten der Verhaltensforschung*, 1970; *idem*, *Die Biologie der Zehn Gebote*, 1971.

19 Cf. W. Lepenies, "Schwierigkeiten einer anthropologischen Begründung der Ethik," *Concilum* VIII (1972), 321ff.

20 E. Cassirer, *Was ist der Mensch?*, 1960; E. Rothacker, *Probleme der Kulturanthropologie*, 2nd ed., 1965; *idem*, *Philosophische Anthropologie*, 1964.

21 B. Pascal, *Pensées*, 294.

22 Cf. the survey of Process Philosophy by John B. Cobb, Jr., "Man in Process," *Concilium* VIII (1972), 328-337.

23 I. Kant, *Anthropologie in pragmatischer Hinsicht*, ed. Weischedel, VI, 399.

24 H. Plessner, "Anthropologie," *Die Religion in Geschichte und Gegenwart*, 3rd ed., I, 412a.

25 Cf. G. von Rad and G. Kittel, "*eikon*," *Theological Dictionary of the New Testament* II, 390-397; H. Renckens, *Urgeschichte und Heilsgeschichte*, 1959, pp. 92-112; J. Jervell, *Imago Dei: Gen 1, 26f. im Spätijudentum, in der Gnosis und in den paulinischen Briefen*, 1960; St. Otto, *Gottes Ebenbild in Geschichtlichkeit*, 1964.

26 J. Moltmann, *Mensch*, p. 12.

27 Cf. Th. C. Vriezen, *An Outline of Old Testament Theology*, 1960, p. 145.

28 Cf. U. Sonnemann, *Negative Anthropologie: Vorstudien zur Sabotage des Schicksals*, 1969; K. Rahner, "Christlicher Humanismus," *Schriften zur Theologie* VIII, 247.

29 K. Rahner, "Über den Begriff des Geheimnisses in der katholischen Theologie," *Schriften zur Theologie* IV, 67ff.; *idem*, "Zur Theologie der Menschwerdung," *ibid.*, 139ff.

30 For the concept of freedom see the good survey by M. Müller, "Freiheit," *Staatslexicon*, 6th ed., III, 528-544.

31 J. B. Metz, *Christliche Anthropozentrik: Über die Denkform des Thomas von Aquin*, 1962; *idem*, "Freiheit als philosophisch-theologisches Grenzproblem," *Gott in Welt* (Festgabe für Karl Rahner) I, 1964, pp. 287-314.

32 H. Plessner, *Die Stufen des Organischen und der Mensch*, 2nd ed., 1965, pp. 288ff.; *idem*, *Philosophische Anthropologie*, 1970, pp. 41ff.

33 W. Lepenies, "Experimentelle Anthropologie und emanzipatorische Praxis: Überlegungen zu Marx und Freud," *Concilium* VIII (1972), 16, 26, 53, 58.

34 M. Scheler, *Man's Place in Nature*, p. 55.

35 J. Moltmann, *Theology of Hope*, 1967; *idem*, *Umkehr zur Zukunft*, 1970; *Diskussion über die Theologie der Hoffnung von Jürgen Moltmann*, ed. W. D. Marsch, 1967.

36 A. Camus, *Der Mensch in der Revolte*, 1964, pp. 223ff.

37 G. Rohrmoser, *Das Elend der kritischen Theorie*, 2nd ed., 1970, p. 23; J. Moltmann, *Mensch*, p. 57.

38 M. Heidegger, *Nietzsche* II, 1961, pp. 31-256, 335-398.

39 E. Käsemann, *Jesus Means Freedom*, pp. 62ff.

40 K. Rahner, "Experiment Mensch: Theologisches über die Selbstmanipulation des Menschen,;; *Schriften zur Theologie* VIII, 281f.

41 H. Marcuse, *One Dimensional Man*, pp. 255, 257.

42 P. Schutz, *Parusia, Hoffnung und Prophetie*, 1960, p. 637.

43 J. Moltmann, *Mensch*, p. 169.

44 K. Rahner, "Christlicher Humanismus," p. 248.

45 M. Müller, *Existenzphilosophie im geistigen Leben der Gegenwart*, 3rd ed., 1964, pp. 160-183.

46 Boethius, *De duabus naturis* 3 (*PL* 14, 1343); Thomas Aquinas, *Summa theologiae* I q. 29 a 1; cf. J. Ratzinger, "Zum Personverständnis der Dogmatik," *Das Personverständnis in der Pädagogik und ihren Nachbarwissenschaften*, 1966, pp. 157-171; R. Guardini, *Welt und Person*, 2nd ed., 1950; M. Müller, "Person und Funktion," *Erfahrung und Geschichte: Grundzüge einer Philosophie der Freiheit als transzendentaler Erfahrung*, 1971, pp. 83-123; A. Halder, "Person," *Lexikon für Theologie und Kirche*, 2nd ed., VIII, 287-290; M. Müller and A. Halder, "Person," *Sacramentum Mundi* III, 1115-1127; W. Pannenberg, "Person," *Die Religion in Geschichte und Gegenwart*, 3rd ed., V, 230-235; J. Möller, *Zum Thema Menschsein*, pp. 41-51.

47 I. Kant, *Kritik der praktischen Vernunft*, ed. Weischedel, IV, 210.

48 "Pastoral Constitution on the Church in the Modern World," Ch. IV, Art. 41.

49 R. Guardini, *Das Ende der Neuzeit: Ein Versuch zur Orientierung*, 1950, pp. 66ff.

50 H. R. Schlette, "Utopisches Denken und konkrete Humanität," *Concilium* VIII (1972), 355-362.

51 Hegel, *Phänomenologie des Geistes*, ed. Hoffmeister, pp. 141ff.; *idem, Grundlinien der Philosophie des Rechts*, ed. Hoffmeister, 36, 48, 57, 71; *idem, Enzyklopädie der philosophischen Wissenschaften im Grundrisse* (1830), ed. Nicolin-Pöggeler, 484,490.

52 M. Heidegger, *Nietzsche* II, 1961, pp. 329ff.

53 Cf. J. Moltmann, *Mensch*, pp. 30ff., 160ff.; B van Ersel, "Das normative Menschenbild des Evangeliums," *Concilium* VIII (1972), 337-343.

54 For this understanding of Christian revolution cf. J. Ratzinger, *Einführung in das Christentum: Vorlesungen über das apostolische Glaubensbekenntnis*, 1968, pp. 112, 144, 205ff., 253.

55 Cf. H. Schlier, "*eleutheros*," *Theological Dictionary of the New Testament* II, 496-502.

56 Cf. J. Möller, *Zum Thema Menschsein*, p. 34.

PRIESTS, PROPHETS, MACHINES, FUTURES:

1202, 1848, 1984, 2001[1]

Benjamin Nelson

I. FROM JOACHIM OF FLORA TO THE "PROTESTANT ETHIC"

One could, if one wished, start the first installment of the story I have chosen to tell here now with the year 1202. Those who have strong memories will recollect that year for at least two reasons. That was the year in which there died the famed Abbot Joachim of Flora, a visionary exegete of Scripture, who was cited by Spengler as the spiritual source of the new image of time which came to prevail in the era of *Faustian* man and culture. In his own day, Joachim's commentaries echoed loudly in a new sense of Apocalypse and realizable eschatology. It was also the year Europe was to become acquainted for the first time with the Hindu-Arabic numeral system including the all-important zero. The source was the *Liber abaci* of Leonardo Fibonacci of Pisa. That event, claimed Werner Sombart, might be said to mark the birthday of modern capitalism. Given the zero, it was possible to innovate in spheres of major importance in the worlds of practical life and science. The zero came to play a large part in the rationalization of economy of the household, the rationalization of the activity and exchanges of firms of every sort, the rationalization of the administrative and public statistics.

I do not claim that the year 1202 or any other dates can be called the Archimedean points of world history; I am simply suggesting that many notable future developments of critical relevance to the present essay need to be traced back to the historic crossings — I include fusions and conflicts alike — of the cultural themes associated with the works of the Calabrian Abbot and the Pisan enterpriser.

of the productions and distributions of warheads, wastes, and noxious pollutants on land, sea, and in the air? To questions of this kind comprehensive and secure answers are not now available. Neither social scientists nor humanists have gotten far enough in their studies of these matters to permit us to speak with any authority.

I can here only hazard selected comments which address several particular issues which have a continuing excitement for men of the Western world. The first addresses itself to the question of how man is responding to the continuing stress on such images as those of infinite universes and life on other planets.

We will recall that the late Arthur O. Lovejoy and Alexandre Koyre have helped us see that the vision of an infinite universe which contained an infinite number of worlds like our own was the key element in spurring the new sensibility of the seventeenth century. The discovery of hitherto unknown stellar events disclosed by the new telescope doubtless involved a struggle to reshape images of the system of the world, recalling to mind the drama involving Galileo, Cardinal Bellarmine, and the Holy Office; but it was Bruno's vision even more than Galileo's *Dialogue of the Two Chief Systems* which implied deep changes in the way Everyman experienced himself in the cosmos.

From the writings of Donne, Pascal, and others we are aware that there was a sense of anguish that all "coherence" — secular as well as sacred — might be irrevocably gone. Who can forget Pascal's great cry from the depths in his *Pensees* when he confesses to his anxiety over the fact that now man saw himself a speck of dust tossed on the oceans of two infinities, the infinitely vast unveiled by the new telescopes and the infinitely minute revealed by the new microscopes?

As far as our manifest behavior in our working states goes, issues of this sort rarely appear to trouble us today. Few are found who openly express dread over the meaning of the new technoculture for the drama of God's Grace and man's redemption. Few seem to concern themselves unduly about the uniqueness of man's place in the cosmos.

I would doubt that very many of the participants or onlookers in successive space efforts have felt that the case for the three-story universe was truly weakened by the achievements of Armstrong, Aldrin, and other astronauts. As far as manifest effects of the descent on the moon are concerned, the world, no less than the moon, is still "Tranquillity Base."

There is, however, another side to this matter.

The care taken to guarantee the homespun religiosity of the American astronauts· surely implies a strong sensitivity to these

Middle Ages. From this point of view, Roger Bacon, Leonardo da Vinci, Galileo, and Kepler have a great deal more in common than is generally realized.

The deeper subterranean urges toward the drive to know nature and expand human productive powers are eloquently evoked by the recent writings of Paolo Rossi of the University of Florence. The union of theology, science, and magic arts is asserted again and again in the Promethean image of Renaissance engineers and artists.

Although Henry Adams' nostalgic phrases clearly exaggerate the extent of unity of the various sectors of the life of Christian society, it is nonetheless the case that some of the most striking abbeys and cathedrals could not have been built without the cooperation of all sectors and segments of the population. *Mont-Saint-Michel and Chartres* offers us the most eloquent account yet rendered of the power of the Virgin in winning the love and hearts, the faith and trust of men to proceed to transcendent achievement. In that work he writes:

> The Queen Mother was as majestic as you like; she was absolute; she could be stern; she was not above being angry; but she was still a woman, who loved grace, beauty, ornament — her toilette, robes, jewels; who considered the arrangements of her palace with attention, and liked both light and colour; who kept a keen eye on her Court, and exacted prompt and willing obedience from king and archbishops as well as from beggars and drunken priests. She protected her friends and punished her enemies. She required space, beyond what was known in the Courts of kings, because she was liable at all times to have ten thousand people begging her for favours — mostly inconsistent with law — and deaf to refusal. She was extremely sensitive to neglect, to disagreeable impressions, to want of intelligence in her surroundings. She was the greatest artist, as she was the greatest philosopher and musician and theologist, that ever lived on earth, except her Son, Who, at Chartres, is still an Infant under her guardianship. Her taste was infallible; her sentence eternally final . . .

> The palaces of earthly queens were hovels compared with these palaces of the Queen of Heaven at Chartres, Paris, Laon, Noyon, Rheims, Amiens, Rouen, Bayeux, Coutances — a list that might be stretched into a volume . . .

This extraordinary unity of conception and design — this marriage of all the arts, including the practical arts, in the celebration of the faith in the Trinity and in the Virgin — was not to go without rupture. Again, Adams needs to be quoted:

> The architects of the twelfth and thirteenth centuries took the Church and the universe for truths, and tried to express them in a structure which would be final . . . and this is true of Saint Thomas's Church as it is of Amiens Cathedral. The method was the same for both, and the result was an art marked by singular unity, which endured and served its purpose until man changed his attitude toward the universe. The trouble was not in the art itself which presented different aspects as man moved. Granted a Church, Saint Thomas's Church was the most expressive that man has made, and the great Gothic cathedrals were its most complete expression.

The split between other-worldliness and inner-worldliness did less to inhibit the development of technology either in the monasteries or in the world itself than many have supposed. Although the prevailing dualism did function so as to place those who had chosen the triple vow of poverty, chastity, and obedience in a grade much above that of anyone who lived within the world — the so-called "status of perfection" — medieval Christianity was not world-denying or acosmic. As Max Weber was to perceive, the monks of the Middle Ages were in a decisive sense spiritual progenitors of the ethic of "inner-worldly asceticism," the spiritual foundation of the vocational ethic of modern Occidental rationalism.

The monastic emphasis on a methodical life strictly lived in discipline under a rule — a life measured by a standardized community time — is the nucleus of the so-called "Protestant ethic" which has played so fateful a part in the life of the modern world.

II. THE RELIGIOUS-SCIENTIFIC-TECHNOCULTURAL REVOLUTIONS OF THE SIXTEENTH AND SEVENTEETH CENTURIES: NEW PERSPECTIVES

The developments between the fifteenth and eighteenth centuries need to be seen from a number of related distinct perspectives. The linkages among these have to be spelled out in some detail in order to make clear the tangled character of the development of the forms of mastery of nature.

Great leaps forward were made in the sciences and technology. There also occurred exceptional changes in the structures of orientation, notably in the spheres of religion and polity; great changes in the organization of action and administration.

I will speak of these now in turn beginning with the so-called religious-scientific-technocultural revolutions of the sixteenth and seventeenth centuries. Some of the perspectives which I shall suggest on these matters may seem novel: they grow out of specialized research I have done in recent years.

The Protestant Ethic as described by Weber and others cannot be identified as the main spur and goad to the emergence of the modern scientific revolution. The key facts about the relation of Protestantism to the new science and technology are more complex than many suppose: (1) Very few of the major theologians and leaders of the Protestant churches looked with favor upon the spread of the new science. (2) The main concentration of Protestantism was on the elimination of the medieval casuistical theology — moral theology even more than natural theology — of the Roman Catholic Church; in the same way the Protestant Reformers protested the inherited concepts of church, faith, grace, God's sovereignty, the sacraments, and so on. The net effect of their instruction was to give support to the breaking down of invidious dualisms between religion and world, and the promotion of a wider rationalization of conduct in the form of the spread of self-reliance and self-control. The weakening of an all-powerful hierarchy did indeed make it possible for there to appear social and professional circles which regarded the pursuit of practical knowledge with greater favor than did the Catholic Church.

The thrust toward experiment, while not originating in Protestant lands, was stronger in Protestant culture areas where it encountered less resistance. It therefore becomes necessary to see the distinctions in the particular blends of religion, science, philosophy, and technology which occur in different lands and different areas.

Elsewhere I have indicated that the critical moments in the passage to the scientific revolution of the early modern era are associated with the attacks by the pioneers — mostly Catholic in background — of early modern science and philosophy upon the inherited logics and decision-procedures of the traditional sciences and disciplines. There was a new impatience with every form of probabilism and exegetical casuistry of opinion, a new hunger for certainty and certitude, a new urge to achieve mathematical precision in the rendering of the *Book of Nature*. Fictionalist views of scientific theory lost ground to emphases on the truth of natural laws discovered in observation and controlled experiment.

The extent to which experiment guided this process has been greatly exaggerated. The principal thrust was toward the uncovering of formal mathematical expressions for patterned regularities observed in the numbered *Book of Nature*. In this respect, as we

39

have hinted above, the most critical advances had their origin in Catholic culture areas among men trained in Catholic settings. It is in truth in these areas that the formal sciences, especially analytic geometry and calculus, make very great headway in the sixteenth and seventeenth centuries. Only a very few writers have correctly assessed the extent to which the new technology and science depended on advances in mathematical analysis — on pure rather than applied mathematics. John U. Nef is one of the few scholars to appreciate the importance of developments in mathematics for the later developments of large-scale industry and precision engineering.

III. TOWARD THE ACTUARIAL WORLD-VIEW AND REGIME: *MATHESIS UNIVERSALIS* AND POLITICAL ARITHMETIC

Elsewhere I have laid stress upon a distinction between two central structures of orientations and rationales which have had long histories in Western civilization. Following a maxim of Piaget based on Durkheim, I have called the schemas "the moralities of thought" and "the logics of action." Since the Middle Ages, both of these structures have regularly rested upon a single hinge, namely, the notion of *conscientia* which had the combined senses in Latin and other languages of "conscience" and "consciousness." These were the grounds on which many central institutions with the Church, the university, law, and polity rested.

From this perspective, the central fact about the Protestant Reformation was the breakthrough it fostered in the inherited images of action. The Reformation stress on conscience was a momentous challenge to the established organization of the systems of spiritual direction, the so-called Forum and Court of Conscience of the medieval period. New openings could now develop for re-constitutions of structures of self, action, association, polity, law, liberty, and other horizons and milieux of life, public and private alike.

In the main, the medieval ethics achieved elaboration through a structured casuistry reared on the bases of Canon Law and Moral theology which were themselves rooted in Scripture (Old and New Testaments), Greek philosophy, and Roman law. At the root the central suppositions of the casuistry were stubbornly inter-personal rather than super-personal or collectivistic. Already in the later Middle Ages, however, we note strong thrusts coming from many quarters to substitute an outlook which was in the end to shatter the medieval rationales of conscience and their institutionalized expressions in moral casuistry, the dialectics of opinion and the cure of souls in large parts of the world. These thrusts gathered ever accelerating momentum in the Renaissance and the Reformation, and entered into new orbits in the seventeenth century.

The new world-view may be given the name of political arithmetic. This new view postulates that the only proper norms for legislation and policy have to be derived from the calculated estimations of the probable outcomes of alternative programs in the sense of relative profits or losses to the State. The casuistry of justice between persons gives grounds to the public-political-*collectivistic* point of view. "Reasons of State" come to prevail over dictates of conscience. Findings concerning the balances of power and trade come to predominate in the establishment of rationalized policies assumed to be in the wider public interest and to maximize general utilities.

We are not yet in a position to offer an integrated comprehensive account of the developments in these spheres. Clearly, as once before, we have to note that the newer developments do not begin with Protestant theology nor are they expressions of a Protestant Ethic in action. The thrust toward the new political arithmetic — the new moral arithmetic — occurs strongly in Italy in the fifteenth and sixteenth centuries. The evidence would seem to be that images of the balance of power arise everywhere in response to the new political and religious situations. Geopolitical outlooks come to take precedence over the previous modes of organizing group responses to moral and religious predicaments.

A remarkable and wholly forgotten pre-Soviet Russian study by E. Spektorsky has clearly established that the sixteenth and seventeenth centuries need to be viewed as times in which every subject, every perspective, and every major thinker moved toward metric expression. The two ruling conceptions were *mathesis universalis* and panmetric. Every branch of learning was compelled to take on the form of geometry. The efforts of Descartes, Kepler, Galileo, Spinoza, Hobbes, Leibniz, and others in this field are most memorable.

We do not need to go so far as Cassirer in making Machiavelli the predecessor of Galileo, but there can be little doubt that in his way Machiavelli was eager to substitute a form of policy science for the prior conceptions of the rule of princes.

By the middle of the seventeenth century the passage to political and moral arithmetic — and indeed to individual moral arithmetic — was very far advanced. This was a decisive step on the road to the full rationalization of activity and technique in the management of group and individual life. Probabilities of perplexed and doubtful consciences give way to statistics which have the appearance of

41

precision and which may be offered as mathematically certain demonstrations of the need for one or another policy.

In another connection I have shown how critical this movement was in the legitimation of a notion of an *average rate* of interest — a notion utterly central to the full institutionalization of capitalism. These passages toward political arithmetic and statistical averages are the highway to what I have called the *actuarial society* of the more recent period. The passage from the prescriptive and principial structures to the actuarial ones now began on their fateful way. Where they have led us is clear for all to see on every night's news reports on television.

IV. THE NEW INDUSTRIALISM AND THE MIX OF RESPONSES

The emergence of the so-called "Industrial Revolution" is more than the introduction of a new technology. It involves an immensely complex series of changes in the conduct and the human organization (and disorganization) of human affairs in every dimension of both group and individual life. The enclosure of the common lands, the breakdown of the inherited structures of villages, local communities, and localities were indispensable moments in the passage toward modern industry.

A great number of sources make it plain that the working groups were not as disposed to engage in self-regulation under factory managers as is often supposed. Edgar S. Furniss, Jr., has told the story of the pressures directed against the working groups through the stimulation of inflationary advances of prices over wages. The introduction of labor-saving machinery was a basic element here.

The critical moment in the emergence of a new bio-sphere and eco-environment must be connected with the emergence of new cities which became centers of urban blight in the very hour they became the homes of modern industry. A host of witnesses testify to the outrages committed against nature and man in these new towns and these new factories. Blake, Carlyle, Morris, Ruskin, and many others maintained unrelenting attack on the ravaging of the landscape as a result of the march of modern industry. We may soon expect to have new intensive studies of the extent to which, in the very earliest new towns, problems of littering and pollution came to be critical.

The earliest important attacks on technology and the evil effects of new industrialism came not so much from theologians, as from workingmen, cultural critics, philosophers, and poets. The wider **discontents** of the actual wreckers of machines, the so-called

"Luddites," who had their counterparts in lands other than England, are only now beginning to be studied closely.

The major cultural critics carried on a continuous inquiry into the very important dangers which the new industrialism threatened to the spiritual values of the past and the hopes of the future. Most important among the dangers explored are: the spread of forms of domination and new forms of dependence; the mechanization of spirit and robotism; the permeation of society by crassness and commercialism; the turning of life for many into sequences of boring and repetitive acts; the subordination of ends to means, the dissipation of religious substance, and the cheapening of religious symbols.

If we wish to recover the spirit of these early critiques, we have to recall especially the writings of Blake, Coleridge, and Wordsworth in England; Herder and Lessing in Germany; the great romantics and social philosophers in France.

V. THE RATIONALIZATION REVOLUTION

The story of the rationalization movement has only so far been told in bits and snatches. In truth, engineers close to industrial production had been aware of the fact that the simple installation of machinery was no guarantee that there would be efficient use of the new Prometheus. It was not, however, apparently until the consolidation of the ideas of Frederick Winslow Taylor and Frank Gilbreth in the United States of America that a way was seen toward the introduction of full rationalization. It was only as this occurs that we may speak of the rationalization movement.

Taylor was the poet and the prophet of the new era and it is, therefore, not strange that the phenomenon should be know as Taylorism or Taylorization in many parts of the world. Even Lenin spoke of the need to introduce Taylorism into the new Soviet industry not long after the Revolution. In Germany, the ideas of Taylor came into already existing notions of coordination that had been elaborated in the course of the innovation of high science, high technology, the universities, and so forth. Oddly, Walther Rathenau was one of the most powerful opponents of the ongoing mechanization of spirit. He was a prophet of the total coordination of all resources. How ambiguous was the response to Taylorism may quickly be gathered by reading the profile of him which appears in *USA* by John Dos Passos.

Our attitudes to the perils and promises of technology and science in our own day have become totally transformed as a result of the awareness that everything now operates on a completely new scale.

Nowhere can we be said to possess insulated chambers where new marvels or new horrors may be allowed to take place. The world has become indivisible as it never was before and all events have achieved the character of instantaneity.

We are not yet able to say exactly when the pace began to quicken in such a way as to threaten the present outcome. My own sense is that the future could already be perceived in the extraordinary spirits and integrations of technologies in the first World War. The American mobilization was probably the most extraordinary effort which industrial society had made up to that time. The German mobilization was an extraordinary premonition of it.

Raymond Williams' fine book, which remains our best source for the developments of the attitude of British literary men toward industrialism, correctly stresses that from the time of Coleridge until our own day, every aspect of the relations between culture and economic-industrial function continues to be very problematic. The fullest detail on the plight of industrial workers in the new factories and towns of the first half of the nineteenth century will be found in the careful Reports of the Factory Inspectors and in Frederick Engels' *Condition of the Working Classes in England in 1844*. New strains were to be sounded on the Continent by political economists and publicists such as Sismonde de Sismondi, Fourier, Marx.

In France, the response to the machine was also strong. France was not without its Luddites, but France saw a concerted effort to discover a positive meaning and future worth in the development of scientific knowledge — it is not an accident that both Saint-Simon and Comte did seek to create new religions more congruent with the industrial order than had been the religions of the past. In France, a so-called positivistic position developed after the French Revolution which was, in fact, stronger than any which emerged in Germany.

"The New Christianity" sought to proclaim a kind of credo and even a pantheon for the new scientific-industrial technocratic faith. A similar effort was made by Comte, who claimed a place for a new science, a science which he christened *Sociology*, to which he assigned the responsibility for discovering scientific social laws analogous to Newton's laws. The new science was to be the creed of a new church and a new Religion of Humanity.

For the Germans the most critical fact from the start was the risk which a new mechanism gave to the destruction of the hoped-for Faustian universality of man. It is for this reason that the animus against mechanism was especially strong. The antithesis between mechanism and spirit is everywhere to be found in German thought and, of course, continues in many guises in the writings of Hegel, Marx, Simmel, Weber, and others.

44

VI. THE VIRGIN AND THE DYNAMO

The twentieth century is now in the throes of a total revolt against the spirit and workings of technocultural civilization and the so-called myth of "objective consciousness" on which it is allegedly based.

The first critical expressions of this new mood occur soon after the emergence in Germany and elsewhere of the accelerated drive toward total rationalization.

Already in the first decade of the twentieth century, the new sensibility finds powerful utterance in outstanding writers of many lands and points of departure, including Henry Adams, Max Weber, and Eugene Zamiatin, who recognized the full meaning of the total coordination of all resources in accordance with the principles of instrumental rationality.

By the time Henry Adams had come to write his extraordinary autobiography, *The Education of Henry Adams*, the world seemed many years older than it did while he was writing *Mont-Saint-Michel*. The power of the dynamo now seemed to have attained full expression. In *The Education of Henry Adams*, he tells us that the new world began with the coming of the railroads and the violation of nature's quiet and privacy. Indeed, it was Hawthorne's statement in one of his Notebooks which led Henry Adams to date the new world from the year 1844.

However, it was only the visit of Adams to London in 1900 in which he saw the great dynamos in action which led him to write on the power of the dynamo as being the modern form of the power of the Virgin. He writes:

> . . . Satisfied that the sequence of men led to nothing and that the sequence of their society could lead no further, while the mere sequence of time was artificial, and the sequence of thought was chaos, he turned at last to the sequence of force; and thus it happened that, after ten years' pursuit, he found himself lying in the Gallery of Machines at the Great Exposition of 1900, his historical neck broken by the sudden irruption of forces totally new . . .

> The historian was thus reduced to his last resources. Clearly if he was bound to reduce all these forces to a common value, this common value could have no measure but that of their attraction on his own mind. He must treat them as they had been felt; as convertible, reversible, interchangeable attractions on thought. He made up his mind to venture it; he would risk translating rays into faith. Such a reversible process would vastly amuse a chemist, but the chemist could not deny that he, or some of his fellow

physicists, could feel the force of both. When Adams was a boy in Boston, the best chemist in the place had probably never heard of Venus except by way of scandal, or of the Virgin except as idolatry; neither had he heard of dynamos or automobiles or radium; yet his mind was ready to feel the force of all, though the rays were unborn and the women were dead.

. . . Before this historical chasm, a mind like that of Adams felt itself helpless; he turned from the Virgin to the Dynamo as though he were a Branly coherer. On one side, at the Louvre and at Chartres, as he knew by the record of work actually done and still before his eyes, was the highest energy ever known to man, the creator of four-fifths of his noblest art, exercising vastly more attraction over the human mind than all the steam-engines and dynamos ever dreamed of; and yet this energy was unknown to the American mind . . .

Henry Adams is only one among many writers toward the close of the last century who gives expression to his deep conviction that the doom of Western civilization impended. He conceived that the multiplication in the fire power of guns might eventuate in the mutual destruction of all mankind. This prediction was to be reaffirmed again and again by others as man's power to destroy himself did indeed increase. There is no one who will, in this connection, forget the astonishing premonition of Freud as he closes his *Civilization and Its Discontents.*

There was yet another factor which led outstanding scientists and scholars to share premonitions of the running down and even the end of the world. Talcott Parsons, in one of his reflective insights, speaks of many thinkers as having been in the grip of a sort of "nightmare of entropy" at the end of the nineteenth century. Many of the ablest minds did, in truth, fear the early onset of irreversible tendencies to entropy.

VII. "INFINITE" UNIVERSES,
"PROJECT TRINITY,"
"PROJECT APOLLO," AND GENESIS:
SEVENTEENTH — TWENTIETH CENTURIES

How are the structures of our consciousness now affected by the new science, new technology, new technoculture, and the no less than half-dozen revolutions which have been making their way across the world during the present century? How are Priests and Prophets responding to the expanding proofs that we may be endangering the life of everyone across the world through the effects

46

Joachim sought to give expression to his conviction that the world was on the edge of a new era, a time of an everlasting Gospel, when men should see each other face to face and not as through a glass, darkly. He was convinced that we had already passed the age of the Father, the age of the Old Testament, when all men lived in a state of bondage to their Fathers, and when institutions had a repressive and authoritarian character. He was further convinced that the Age of the Son had been and was being represented by the monastic communities which dwelt in mutual regard, concord, and love, and where they were guided by the New Testament, which was the Book of the Age of the Son.

The Third Age was already upon us — the third age, the third time, the third kingdom — and in this third age, the age of the Holy Ghost, there was to be no longer any mine or thine, no superior or inferior; there was, indeed, to be the time of total undividedness and absolute freedom.

Joachim of Flora merits the accolades which Spengler and others since have heaped upon him. Joachim was preeminently a Trinitarian thinker who clearly had in mind to overcome the divisions among peoples, classes, religions, nations, and to work toward a higher unity. He is a medieval precursor of a thinker like Teilhard de Chardin, one who wishes to speed the advent of a perfect Unity of Mankind, mind, and spirit — a kind of noosphere.

Despite — perhaps because of — the questions raised about his Trinitarian views at the Fourth Lateran Council of 1215, his wider message quickly carried to all who were in favor of the apostolic renewal of the church. His influence was especially strong — indeed, he took on the appearance of a sort of John the Baptist — among all those in the Franciscan order who preached the doctrine of Apostolic poverty and sought to prepare for the New Time. Many of the foremost innovators among the Franciscans counted themselves adherents of the Spiritual Fraticelli, as they called themselves.

From the point of view of this essay, the most striking fact is that many noted leaders of the hunted Spiritual party combined the Joachite emphasis on Apostolic poverty with a philosophy of mystical enlightenment (illuminism) which at one and the same time celebrated the supreme worth of mathematics, the idea of an "experimental" science, and utopian hopes for a new technology.

It is no easy matter to say to what extent the thrust to the new technology may have, indeed, rooted in a mystical enthusiasm for the workings of natural magic. Roger Bacon's writings certainly communicate this flavor. Profound religious impulses may well have played a much larger part than a bourgeois secular spirit in the thrusts toward science and technology in the High and Latter issues. Indeed, if the testing of the atomic bomb at Almogordo was labelled *Project Trinity*, the execution of the space effort at Cape Kennedy could easily be described as *Project Genesis*. The apparent preference of Greek titles for the successive flights and missiles — Apollo, Gemini, and so forth — does not detract from the fact that the astronauts read to us directly from the *Book of Genesis*.

Indeed, the very questions which confront us now call us back in every way to the *Book of Genesis* — and the theme of possible new Beginnings. Actually we have been moving in the margins of Genesis and its images of creation, the world, man, and the dominion of nature from the start of our present essay.

VIII. TOMORROW'S DOOMSDAYS AND APOCALYPSES

The encounters of Faiths, Sciences, and Machines have reached new peaks of intensity in our own twentieth century. We are yet too close to the events to be able clearly to delineate cultural outcomes and to set up rank-orders of their significance. We must be content now to make the following observations.

As far as religious institutions and sensibilities are concerned, advanced science and technology have had mixed effects not easy to compress into linear equations. The three-story universe of traditional Christianity is playing an ever decreasing part in the explicit doctrines of churches and peoples, but we would err if we said that this older image of cosmos has entirely disappeared from the belief structures of everyday men. Few of the changes result from direct explications by astronomers or physicists of the structure of the new universe revealed by the new science.

As might have been expected, the ruling structures of men have proved mainly responsive to the critical horizons of their life-environments, their compelling experiences, and the immediacies — public and private alike — of their historical existences and times. The response of peoples to the new marvels wrought by the new science and technology has, however, been far from unitary or consistent. Those who have not been alienated by the overcommitment of the science to destructive purposes of warfare have come to regard our time as Ages of Miracle and Natural Magic. This is readily illustrated in the scenarios of science fiction which explore the mysteries of interplanetary-travel and the intercivilizational contacts with extraterrestrial populations and polities.

Not surprisingly, the activities associated with nuclear fission, the building of ultimate weapons, and the preparations for Doomsday, have evoked a sense of the cosmic, ever a seedbed of new religious images associated with the creation, origin, meaning, purpose, and destiny of the world and universe. So far, however, the awarenesses which were so frightening to Donne and Pascal — the feeling of man's insignificant lack of centrality in an infinite universe — have had little recurrence in our time. Not many ordinary men of the highly rationalized parts of the world seem to be distressed by images of the removal of the earth from its central position in the cosmos, or even the possibility that other peoples may now be inhabiting other planets. We cannot safely predict, however, what the future will bring in these areas.

The most critical encounters of Science, Faiths, and Machines have occurred in the societal and intercivilizational experience of men today. The sense that the opportunities for man are shrinking at a geometric rate, that his effective freedoms have been set at naught by the omnicompetence of military and political establishments, and the proof that the environments — the air, seas — of mankind are now undergoing pollution at alarming speeds, have contributed to the sense that a civilization believed to be reared on the myth of the indifferent consciousness must not be allowed to endure.

In this era of Doomsday and Apocalypse, new mystery religions, new superstitions, new magics, spread everywhere. Everywhere men seek relief from the ordeals of civilization through instant actualizations.

At the very moment that our Games of Life are taking on the shapes of Dances of Death, hopes multiply that bio-medical engineering and cryonic suspension will offer us a new immortality and even collective resurrection.

EPILOGUE

We allow ourselves only a few words of Epilogue. The more closely we study the evidence, the more it becomes apparent that, in the main, Faiths, Sciences, and Machines reinforced one another in the development of Western civilization. Theological rationalism and mysticism cooperating with a natural science and natural magic helped to produce the new cosmology and technology of the later Middle Ages and the early modern era.

The contemporary technocultural cosmos is the fruit of the fusion at white heats of science, technology, and organization, which occurred in the wake of successive restructurings of rationales of conscience and opinion, and the breakthroughs in the moralities and logics of thought and action since the end of the Middle Ages. Beyond Joachim of Flora and Leonardo of Pisa, the key figures in developing these algebras were: Roger Bacon and Francis Bacon;

Luther and Calvin; Galileo and Descartes; Jeremy Bentham and Benjamin Franklin; Saint Simon and Marx; Frederick Winslow Taylor and Henry Ford; Lord Rutherford and Nils Bohr — and all their heirs and epigones in our modern and contemporary worlds.

Judaism and Christianity made their contribution to the building of Western civilization.

In their own ways Prophets and Priests alike have contributed to its present impasses.

Can they not — will they not — contribute to the building of newer and stronger foundations for the newer and stronger world now waiting to be born?

APPENDIX

OUR ECOLOGIC CRISIS:
ITS HISTORICAL ROOTS
AND THE RECENT STOCKHOLM CONFERENCE

It would be impossible to conclude this paper without taking note of the now renowned essay by Lynn White, Jr., "The Historical Roots of our Ecologic Crisis" (*Science* [March 10, 1967], pp. 1203-1207). Much as I admire its learning and humaneness of spirit, I have to admit that I cannot accept its very turn of argument without some demurrer. I would readily agree with Professor White on his first point:

> . . . Viewed historically . . . modern technology is at least partly to be explained as an Occidental, voluntarist realization of the Christian Dogma of man's transcendence of, and rightful mastery over, nature . . .

His dramatic lines of explanation and assessment seem to me partly right, partly overstated:

> . . . as we now recognize, somewhat over a century ago science and technology — hitherto quite separate activities — joined to give mankind powers which, to judge by many of the ecologic effects, are out of control. If so, Christianity bears a huge burden of guilt . . .

> . . . the present increasing disruption of the global environment is the product of a dynamic technology and science which were originating in the Western medieval world

50

against which Saint Francis was rebelling in so original a way . . .

I cannot agree, however, that the remedy he proposes speaks clearly to all the issues at stake:

> Since the roots of our trouble are so largely religious, the remedy must also be essentially religious, whether we call it that or not. We must rethink and refeel our nature and destiny. The profoundly religious, but heretical, sense of the primitive Franciscans for the spiritual autonomy of all parts of nature may point a direction . . .

It is hard to see how we can make great way in realizing the ends we must pursue by our general acceptance of the principles of Zen Buddhism or adoption of the ways of the Beatniks, whom Professor White describes as the "basic revolutionaries of our time." It is of the utmost importance for the new world in the making that we get beyond "poetic" ways of conceiving the relations of East and West.

We must not be surprised that the contemporary crisis in respect to the so-called bio-sphere and eco-sphere is finding form in schematic versions of historical process which at times take on the hue of Manichean melodrama. Although there is no denying that an exceptional figure like St. Francis of Assisi might set an example of a new sense of cosmic harmonies and the integrity of all creation, we must agree with the sense communicated by Clarence Glacken in his interesting study of nature and culture in Western thought from ancient times to the end of the eighteenth century which he has entitled *Traces on the Rhodian Shore*. Glacken writes:

> It is often said that what distinguishes the modern from the medieval and classical periods is the modern sense of triumph in the control over nature in contrast with an earlier and unrelenting dependence. Such contrasts rest on an underevaluation of the extent of environmental change in classical and medieval times, on the belief that an advanced technology and sophisticated theoretical science are required for extensive and permanent change, and on a too sharp contrast between the so-called industrial revolution and the industry and technology of the past. One may wonder at the failure of the thinkers of the Middle Ages to create a theoretical science comparable with that of Galileo and Newton; fail they did, but they lacked neither an empirical knowledge of forestry, agriculture, drainage, nor a technology permitting them to induce sweeping and lasting changes in their environment. In fact, they made some of the most drastic changes in landscapes in human

51

history up to that time.

An ascetic ideal was the original stimulus in evolving a philosophy of man as a creator of new environments. The early saints purposefully retired from the world, and they fancied that by their clearings they were re-creating the earthly paradise, reasserting the complete dominion over all life that existed before the Fall. The attractive force of these retirements, both to other monks and to the laity, and organized efforts at conversion led to Christian activism, in which taming the wild was a part of the religious experience. One of the many great roles St. Bernard played was to increase the Church's potential for landscape change. Under his influence one can see the Cistercian order changing from remoteness and renunciation to a role of active Christianizing of new and old lands alike. The success of such undertakings depended on practical knowledge and sense like that expressed in the *Instituta capituli generalis of 1134*; "victus debet provenire de labore manuum, de cultura terrarum, de nutrimento pecorum"

In the age of the great defrichements, lay ambition and church ambition alike called for activity and change as a part of economic expansion and of conversion. The result was a yearning, to use a modern expression, for control over nature. In the later Middle Ages the interest in technology, in knowledge for its own sake whether to improve thinking or to better the human condition, in clearing, and in drainage and the like betrayed an eagerness to control nature. As in all epochs of human history, modification of the physical environment is linked with ideas, ideals, and practical needs. The period of great cathedral building embodied a religious ideal; it also meant vast quarrying; probably more stone was removed from the earth in this period than in any comparable period of the past. In the three centuries from 1050 to 1350 stone quarried in France built eighty cathedrals, five hundred large churches, and tens of thousands of small churches. The Christian duties of conversion and lay expansion and colonization meant firing, clearing, burning. The grain and the grape have their practical, their cultural, and their religious history.

The life of Albert the Great provides a clue. He shared with his contemporaries and the Christian thinkers of the past a belief in a designed earth, in nature as a book revealing the artisanry of God, in the need to know nature for religious and practical ends; he thought also of the role of the environment in cultural matters, and he saw the force of clearing, of burning, of domestication, of manuring. That is what it was, a chain from theology to manuring. (*Traces on the Rhodian Shore* [Berkeley, 1967], pp. 349-51. Reprinted by permission of the Regents of the University of California).

As these very lines are being written, spokesmen for 114 nations of the world are gathered in the hope of arriving at some ways of "preserving our small planet." If the intentions of this present essay are on the right track, solutions will not come easy. The tangles are too knotted, the motives too mixed, the ailments too complicated, the remedies too "costly." This is always the case when the interests are so mixed as the ones at stake in Stockholm.

If the world for whose birth we wait can come forth from its present anguish, "miracles" of every description — "social," "political," "religious" — shall have to occur. At the end of a statement such as this, one may be allowed to add without ado: Where "miracles" are awaited, are we not in the sphere of "faith"? Are we not also in need of Wisdom?

The achievement of improved relations of theologies, sciences, machines, and faiths will only come with continuous effort to use wisdom, however gathered, in the melioration of the patterns of human existence and the uses of human knowledge. The day is coming when all men who own and control machines shall have to offer proof that these do not involve social and cultural costs which are prohibitive. This has already begun in some lands, including our own.

There is no possibility of mitigating the problems of the world without effecting improved arrangements of the production and distribution of productive resources. There have to be better ways than we now have of creating wealth and sustenance, and better ways of reconciling differences and avoiding lethal conflict.

NOTES

1   Related aspects of our theme and significant contemporary writings are considered in several of my previously published papers: "'Probabilists,' 'Anti-Probabilists,' and the Quest for Certitude in the 16th and 17th Centuries," *Actes du Xme Congres international d'histoire des sciences (Proceedings of the Xth International Congress for the History of Science)*, 1965, I, 269-273; "The Early Modern Revolution in Science and Philosophy: Fictionalism, Probabilism, Fideism, and Catholic 'Prophetism'," *Boston Studies in the Philosophy of Science, III, ed. R. S. Cohen and H. W. Wartofsky, 1968, pp. 1-40;* "Scholastic *Rationales* of 'Conscience,' Early Modern Crises of Credibility, and the Scientific-Technocultural Revolutions of the 17th and 20th Centuries," *Journal for the Scientific Study of Religion*, VII, No. 2 (Fall, 1968), 157-177; "The Omnipresence of the Grotesque," in *The Discontinuous Universe*, ed. Sallie Sears and Georgiana W. Lord, 1972, pp. 172-185 (originally published in *Cultural Revolutions and Generational Conflicts*, ed. B. Nelson, special issue of the *Psychoanalytic Review*, LVII, No. 3, 505-518); "The Games of Life and the Dances of Death," in *The Phenomenon of Death*, ed. E. Wyschogrod, 1972; "Civilizational Complexes and Intercivilizational Encounters," in *New Visions of the Sacred*, ed. Lorin Loverde, 1972-1973.

LOVE WHICH REJOICES IN TRUTH

Ernst Käsemann

Christian existence is a matter of joining truth and love. Church history shows how difficult this is. Time and again the attempt has been made to reduce the two to one. In former days, the opinion prevailed that whoever stood up for truth was at the same time serving love, since for man nothing would matter more than truth linked to eternity. The more people became aware of their historicity, and liberated from metaphysical thinking, the opposite perspective gained currency: by loving your neighbor, even the most distant, you show forth the power of ascertainable truth. Both points of view may be right, since as a matter of fact truth and love indissolubly belong together in our lives. Not without reason St. Paul says in First Corinthians, chapter 13, verse 6, that "love takes delight in truth." But in saying so, he also distinguishes between the two.

1. My first thesis is that truth and love are not properly known and grasped either when they are separated from one another, or when they are simply identified. In both instances, the result is a dangerous confusion.

We must be frank to state immediately that Christianity on the whole has been more inclined to sacrifice love for the sake of truth than to let faith yield to the claims of love. Its missionary endeavors and its controversy with the so-called heretics give incontrovertible evidence of the intolerance with which millions have been made to knuckle under, and even have been tortured and murdered. Truth advanced in this fashion can only appear as a horrible delusion. In this respect, times of enlightenment when people have been accepted without being coerced into conversion seem particularly bright. For the sake of past, but unforgotten, guilt all who today proclaim and practice the gospel of humanity deserve our sympathy, or at least our respect, even when they do so in the name of a death-of-God theology. Extreme solutions of this sort show how incredible the Christianity of the churches has become. If they merely make us furious, we are clearly unable and unwilling realistically to notice the inhumanity of the world in which we live. Whether consciously or unconsciously, we still presuppose as a matter of course a hierarchy of values created by white men. Thus unfortunately our eyes and our minds are closed to the needs of those who have been, and every day still are, made objects of exploitation and tyranny by our scale of values.

It should be clear that I am not prepared, in the name of a

particular faith and its confessions, theologies, or institutions, to restrict the general obligation to love everyone. This entitles me, however, to remind you of a problem that since Augustine had to be dealt with in dogmatics, a problem that has torn religious communities apart and even today has the power to reveal which side you are on. It focuses in the phrase *fides caritate formata*, which draws upon Paul's comment (Gal.5:6) on faith active in love. This, of course, cannot be denied if, according to the word of the Apostle, all one wants to say is that faith without love is pointless and self-delusory. But what the latin slogan actually means is that faith is merely the temper of love and conversely that love is not only the fulfilment of the law, but also the real intention and substance of faith. Therefore faith first of all gets its truth from love, and thus not only becomes the point of departure for love, but its access road as well. In theological language, this entails ranking sanctification over justification. It is not by chance that Reformation Protestantism has violently resisted this point of view and has expressed its opposition in the antithetical formula: *fides verbo formata* — faith shaped by the Word. Here faith derives its being and its stability entirely from the hearing of the divine Word. Love is here seen as consequence and authentication of this hearing. It is the response of gratitude towards the Gospel message which actively has to be made manifest in the concrete circumstances of our everyday life.

This type of reasoning will strike many who are no longer familiar with the dogmatic tradition of the church as confusing. The repetition of polemical formulas will even seem outmoded. But as an academic discipline theology cannot give up calling attention to controversial tradition if in the jungle of the many opinions it wants to get its own bearings and offer the people a ground to stand on as well. Christian faith must let itself be scrutinized as to whether or not it still is able to represent its own cause, or merely serves old or new morality as nursemaid of the perennially adolescent. Because of the sloth of our heart, the unreasonableness of our mind, and the want of good instinct in our will, it probably will be necessary time and again to say what one should know anyway. Faith does not have to be ashamed of this auxiliary function. Theology, however, is superfluous if our impulses can equally well be directed by common-sense, a general world view, or a particular theory of education. The claims of truth can never be transposed to a *program* of action, not even in the name of love.

2. Therefore my second thesis is as follows: As soon as one enters the realm of the concrete, the actual implications of love and how it is to be manifested are by no means self-evident. The particular situation generally messes up the neatest theory, so that one becomes exposed either to the pattern of convention and its casuistry

or to personal preference. Even though one may have grasped something as inescapable at the present moment, one still does not escape the ambivalence which dogs even correct insight, good will, or the deed to be done. All love pertains to relationships. The fatal thing about them is that they can always be manipulated, misused, or rejected by the partner. Love — more than by our *intentions* — is determined by our *need* for it to be accepted. A disciple of the Crucified One at least has no illusion as to how seldom even true love reaches its goal. Psychoanalysis perhaps -even denies the possibility of selfless love. At any rate, all of us are familiar with the phenomenon of misguided, desperate, and falsely interpreted love. This does not apply merely to the personal sphere. Revolutions prove that the proclamation of universal brotherhood can lead to the bloody reign of terror. In ordinary life, brotherhood often turns out to be no more than a beautiful dream which disintegrates as soon as we dislike a person or have to live a longer time with him. The many tomes written on the subject are obviously an indication that it is not all that easy and self-evident as people generally claim. Love is a many-splendored thing with many shades of meaning — and is often a pseudonym for our own egoism and delusion. It cannot escape further definition in terms of what we call truth. St. Paul lauds it as the highest charism, and then adds by way of explanation: "love delights in the truth."

That sounds like a bit of homily, and probably has been understood that way most of the time. The theologian, however, cannot be satisfied with an easy answer. His job is reflection, and he should not be afraid that others might consider his distinctions hair-splitting. Whoever, in speculative or pragmatic somersaults, leaps across experience — as contained in the dogmatic tradition — lands in his own dream world rather than reality, which is always complex. Man of course depends on love, and weddings seem to suggest that it is the simplest thing in the world. Comedy and tragedy, however, reveal the embarrassment and mistakes, as a result of which the most necessary and apparently self-evident things in our lives are frequently the most difficult and unfathomable. Here as nowhere else man's humanity is at stake, which cannot be left to theories and experiments. Humanity is not something we *have* as a firm possession. If we do not deceive ourselves we realize that at best we are on our way toward it. Our relationships — and therefore we ourselves — are dominated more by inhumanity and bestiality than by truth and love, which not by chance in the New Testament are regarded as eschatological gifts of salvation. If Ernst Bloch opposes Christian statements about the hidden God (*deus absconditus*) with his utopia of the hidden man (*homo absconditus*), it is atheistic *only as alternative*. Theologically both belong together.

We are not yet what we shall be, according to I John, chapter 3, verse 2. We await, according to Romans, chapter 8, verse 23, together with the unredeemed creation, the revelation of the glorious freedom of the children of God. One of the worst mistakes of the traditional doctrine of man has been "to nail man down" on the category of being rather than becoming. We still do this even in our talk about evolution, which fails to do justice to all that is fragmentary, dissonant, and discontinuous in our lives. The disorders are normally thought of as abnormal. But whenever one assumes to know what is normal, he leaves insufficient room for the unforeseen. In the age of the computer we cannot do without statistics and programmers. The specifically human, however, retains its place in the uncalculable, regardless of whether or not one considers this a bane or a boon. No one can escape the theoretical and practical dilemma of bringing truth and love to concord instead of driving them to discord, of leveling their dialectical relationship, or, according to circumstances and opportunity, of preferring sometimes the one and sometimes the other. In this dilemma the most profound crisis of humanity articulates itself, the crisis of a humanity which is forever threatened and must always find itself anew.

3. My third thesis serves as a step toward resolving the aforementioned dilemmas. The relationship between truth and love must, in Christian theology anyway, be determined on the horizon of freedom. I realize that taken by itself this concept also is no less problematic than the other two. It gains firm contours only in relation to them, that is, when it marks the point where conflict between both may arise. It is often assumed that the theologian ought to move within the realm of harmony, not conflict, and that he is bound to act accordingly also when he speaks of freedom. I can only repudiate the assumption and insist that in this instance he cannot communicate the message of freedom at all. Freedom exists only concretely, that is, only within the realm of tensions. Other people may find their pleasure and pain in abstractions. The theologian is professionally bound to cope with conflict. He authenticates his humanity by never evading it in any respect. Otherwise he had better not use the word freedom at all.

To clarify the point I return to a passage already referred to, Galatians, chapter 5, verse 6, which speaks of faith active in love. One really cannot call the context "loving" in this case. The whole letter is a bitter polemic against an aggressive Judaizing, written in behalf of the freedom of a Gentile church. The argument with Peter, the chief apostle, given as an example, is in Galatians, chapter 2, verse 14, summed up in the phrase "the truth of the gospel." The Galatian Christians are instructed in every way that this truth stands or falls with the freedom from the law of Moses which they have been granted. Concessions, like those Peter made in Antioch, evidently under strong personal pressure and with the best of intentions, are a betrayal of the Gospel, even when their purpose is to prevent an irreparable break. They are subject to the curse solemnly pronounced in chapter 1, verses 8f., as applying even to angels. So St. Paul recognizes an immovable limit to the love which is so rapturously praised in First Corinthians, chapter 13. The same limit is also introduced in regard to the Corinthian enthusiasts who boast of their Christian freedom and practice it in a radical way. A freedom which results in injury to the neighbor's conscience or which interferes with the building up of the community is but plain arbitrariness. So St. Paul is engaged in a battle on two fronts: against legalists and against enthusiasts. Truth must not be tampered with for the sake of love, nor love for the sake of truth, if we are not to lose both.

To this insight corresponds a peculiar approach of the Apostle to means repudiated on principle; it is in fact often suggested. First Corinthians, chapter 9, verses 19ff., describes in moving words how he is ready to serve all men, explicitly including Jews under the law. The Jewish Christian, without interference, is allowed to remain true to the tradition of his fathers while its acceptance is prohibited the Gentile Christian. Conversely, eating meat sacrificed to idols seems for St. Paul personally to offer no problem. At the same time, however, the enthusiasts who appeal to this gnosis are emphatically enjoined to abstain when they are in the presence of church members with tender conscience. Although he himself is a resolute ascetic, he allows marriage relations, and even, where desired by a non-Christian partner, divorce. In Romans, chapter 14, he relativizes existing taboos, but in First Corinthians, chapter 15, verse 29, he at any rate omits to rebuke the superstition of those who are baptized in magical substitution on behalf of dead relatives. One might almost say that in essence the Apostle always agrees with the strong, but in fact usually takes the side of the weak. Is that not a flamboyant opportunism and self-contradiction? How can one radically affirm truth to the point of cursing those who depart from it, and at the same time demand constant attention to, and love for, those who are anxious? Are conflicts here not being resolved arbitrarily and casuistically fogged? Since this ambiguity is nowhere in the New Testament more visible than in St. Paul, we can discuss our theme in reference to him. Does not his view of love taking delight in truth remain a beautiful illusion, or even worse, a mere preachment, when it gets specific and complicated, i.e., when we are confronted with reality?

These questions have to be raised in order to explain why I am injecting the notion of freedom. Without it we find ourselves arguing in a circle, and we never get beyond the conflict between truth and love in the Christian life. It must of course be first repeated that in Galatians, chapter 2, verse 14, as in the whole epistle, St. Paul identifies the truth of the Gospel with freedom. Precisely that is confirmed when in First Corinthians, chapter 3, verse 21, he takes up the slogan of the enthusiasts: "All is yours." He then sharpens this and interprets it in cosmic dimensions: "Paul, Apollos, Cephas, world, life and death, present and future — all belong to you. But you belong to Christ." Thus freedom for the Apostle is not simply belonging to the kingdom of Christ, but it is its earthly manifestation: a confident, but prejudiced life, which can accept and make use of everything. It is, however, not sustained at the deepest level by anything except Christ. Freedom can be all this only and always in a context of conflicts, threats, and anxieties, and in regard to the danger of arrogance. For in this situation the Corinthians find themselves, split up as they are in different cliques. No doubt the Gospel could be equally well characterized as righteousness, redemption, peace, joy, sonship, sanctification and much else. But these are all marks of Christian humanity which do not sharply enough characterize it in its vulnerability. Freedom exists only in the encounter with the powers and principalities which dominate the earth, which St. Paul also sees summed up in the triad of law, sin, and death, and to which in his view we are subjected in our existence of flesh. With this ilk, theories won't do. Law, sin, and death can only be overcome in the thick of life. That is why all theological concepts are only meaningful as pointers to, and horizon of, actual life. Otherwise they are utterly worthless, or at best merely building blocks in the construction of a Christian ideology. But since law, sin, and death implicate the whole world, they circumscribe the status quo in which we continually live.

Christian freedom is therefore always the exodus from the familiar and the apparently obvious. Even when on the surface this freedom agrees with tradition and convention, it will leave room for surprises, so that people may say: "Look! A human being!" Far more often, however, it will give the sort of offense that generally accompanies any exodus from the average perspective and normal behavior patterns. It breaks through role expectations. It is never a clear case that the liberated Christian will feel constrained to become partisan to a definite party, to prevailing opinion, or certain principles and norms. Where he does this for a limited period of time, his solidarity will remain critical, and will frequently involve opposition and protest against the majority view. He will have to distance himself from the popular trend and will often become a "thorn in the flesh" of his community, an irreplaceable individual who evades manipulation.

To be consistent we have to put that even more sharply. If law, sin, and death really are the profoundest indicators of the status quo on earth, producing reaction and revolution and technological society with its exploitation and conformism, then every status quo in bourgeois or Marxist society will always be questioned by Christian freedom, as characterized by the Exodus call. Unfortunately, on the whole, church history confirms this only insofar as it is the history of heretics. Usually Christianity could be regarded as tied to conservative tradition and as state-conserving power, and thus subsidized, not by chance, by the state. Therefore revolutions have always been connected with attacks on ecclesiastical institutions and even the Gospel itself. In all fairness it should be granted that human history is no different. Here too humanity is always denied more than affirmed. If one is not led by such experiences utterly to despair in mankind, then neither should the Gospel be judged and condemned simply on the basis of history. As soon as philosophical theory is set aside and historical reality considered, man cannot be defined a priori as rational animal. For this very reason the historical shame of Christianity is no final argument against the truth of the Gospel. It only shows that Christian freedom cannot be inherited, nor can it be secured by institutions. This freedom reaches only as far as the message of the Gospel is followed in an ever new *metanoia* and exodus. In *metanoia* and exodus it of course happened time and again that gods and demons were deposed and that the social and political status quo could no longer be taboo and became shaky. In regard to every possible risk it must candidly be stated that, in our world more than ever before, Christian freedom has to be understood in terms of this promise and this task. The trumpet must be sounded for attack, not defense. Today the individual can only be helped by battling and resisting the powers of the world. Concern for man today is concern for the earth.

This brings me to the other side of our problem. The truth of the Gospel is shown in the freedom of a Christian man over against the prevailing powers, opinions, groups, and society conventions. But what about love? Is it not bound to deny freedom by accommodating itself and making concessions and compromises? Have not the churches invariably, in the name of love, discovered Christian obligation to reside in compromise agreements or in strict neutrality between the two sides, restricting their engagement to declarations while in fact indulging in opportunism? Did not even St. Paul fall into self-contradiction when he relativized correct insights in concrete situations? Does one not inevitably land in theological schizophrenia in attempting to combine truth and love? Whoever does not ask these radical questions is just whisking up froth and he is incapable of clear thought.

To return again to First Corinthians, chapter 3, verses 21ff.: there the freedom of a Christian is grandiloquently based upon the fact that he belongs to the kingdom of Christ and that he manifests this on earth. Everything here depends upon the abrupt switch at the end of the verse: "Everything is yours; but you are Christ's." Freedom is here described *sub contrario* as a matter of being subject to a Lord. Romans, chapter 6, verses 12ff., sharpens this even more by speaking of freedom as a way of obedience and even of slavery. This must be seen as the key to our problem. It dare not be given an idealist twist. It is not that obedience is a variation of Christian freedom. Rather, freedom is the actual practice of obedience. Similarly, the truth of the Gospel cannot be made into a system of particular truths which could be derived from a general principle and spelled out casuistically. The truth of the Gospel according to First Corinthians, chapter 15, verses 1ff., for example, is nothing other than the risen Christ distinguished from other redeemers by the marks of the Crucified One, who creates on earth a community of those who follow him. One only possesses him when he possesses us, i.e., when he is our Lord. Obedient faith is the only genuine relationship to him. When salvation, peace, justification, reconciliation, grace, joy, or sanctification are talked about, what is being described is the experience of discipleship. The decisive thing for a disciple, however, is that he must listen continually to the voice of his Lord and so continue the earthly path of the exalted one.

As this Lord gives himself in the fullness of his gifts, so conversely does he claim us precisely by being and remaining our Lord, with an exclusiveness that nothing can relativize. The first commandment is taken up in the New Testament christologically: "I am the Lord thy God. Thou shalt have no other Gods but me." It is only by letting the Christ and no one else become and remain our Lord that we can be free of the powers of the world which ever anew are laying hold of our existence in the flesh. This means of course that we are inevitably pitched into a lasting conflict with these powers and their pressures, so that we become troubled while simultaneously we are summoned to the exodus away from their power and every earthly status quo, whatever it may be. This is how we demonstrate our membership in the kingdom of the Risen One, and at the same time suffer the fate of the Crucified One, the birthpangs which produce the new humanity of God's children. For where God appears in Christ he creates — as in the first creation — men who are nothing but real men and who desire to be nothing else. His freedom as the earthly realization of his Lordship liberates us at the deepest level from that self-care which throws us into despair and presumption, and therefore opens us for our neighbor and for care for the earth. A person who no longer has to worry about himself has time and strength to interest himself in other people, and cannot keep freedom to himself, but has to pass it on to others. This is what Christian love means: creating freedom for the neighbor and making the earth the space for open life. Again, that demonstrates participation in the kingdom of the Risen One as well as in the suffering of the Crucified One. For the breakthrough to co-humanity occurs under the same promise, the same danger, and the same pain as the birth in which one becomes a man who belongs to God. Love is the freedom of the children of God directed to every neighbor. It is the truth of the Gospel in the mode of participation and communication. There is no conflict between truth and love, as certainly as both can be misunderstood and falsified, as certainly as both can only be preserved in a situation of ongoing conflict. Both are one, since in each case their content is Christ in his relationship to man. Both are distinct in that the Lord who gives himself does not give us freedom simply as his gift meant for us, but at the same time as task of our self-authentication — and herein liberated humanity can embody itself only in co-humanity.

This leaves still unanswered a final question: is it not the case that what was theologically clarified in its connection and differentiation, in the concrete situation nevertheless collides and gets confused? We have in mind here the rigorous dogmatism which separated confessions and condemned heretics just as much as the love which does not want to hurt anyone and thus relativizes truth. To be a disciple of Jesus is never a *fait accompli*. The temptation of the flesh and the coercion of the powers that threaten us cannot be denied. Humanity and humaneness are on earth always provisional. Their perfection is something for the future. The main thing is to listen and to experience that the Lord never gives himself to his disciples once and for all, and he is always out ahead of them. We do not control him when we call ourselves by his name. The decisive issue is how far he draws us time and again into his power, how far the Gospel takes hold of us ever anew and forms us in his image and liberates us for his service. This shows both the promise and the limits of being a Christian, which concerns both truth and love. Put in theological language: the primacy of Christology is not merely dogmatically, but also practically the hinge of our existence. This means that when we give an account of the Lord who is determinative for us and of the freedom he has granted us as the earthly realization of his Lordship, no kind of concession or compromise is possible or permissible. At this point every other obligation ceases, the inescapable conflict with the world and false Christianity begins, and freedom issues in offense and the cross. The Christian can sacrifice everything except his Lord and the freedom which is the sign of his Lordship on earth. Otherwise he becomes the victim of idolatry and will no longer be identifiable as a Christian, and will have betrayed the Gospel of truth.

If, however, these are safeguarded, everything else is permissible and possible for him. Someone who is captured by the one Lord will in the end no longer let himself be captured by principles, norms, conventions, and society structures, thus also not by dogmatic theories or ecclesiastical and confessional forms of community. To the extent that these things have value as they have indeed, it is stimulation to reflection and experiment, no more and no less. Without reflection and experiment there is no life. Everyone has his particular place, his own abilities and weaknesses. Everyone lives on grounds of inherited traditions and institutions and is dependent on cooperation and representation. If faith lacks association with others, it withers, and in the course of time and with changing situations also alters its thrust. Since it is concerned with man and the earth, it can accommodate itself as well as run counter to things antiquated. It will, however, not let itself be regimented because it has to serve, and will not regiment others because it has to bring freedom. Love respects human differences, since it realistically orients itself in concrete cases, and it detests rigid conformism, since it sides in favor of man as individual being. Its sole limit is its Lord. He associated with every man exactly wherever he was, and was forever breaking taboos for the sake of individual lives. As long as his freedom to remain our Lord is not tampered with, we can and even must sacrifice our own freedom.

Finally, this can be sharpened by saying that faith has to develop reason and imagination, today more than ever. According to Romans, chapter 12, verse 2, a renewed mind is both promise and presupposition of Christian worship in everyday life. It is a mind raised by Christ out of spellbound anxiety beyond the powers and coercions of this world, and so a mind no longer determined in concrete situations by self-concern or arrogance. A liberated faith devotes itself in concrete situations to the service of its Lord and the well-being of the neighbor. That is, it makes room for the needs and opportunities of the moment. Love is allowed to be practical and to act. All the churches, in solidarity with the modern world, are undergoing one of the most dangerous crises of their history. It cannot be disputed that they all are in urgent need of reform and of an exodus which will get them out of the old ruts. But their emergency is overshadowed by the crisis of reason itself, which everywhere is found to be subject to and very largely helpless against the mechanisms, structures, and coercions of the economic, technical, social, and political facts of life. To come to its aid with the utmost energy and with all the inspiration that love can muster, even to the point of sanctioning the most extreme methods, is the demand of the hour as well as of the faith which confesses Christ as the salvation of the earth. The struggle against stupidity is even more strenuous and apparently more hopeless than the struggle against obvious wickedness, since it is conducted below the surface of society and arouses hostility among the majority of the people.

64

Without reason and imagination the earth will sink back into chaos, humanity will be lost, and brutality will forever claim new victims. Because of the Crucified One it is impossible for the churches and their members to avoid taking sides. They must unmask injustice wherever it occurs and cooperate in its elimination. This is how today "love rejoices in truth."

ŚŪNYATĀ AND PLĒROMA:

THE BUDDHIST AND CHRISTIAN RESPONSE

TO THE HUMAN PREDICAMENT

Raimundo Panikkar

"The first and essential step is to confront this issue [of Religion and the Humanizing of Man, says the invitation to this Congress] clearly and honestly, in its acute form." *Honesty* requires that we do not overlook traditional religions when speaking about religion. No amount of benevolent hermeneutics can edulcorate the fact that religions have not always been humanizing factors. *Acuteness* suggests we deal with the orthodox Buddhist and Christian conceptions, for it is hard to find a more acute formulation of opposite attitudes, both mutually and regarding the humanistic trend of our time. *Clarity* demands brevity and concentration on one single point so as not to blur the issue with accidental considerations.[1]

I. THE HUMAN PREDICAMENT

In spite of the scores of attempts at defining religion I may venture the simple and brief statement: Religion is the path man follows in order to reach the purpose of life, or shorter, religion is the *way of salvation*. One has to add immediately that the two words do not claim to have any particular content; rather they stand for the existential pilgrimage man undertakes believing that this enterprise is what will help him to reach the final purpose or end of life.

In other words, every human culture, under the particular perspective which we may call religion, presents three elements: (1) a vision of man as he actually appears to be (*hic et nunc*); (2) a certain more or less developed notion of the end or final station of man (*illic et postea*); and (3) the means for going from the former situation to the latter.

The first element may be called the *human predicament*, i.e., the particular view of how man is seen and evaluated. We use this expression rather than the more common one of "human condition" in order to stress that not all religions view the factual situation of man along the lines suggested by the expression "human condition." Man is not independent of what he takes himself to be and the human condition is precisely such because it is conditioned by man's own view of it. By human predicament we mean the factual status of man as it is evaluated in a particular conception which is part of the factual status itself.

It goes without saying that no religion, and much less those we are proposing to consider, can be treated as a monolithic doctrine, as if one single doctrine could sum up all that they stand for. This paper will choose only a pair of notions, one in each tradition, as representatives of an orthodox view in the respective religions.

The human predicament as it is seen by the Buddhist tradition could be summarized: (1) in a philosophical presupposition, the *anatmavāda*;[2] (2) in a theological statement the *āryasatyāni*,[3] expanding the cosmoanthropological intuition of *sarva duḥka*;[4] and (3) in a moral injunction, best rendered by the last words of the Buddha: "Work out your salvation with diligence."[5]

The human predicament as it is seen by the Christian tradition could be summarized: (1) in a philosophical presupposition, the creation of the world;[6] (2) in a theological statement, the redeeming or saving power of Christ,[7] expanding the theocosmoanthropological intuition of the incarnation;[8] and (3) in a moral injunction, best rendered by the very words of Christ summing up the Law and the Prophets: "Love the Lord your God with all your heart and soul and strength[9] . . . Love your neighbor as yourself.[10]

We may try to express in our own words the gist of this double vision It should be remembered that an immense majority until recent times has had a similar notion of the human predicament. Rightly or wrongly these two traditions seem to agree in saying that man is endowed with a craving — literally a thirst[11] — or with a lust — literally a desire[12] — which is the cause of his unhappiness. Further theological elaborations will speak of an Ignorance or a Fall, requiring thus enlightenment or redemption to overcome the human predicament. In any case the human predicament is neither as it should be nor as it could be. The Buddha[13] and the Christ[14] claim to put a remedy to such a situation. Man has to transcend his present condition in order to be freed, i.e., to get disentangled from the wheel of *samsāra*,[15] from this *kosmos*.[16] Both traditions stand for the liberation of man.[17]

Both traditions express here an almost universal human experience. Both are convinced that man is a not yet finished being, an unachieved reality, growing, becoming, on the way, a pilgrim. This is the human predicament. What constitutes the real problem is the response that these two world religions give to it.

II. THE BUDDHIST AND CHRISTIAN RESPONSE

1. *Nirvāna and Sōtēria.* The second element of all religions, as we said before, is the notion that there is an end or a final station of man. Man, this unfinished being, is not to remain as he is but has to undergo a more or less radical transformation, a change, in order to reach that state which Buddhism calls *nirvāna*[18] and Christianity *sōtēria*.[19] Religion is the dynamism towards a *terminus ad quem* out of disconformity with the status quo.

Significantly enough, the canonical writings of both traditions seem not to want a limiting description of the nature of the terms *nirvāna* or *sōtēria. Nirvāna* is simply the cessation of becoming,[20] of all *samskāras*,[21] of all links,[22] of every thirst.[23] It is the blowing out of all the *karmas*,[24] the indescribable term of which not even being can be predicated,[25] the radical originating power of everything,[26] the end with neither way in nor out.[27] It is beyond all dialectic[28] and thinking,[29] without a subject and object.[30] The whole effort is laid upon the reaching and not the describing or understanding of it.[31] But again this sentence is false if understood as in any way linking *nirvāna* with our will or imagination.[32] *Nirvāna* is "unborn, unbecome, unmade, unaggregated."[33] *Nirvāna* is not transcendent in the common sense of the word, because if it would transcend anything it would already be transcendentally linked with what it transcends.[34] *Nirvāna* is the mere destruction or rather the unmaking[35] of all that there is, which, by the very fact that it can be undone, destroyed, and negated, proves its non-reality, so that *nirvāna* is the most positive "thing" because it destroys nothingness.

The same vagueness seems to be the case with the Christian scriptural idea of *sōtēria*. It is salvation from perdition,[36] from death,[37] through Christ,[38] who is the leader to salvation.[39] It seems to be eternal[40] for it is the salvation of our lives.[41] Often salvation is used without further qualifications — in apparent acceptance of the common use of the term.[42] There is a way,[43] a word,[44] and knowledge[45] of salvation. Jesus is the savior,[46] he saves the people from their sins,[47] and there is salvation in no one else.[48]

In other words, neither *nirvāna* nor *sōtēria* has developed cosmological or metaphysical underpinnings. *Nirvāna* is the extinction of the human condition and *sōtēria* the freeing from sin.

69

②. *Śūnyatā and Plērōma.* It would require an entire volume to render even cursorily the different interpretations of these two central notions. We shall, as already indicated, alleviate the difficulty by choosing two significant examples and offering only the bare sketch of their doctrines. The two key words here are *śūnyatā*[49] and *plērōma*,[50] emptiness and fulness. Both are radical and both could be said to represent most emphatically the quintessence of their respective traditions. Furthermore, both terms seem to be at total variance, as the prima facie meaning of the very words suggests, not only with each other, but also with the modern humanistic traditions.

The end of the journey, the goal of man, is by definition *nirvāna* and *sōtēria*, but the nature of this goal is supposed to be *śūnyatā* in the former case and *plērōma* in the latter, according to some schools in the respective traditions.

In complete harmony with the Buddhist central *nairātmyavāda*, or doctrine of the ultimate unsubstantiality of all things, the concept of *sunyata* (vacuity, voidness, emptiness) tries to express the very essence of the absolute, of the ultimate reality or the ultimate nature of all things.[51]

Sūnyavāda is not philosophical nihilism or metaphysical agnosticism, but a very positive and concrete affirmation, one of the deepest human intuitions regarding the ultimate structure of reality.[52] It says that everything, absolutely everything, which falls under the range of our experience — actual or possible — is void of that (superposed and thus only falsely appearing) consistency with which we tend to embellish our contingency. All is under the grip of contingent flux, including our reason, by means of which we express this very idea. The other shore of the recurrent Buddhist metaphor is so totally transcendent that it does not exist, and the very thought of it mystifies and negates it.[53] "*Nirvāna* is *samsāra* and *samsāra* is *nirvāna*," says one well known formulation,[54] repeated again and again in different forms.[55] There is no way to go to the other shore because there is no bridge and not even another shore. This recognition is the highest wisdom, the advaitic or non-dualistic intuition or the *prajñāpāramitā*. To recognize *samsāra* as *samsāra*, i.e., as the flux of existence and the same existence as being in flux, is already the beginning of enlightenment, not because one transcends it (for there is no other "place" behind or beyond) but because this very recognition sweeps away the veil of ignorance, which consists precisely in taking as real or as substantial what is only pure void and vacuity.[56] That is why only silence is the right attitude — not because the question has no answer, but because we realize the nonsense of the question itself, because there is no question of the unquestionable (it would be a contradiction) and there can be no

70

answer when there is no question.[57] Who can question the un-questionable? Certainly not the unquestionable itself; and from the questionable world there can be no question about that which cannot be questioned. Everything that can be questioned is certainly not unquestionable. Thus the ontic silence of the Buddha.

In complete harmony with the central Christian doctrine of the *Incarnation*, the concept of *plērōma* (fullness, fulfilment) expresses the very end of man and of all creation.[58] Not only the Redeemer came at the fullness of time,[59] but he let all those who believe in him be filled with his own fullness,[60] for of his fullness we all have received,[61] and in him the fullness of the deity dwells bodily.[62] It is then the fullness of God[63] which fills up everything, though there is a distention, a period of expectation and hope until the restoration of all things.[64] Once the whole world is subjected unto him to whom all has been subjected, then he will subject himself fully to God, so that God will be all in all.[65]

Apart from the possible hermetic, gnostic, and other uses of the word *plērōma*, Christian tradition has understood this message as one of being called to be as perfect as the heavenly Father[66] — as being one with Christ,[67] as he is one with his Father,[68] and thus becoming not like God, as the Tempter offered,[69] but God himself,[70] by means of man's union with the Son by the work and grace of the Spirit.[71]

Theiosis, divinization, was the technical word used during long centuries of Christian tradition, and the simplest formula was that of saying that God has become man in order that man become God.[72]

The whole of the Christian economy is the transformation of the cosmos until the new heaven and the new earth,[73] which includes the resurrection of the flesh.[74] The destiny of man is to become God, to reach the other shore where the divinity dwells by means of the transformation which requires a new birth in order to enter into the kingdom of heaven.[75] *Metanoia*, change of heart, of life, and ultimately a passage from death to new life, was the central topic of Christ's proclamation,[76] already prepared by the prediction of John the Baptist, the forerunner.[77]

We should try now to understand what these two words symbolize within their own respective traditions.

Without *śūnyatā* thought is bound.[78] In fact, neither is the bound one released nor the unbound one not released.[79] To realize the emptiness of all things is the culmination of wisdom (*prajñā*), and this leads to the discovery of the radical relativity of all things (*pratītyasamutpāda*), which is the beginning of the realization of *nirvāna*. In point of fact there is more a sense of equality than of gradation between these four notions.[80] We are not describing four steps, epistemological or ontological, but rather four ways of

71

conveying one and the same realization. The realization that there is no-thing definitive in this world and that any other possibility, even the thought of it, is still linked with our "this-wordly" experience and hence also conditioned, dependent, not definitive — in one word, empty. Were it not for this emptiness things could not move; change would be impossible since material bodies could not move if there were no space between them. Emptiness is the very condition for the proper type of existence things have. And there is no-thing else, because any-thing which there could be besides, would be affected by the same emptiness, by the very fact that we consider them as possible and thus as an object of our thought.

> There neither water nor earth,
> neither fire nor air can subsist,
> there the stars do not shine nor the sun illumine
> there the moon is not bright nor darkness exist.[81]

Without *plērōma* there would not be place for God, there would be no sense to human existence. Man is more than man and when man wants to be merely man he degenerates into a beast.[82] He is destined to higher things.[83] When he is in a state of disquietude,[84] when he is searching for something higher, it is because God is already calling him.[85] The divine transcendence is safeguarded because the Christian divinization is, properly speaking, more a "filiation" than an indiscriminated fusion with the Father. The Christian Trinity is here the warranty for the necessary distinction without separation. Man and with him the whole universe becomes one with the Son by the power and grace of the Spirit, and, as such, he is one with the Father, but never becomes the Father. Even more, orthodox Christian thinking will stress, in one way or another, that while the Son *is* God of God, Light of Light, Man *becomes* one with the Son and thus reaches the Godhead in and through the Son. The scar of man's temporality, as it were, ever remains in the very heart of his being. Divinization, Christian tradition will stress, does not represent human alienation precisely because man is of divine nature.[86] Man is called upon to share God in a fuller way, going home to his primordial nature and origin. Divinization re-establishes the distorted image and really makes man what he ultimately is called upon to become. Divine sonship is the very vocation of man. What Christ is by nature,[87] is what Christ, who is man's brother,[88] has effected man to be by adoption: to share in the same sonship for us,[89] based on a new generation,[90] on a rebirth in water and the Spirit.[91]

72

III. RELIGIONS AND THE HUMANIZING OF MAN

It was a Greek who said that man is the measure of all things.[92] But it was another Greek who refuted him[93] and further affirmed that it is God and not man who is the measure of all things.[94] So that his disciple could say that man, though mortal, should not satisfy himself with mortal things, but strive to become immortal.[95] They all might have remembered one of their great ancestors saying: "The idiosyncrasy of man is his *daimon*."[96]

It was from a Hebrew inspiration that it is written that God created man in his own image and likeness,[97] and again it was from the same source that the sentence was often reversed and considered to be more the definition of God than the description of man: God would then be in the image of man.[98]

It was a Jew influenced by Greek culture and by a unique event according to his faith, who wrote that it was the divine Word dwelling with God that became flesh,[99] and a Roman who presented the same person as the Man.[100]

And it was another man who refused to speak about God and declined to indulge in merely theoretical speculations.[101] It was this same man who was directly and exclusively concerned with giving concrete and effective advice as to how to handle the human predicament.[102] Reacting against the religious inflation of his time, and reacting against the deleterious human condition of the people of his surroundings, he centered all his life in showing the way to get rid of the almost all-pervading human disquiet and anxiety, refusing even to undergird his teachings with any anthropology.[103] He was echoing the same tradition of his own culture which had stressed with great emphasis that:

> The Man, indeed, is the All,
> What has been and what is to be,[104]

because the primordial man is the supreme reality.[105] No wonder Buddhism was to flourish in the humanistic soil par excellence, the Confucian world, and in the Chinese culture at large.[106]

Following up the functional description we have already given of religion, we may still add that religion is the way in which man handles his human predicament in order to steer it towards a somewhat better situation. Modern man has an acute awareness of the urgency and difficulty of performing such a task. It is here that the sketch of two great religious traditions could prove of some value. We are, by this very fact, saying that Comparative Religion, far from being a mere comparison of religions or a historical discipline regarding what it has already been, is, in fact, a study of ultimate human problems — i.e., of religious situations — with the aid of more than one religious tradition, so that, illumining the concrete human predicament with the accumulated experience of mankind, we may be in a better position to understand the human predicament.

1. *Buddhism, Christianity, and Humanism.* It is in this light that we may draw our attention to the contemporary humanistic situation. Humanism has become for some decades a powerful word.[107] It expresses a valuable myth which in traditional countries of Christendom can be understood as a reaction against a certain devaluation of the human in favor of the supernatural in one way or another.[108] The twentieth century has seen the birth of all possible humanisms: atheistic, integral, Christian, religious, scientific, critical, Marxist, authentic, new, classical, modern, medieval, social, and even hyperbolical. Even isolated voices were raised in favor of Hindu and Buddhist humanisms. It is difficult to figure out what is not a humanism, except some exaggerated and obviously inhuman tendencies in several ideologies. Man is weary of certain dehumanizing trends in established religions. Humanism may be a healthy reaction. Currently, modern ideologies and ways of life, so-called technocracies of all types, have also been seen to be forces of dehumanization. Not only a transcendent heaven and an eternal hell are now seen as dehumanizing factors, but also society, techniques, modern cities, etc., are seen as having a deleterious effect on man. It is in this context that some would like to challenge traditional religions in order that they be now at the service of this task of humanizing man. And it is here from the viewpoint of Buddhism and Christianity that we may add some reflections.

To begin with, religions are very sensitive about being dictated to from the outside or told to be at the service of anything, for they think of themselves as above any servitude. What matters is not the "saving" of the human predicament according to men's individual opinions, they will say, but to see the true situation, as it really is, in the light of the religious tradition. Perhaps what one calls the "humanizing of man" is nothing but his entanglement and damnation.

Avoiding those touchy attitudes, which come only from superficial approaches, we would like to approach the problem from the perspective of the Philosophy of Religion or Comparative Religion, as defined above.

The roughly seven thousand years of man's historical memory on earth show a common pattern present almost everywhere: man's desire for immortality. Overcoming death has, in point of fact, been one of the central religious and human concerns. As to the how and the figurations thereof, religions differ. From the point of view of History of Religions one could be inclined to interpret the thrust toward divinization as a means to rescue man from the clutches of death as well as from the fear of nature or from the grip of the whole cosmos. The fundamental trait of divinization, in almost all religious traditions, is immortality. Men are mortal and the gods are immortal. The human predicament is that mortal man has to overcome this situation by the diverse manners offered by the most different religions. In one way or another traditional religions want to overcome the human condition by reaching the unconditioned. Divinization could appear here phenomenologically as the unconditioning of the human condition. Man reaches the divine (which may be interpreted in the most variegated ways) once he has overcome his mortal condition. Christianity would be a peculiar case of this attitude. Its doctrine of the Trinity makes it possible to defend a total civilization (union with the Son) without destroying the God-man difference.

Buddhism offers a different attitude. It does not want to uncondition but rather to de-condition man; it is not concerned with reaching transcendence, but with overcoming immanence; it does not care as much about God as about de-conditioning man in a radical and ultimate way. Man has to cease to be what he *is*, not in order to become another thing, not even God, but in order to negate totally the human and worldly situation. Buddhism shatters the human dream of any type of imaginable or thinkable survival.

Over against these two types, present-day secularism could be said to represent a new attitude which considers time, i.e., the temporal universe, to be real and positive, so as not to be transcended.[109] Secularism stands not for the unconditioning or de-conditioning of the human predicament, but for a sober recognition of it as it appears, without allowing for any escapism which would tend to deny this human situation. To make man really man and nothing but man is the driving force behind any humanism. And man, humanism would say, does not need to be afraid of being man, and should get rid of any fear of the world and the superworldly powers. Man has come of age. But man, who may have overcome the fear of nature and of God and gods, now begins to feel fearful of himself and of his societal reality, and thus the whole problem begins all over again. Furthermore, what is man that he has to be made man? What is that being that needs to be made or to become what he is not yet?

2. *Homo viator.* A study in depth of these three types of answers may perhaps furnish modern man with a more elaborated model

than any of the one-sided solutions so far proposed.[110] This would be Comparative Religion really at work.[111]

We may observe a common double assumption: (1) man is an unachieved being; (2) this achievement is the real Man.

The first part of the assumption is almost a matter of course. The human status quo is not (never) the definitive one. There is always place for change, growth, repentance, hope, enlightenment, salvation, betterment, and the like. The human predicament is infinite, because it is not finite, finished. Man is an open being; he is not finished: he "ek-sists" by stretching out his being along time and space at least.

The second assumption is less apparent and yet nevertheless equally common to the three fundamental attitudes under analysis. No human tradition, religious or secular, endorses the alienation of man. To convert man radically into an altogether different being would not only be heterodox and foreign to any tradition, but nonsensical too; any difference has only meaning within and over against an underlying identity. An absolute change is a contradiction in terms, for nothing would remain of what is supposed to have changed.

If Buddhism wants to annihilate man, to de-condition his human condition, to extinguish in him all *samsāric* existence, all remnants of creatureliness, it is because it presupposes that man *is* not, that there is no *ātman*, so that the blowing out (*nirvāna*) of all spatio-temporal and experiential structures is then the "true realization of man's authentic 'nature'." The destruction of all our constructions is the real liberation of man. And this is not against the orthodox central Buddhist attitude of universal compassion (*karunā*)[112] or unlimited friendliness. You can only embody the serene, joyful, and even pragmatically effective loving attitude, once you have realized the *śūnyatā* of all things.

If Christianity wants to divinize man, to let him share the divine nature and return through Christ to the Father, it is because it presupposes that divine nature is the ultimate and most intimate constitution of man.[113] Man is an offspring of God[114] and has to go back to the Father in order fully to realize what he is.[115] And this is not against the distinction between God and man, nor against the Christian emphasis on death and resurrection, new birth and total repentance. The risen Christ, as the risen Christian, is certainly a new creature,[116] but not another one (*aliud non alius*). The person is the same.[117] Or, in scholastic terms: "gratia non destruit, sed supponit et perficit naturam."[118] God does not become God, yet man becomes what he is not yet.

Similarly, if humanism wants to humanize man by making him recognize and accept his human condition, and to help man resist the temptation of escaping into realms of unreality, it is because it presupposes that the future of man *is man* and that his authentic dignity consists in affirming his humanness in spite of all allurements from above and from below. Man has to face his future with daring and dignity, and, even when confronted with the absurd or the meaningless, he will have to accept and affirm himself.[119] This attitude does not contravene the humanistic dogma of denying any substantial instance superior to man, for not only does the secularized future play many of the roles of the monotheistic God, but also humanism, as much as any other belief, requires a proper belief in man, which is of the unseen. Humanism demands of man as much an heroic position as any other traditional religion.

Nevertheless, in spite of all the structural similarities between these world-views, we cannot overlook the different anthropologies, i.e., the different underlying conceptions of man and, in the last instance, of reality. Nothing is more barren and dangerous than superficial agreements and merely tactical compromises. The injunction of Humanizing Man, which practically everybody could admit, means diverse and often opposite things to different world-views and religious traditions. The real encounter takes place when we cease to analyze structural patterns and concentrate on the nature of the purpose itself. What is humanizing? We cannot do more here than merely to ask the question.

3. *The Crossing of the Ways.* If the study of religion means anything today, it is to this problem that it has to address itself. A whole new methodology is required because we can no longer put the problem in a limited and particular way as has been done so far, due to the fact of the cultural compartments in the world. Even modern humanism is, by and large, as provincial and limited to a very peculiar conception of man and reality as many of the more traditional cultures it criticizes. Nobody can decide a priori what is the enterprise of humanizing man, nor can this be totally dependent on a single anthropology. It requires a methodology of its own, which makes its way in and through the mutual interaction and possible cross-fertilization of the different religions and cultures. What is necessary here is a dialogical dialogue, which is different from a dialectical one. This dialogical dialogue rests on the assumption that nobody has access to the universal horizon of human experience, and that only without postulating the rules of the encounter from one single side can man proceed toward a more universal and deeper understanding of himself and thus reach closer to his own realization. To want now to humanize man according to some preconceived scheme, even if convincing for some, would amount to repeating the same fault that so many religious traditions

have made under the conviction that they possessed the truth or had the duty and thus the right to proclaim their message of salvation. No man can be excluded from the task of humanizing man; no human tradition should be silenced in this common task.

A final thought may be added. It is the distinction between eclecticism and syncretism. The former is an uncritical mixture of religious traditions and an agreement among them obtained by chopping off all possible discrepancies in favor of an amorphous common denominator. Syncretism is the result of mutual and free interaction between cultures and religions, allowing for a possible assimilation of elements, by virtue of which those same elements cease to be foreign bodies, so that organic growth within the respective traditions is possible, and furthermore fecundation of religious traditions becomes a genuine option.

Avoiding eclecticisms, but having in mind possible interactions — though we should not minimize the existing tensions, either philosophical, theological, or religious, which exist between the religious traditions under consideration — we may envisage corrections, warnings, and complementarities which may not only allay mutual suspicions and soften one-sided positions, but also help toward a real human growth and thus positively contribute to a concrete humanization of human life on earth.

Let us indicate a few points of study. The Buddhist central concern will be a timely reminder both to Christianity and to all humanisms that no amount of "revelation" or of "reason" justifies the manipulation of man under the shield of the "will of God" or the "demands of reason" in order to steer man and the world to clearly defined goals. The ultimate goal is always so ineffable that even it does not exist. Buddhism is the thorough defense of the ultimate, absolutely ungraspable, mystery of existence. The mystery here is immanent.

The Christian central concern will be a timely reminder both to Buddhism and to all sorts of humanisms that no amount of self-effort and goodwill suffices to handle appropriately the human predicament, so that we have to remain constantly open to unexpected and unforeseeable eruptions of reality itself, which Christians may want to call God or divine Providence. Christianity stands here for the unselfish and authentic defense of the primordial rights of reality itself of which man is not the master. The mystery here is transcendent.

Humanism will be, further, a timely reminder both to Buddhism and to Christianity not only that traditional religions have often forgotten their own sayings like the non-authority of the Buddha[120], who may become the greatest obstacle even to reach Buddhahood,[121] like the sabbath made for man and not vice-versa,[122] and the freedom

78

of the children of God,[123] made free by truth itself,[124] but also that the Humanizing of Man cannot lose sight of the concrete man to be humanized, and that no amount of pointing out the way or proclaiming the message will suffice if the conditions are not given and worked for. Secularism is the awareness of the full responsibility and coming of age of man. The mystery here is the point of intersection between immanence and transcendence.

Even at the cost of possible misunderstanding (if the meaning of my words is interpreted only in one scale), I would try to express what can be considered a true humanization of man within the framework of these three major human traditions. Humanizing man means to make him truly man, but the expression is treacherous and ambivalent, because this gerund is neither merely transitive nor merely intransitive. It is not as if somebody else were humanizing man or as if man himself would achieve what he is not yet. Humanizing man means rather this plunge into reality and participation in the overall destiny of all that is, taking place inside and outside man. It is a process by which man becomes truly a person, sometimes dropping off the image he has of himself, dying, disappearing, transcending himself, sometimes affirming his being threatened by alien forces, in all cases entering into a deeper *ontonomic* relationship with reality — whatever this may be or not be. It is touching not only the shore of gentleness, power, and wisdom, but also the depths of despair, nothingness, and death. It is to become all that man is capable of in a unique way; thus it cannot be compared to anything else. Each person is a unique knot in the universal net. It means to reach the heights of the godhead if such is the model man has of himself, provided this vocation is not a mere wishful projection of lower unfulfilled desires. It means to touch the shore of nothingness, provided he does not rest on that unexisting place. It means to develop all the potentialities man is capable of, provided these are not artificially concocted dreams. It means finally to know and accept the human predicament and at the same time recognize that this very human predicament carries with it the constant overcoming of all that man actually is.

It is in this sense that the sincere and totally (because disinterestedly) committed *studium* of religion today, with all its attendant risks, uncertainties, and joys, is perhaps one of the most authentic religious acts — at least for some of us.

NOTES

1 The nature of this paper justifies, I hope, the omission of the so-called secondary literature, otherwise so valuable, and the limitation of quotations to merely indicative samples. Most of the citations are taken from the author's books: *El Silencio del Dios*, 1970, and *Humanismo y Cruz*, 1963.

2 I.e., the doctrine of the non-self or ultimate unsubstantiality of the real. Cf., for example, *Saṁyutta-nikāya*, III, 66; *Dīgha-nikāya*, II, 64ff.; *Milindapañha* II, 1, 1 (or 251); II, 2, 1; III, 5, 6; *et al.*

3 The four noble truths or *aryasaccāni* (or, in Sanskrit, *āryasatyān*), namely: the universal fact of sorrow, the different cravings as cause of sorrow, the stopping of all cravings as the stopping of sorrow, and the eightfold path leading out of sorrow: right vision, right intention, right discourse, right behavior, right livelihood, right effort, right memory, and right concentration. Cf. *Samyutta-nikaya* V, 420ff.

4 Cf. *Mahāparinibbāna-sutta* VI, 10; III, 66; *et al.* Cf., incidentally, Phil 2:12: "You must work out your own salvation in fear and trembling."

5 I.e., all is sorrow. Cf. *Dhammapada* XX, 6 (Nr. 278). Suffering, uneasiness, turmoil, etc., are other versions of *duhkham* (from the root *dus*, deteriorate).

6 Gen 1:1ff.; 1:31; *et al.*

7 Cf. Luke 2:11; Acts 13:23; *et al.*

8 Cf. John 1:14; *et al.*

9 Cf. Deut 6:5.

10 Cf. Matt 22:37-40.

11 The Pāli *tanhā* corresponds to the Sanskrit *trsnā*, meaning thirst. Besides the text already quoted, cf. *Aṅguttana-nikāya* III, 416; IV, 400; *Saṁyutta-nikāya* I,1; I,8; *Majjhima-nikaya* I, 6; II, 256; *Itivuttaka* 30; 50; 58; 105; *et al.*

12 The New Testament term is *epithymia*, which Latin theology translated by *concupiscentia*. Cf. 1 John 2:16-17; 2 Pet 2:18; Gal 5:16; Rom 6:12; 2 Tim 3:6; *et al.*

13 Cf. *Majjhima-nikāya* III,6: "The Tathagata limits himself to show the path;" *et al.* (cf. also *Majjhima-nikāya* I, 83).

14 Cf. John 10:9; 14:6; *et al.*

15 Cf. *Milindapañha* 326; *et al.*

16 Cf. John 16:8ff.; 17:9ff.; *et al.*

17   Cf. *Udāna* V, 5: "As, O Bhikkus, the great ocean has but one single taste, the salty taste, even so, O Bhikkus, the discipline of the teaching has but one single taste, the taste of liberation. That the discipline of the teaching, O Bhikkus, has a single taste, the taste of liberation, this is, O Bhikkus, the sixth marvelous and extraordinary thing of the discipline of the teaching." Cf. the same metaphor in the *Chāndogya Upanisad* VI, 13 for a different, but related, teaching. Cf. also John 8:36; 1 Pet 2:16; Rom 8:21; *et al.*, for the Christian side.

18   The word is not exclusive to Buddhism, as is proved by the *Gītā* II, 72; VI, 15; the *Mahābhārata* XIV, 543; *et al.*; and confirmed by the discussions on the non-Buddhist meaning of the term in *Dīgha-nikāya* I, 3; 19; etc.

19   The word is, on the one hand, the Greek rendering of the Hebrew words *yeshuah, yesha* and *teshuah,* and, on the other hand, the Christian rendering of the same word of classical antiquity; often ambivalent, i.e., applied to gods and men alike.

20   Cf. *Saṁyutta-nikāya* II, 68.

21   I.e., "of all this-worldly elements," "of all creatureliness" one could venture to translate. Cf. *ibid.* I, 136.

22   Cf. *ibid.* I, 210.

23   Cf. *ibid.* I, 39.

24   Cf. the etymology of *nirvāna* from the intransitive verb *nirvā,* to be extinct, quenched, consumed. The root *vā* means to blow and *vāta* means wind (cf. *spiritus, pneuma*). *Nirvāna* is the extinction of all combustible (mortal, contingent, temporal, etc.) material.

25   Cf. *Kathavatthu* XIX, 6.

26   Cf. *Itivuttaka* II, 6 (or 43); *Udāna* VIII, 3.

27   Cf. *Udāna* VIII, 1.

28   Cf. Nagarjuna, *Mūlamādhyamikakārikā* XXV, 1ff.

29   Cf. Candrakīrti, *Prasannapada* XXIV, *passim.*

30   Cf. the whole chapter III or *suññatavagga* of *Majjhima-nikāya.*

31   Cf. the famous parable of the man wounded by the arrow, who dies for being inquisitive over such unnecessary details as who shot it and why, in *Majjhima-nikaya* I, 426ff.; *Aṅguttara-nikāya* IV, 67ff.

32   Cf. *Majjhima-nikaya* (Vol. III, p. 254 of the Pali Text Society), where concentration is called void, signless, and aimless.

33   *Udana* VIII, 3. Cf. also Chandrakirti, *Prasannapada* XXV, 3 (ed. La Vallec Poussin, p. 521; tr. R. H. Robinson): "Nirvana is defined as unabandoned, unattained, unannihilated, non-eternal, unextinguished, and unarisen."

34   This could be considered the quintessence of Nagarjuna's insight.

35   Cf. the important concept of *asaṃskrta*, the non-constructed. The notion of *akata* (*akrta*), the not-done, -made, -created, stands in contraposition to the *saṃskrta*, the constructed of the Indian tradition. Cf. *Dhammapada* VII, 9 (97).

36   Cf. Phil 1:28.

37   Cf. 2 Cor 7:10.

38   Cf. 1 Thes 5:9; *et al.*

39   Cf. Heb 2:10.

40   Cf. Heb 5:9.

41   Cf. 1 Pet 1:9-10.

42   Cf. John 4:22.

43   Cf. Acts 16:17.

44   Cf. Acts 13:26; *et al.*

45   Cf. Luke 1:77.

46   Cf. Luke 2:11 and the very name of Jesus (Yoshua), meaning salvation.

47   Cf. Matt 1:21; Acts 5:31.

48   Cf. Acts 4:12.

49   The root *śū* (or *śvid*) means "to swell," and the term *śūnya* (empty or void) exists already in the ancient pre-Buddhist and non-Buddhist literature. Cf. *Atharva Veda* XIV, 2, 19; *Satapatha Brāhmana* II, 1, 9; *Taittirīya Brāhmana* II, 1, 2, 12; and many *Upanisads*. An interesting compound is *śūnyāgāra*, the deserted, empty house (*Jabala Upanisad* VI), signifying the house where the *sannyasis*, or Hindu monks, were supposed to live (or also in a dwelling-place of the god, a temple: *devagrha*). Cf. also *Maitrī Upanisad* VI, 10.

50   There is no need to stress that the word *plērōma*, i.e., that which fills (up), is of pre-Christian origin, and has its full meaning in Greek literature.

51   Cf. the beginning of Nagarjuna's *Mūlamadhyamikakārikā* I, 1: "Neither out of themselves, nor out of something else, nor out of both, nor out of any cause, do existing things arise."

52   Cf. the expression *svabhāvaśūnyatā* (emptiness of [in] its own being) as one of the modes of emptiness described in the *Pañcavimśatisāhasrikā* (one of the later *Prajñāpāramitā-sūtras*), or the expression *svabhāvaśūnya* in the quintessence of the *Prajñāpāramita* (the so-called *Heart-sūtra*) 1. Cf. also the *dharmaśūnyata* of Santideva's *Siksāsamuccaya* XIV, 242; and the *śūnyabhutah* (void of being) of the *Maitrī Upanisad* VI, 23.

53 The simile of the other shore is recurrent in Buddhist literature. Cf. *Aṅguttara-nikāya* II, 24; IV, 13; IV, 160; *Itivuttaka* 69; *Saṁyutta-nikāya* IV, 175; *Prajñāpāramitā-sūtra* IX, *et al.*

54 Cf. Nagarjuna, *Mūlamādhyamikakārikā* XXV, 19.

55 If there were to be any difference between the two, this difference would have to be either *samsara* or *nirvana* or a third kind, each which is contradictory.

56 Cf. *Lalitavistara* XII, 175ff. *Majjhima-nikaya* I, 297 stresses that the world is empty (*sunna* in Pali) of self and of what pertains to the self (*attā* and *attaniya*). Cf. also *Saṁyutta-nikāya* IV, 54 and 296; *et al.*

57 Cf. *Samyutta-nikaya* III, 189.

58 Cf. Eph 4:13; *et al.*

59 God sent his Son at the fullness of time (*chronos*) (Gal 4:4), but in the fullness of times (*kairos*) he will gather all things in Christ (Eph 1:10).

60 Cf. Eph 1:23.

61 Cf. John 1:16.

62 Col 2:9.

63 Cf. Eph 3:19.

64 Cf. Acts 3:21.

65 Cf. 1 Cor 15:28.

66 Cf. Matt 5:48.

67 Cf. John 15:1ff.

68 Cf. John 6:56-57; 17:23; *et al.*

69 Cf. Gen 3:5.

70 Cf. John 1:12 (and 10:34-35 with qualifications); *et al.*

71 Cf. John 14:17; 15:26; *et al.*

72 Cf. Clement of Alexandria, *Protrepticus* I, 9 (using here the term *theopoiein*, which was generally used for the making of idols); Irenaeus, *Adversus haereses*, Praefatio (*PG* 7, 1120); III, 18, 1 (*PG* 7, 937); III, 19 (*PG* 7, 939); Gregory of Nazianzus, *Oratio theologica* III, 19 (*PG* 36, 100); Athanasius, *De Incarnatione Verbi* 54 (*PG* 25, 192); *Oratio 4 contra arrianos* VI (*PG* 26, 476); Augustine, *Sermo* 128 (*PL* 39, 1997); *Sermo de Nativitate* 2 and 11 (*PL* 38, 999 and 1016); "Propter te factus est temporalis, ut tu fias aeternus," says Augustine again with his lapidary style, *Epist. Io.* II (*PL* 35, 1994); "Quod est Christus, erimus Christiani," repeats Cyprian, *De idolorum vanitate* XV (*PL* 4, 603); *et al.*

73   Cf. Rev 21:1.

74   Cf. 1 Cor 15:12ff.

75   Cf. John 3:3ff.

76   Cf. Matt 4:17; *et al.*

77   Cf. Matt 3:2; *et al.*

78   Cf. Santideva, *Bodhicaryāvatāra* IX, 49.

79   Cf. Chandrakīrti, *Prasannapada* XVI, 8 (ed. La Vallée Poussin, p. 293).

80   *Prajñā, śūnyatā, pratītyasamutpāda, nirvāna.*

81   *Udāna* I, 10.

82   Cf. the famous saying of Pascal, *Pensées*, 358.

83   Cf. the often-quoted passage, "Agnosce, O Christiane, dignitatem tuam: et divinae consors factus naturae, noli in vilitatem degeneri conversatione redire. Memento cuius veterem capitis et cuius corporis sis membrum," Leo I, *Sermo* 21 (*PL* 54, 19922).

84   Cf. the famous Augustinian "irrequietum est cor nostrum donec requiescat in te."

85   Cf. Maximus Confessor, *Ambigua*, "God has inserted in the human heart the desire of him" (*PG* 91, 1312); or, accepting the idea that the purified *epithymia* (concupiscence) can become the burning desire of him, *Quaest. ad Thal.* (*PG* 90, 269). Cf. the Christian commentary to John 6:44: "Nemo te quaerere valet, nisi qui prius invenerit" (Bernard of Clairvaux, *De diligendo Deo* VII, 22 [*PL* 189, 987]); also; "Console toi, tu ne me chercherais pas, si tu ne m'avais pas trouve" (Pascal, *Pensées*, 552).

86   Cf. 2 Pet 1:4; *et al.*

87   Cf. Rom 8:29; *et al.*

88   Cf. Heb 2:11; *et al.*

89   Cf. Gal 4:5; *et al.*

90   Cf. 1 John 2:29; *et al.*

91   Cf. John 3:5; *et al.*

92   *Panton chrematon anthropos*, Protagoras, *Frag.* 1.

93   Cf. Plato, *Cratylus*, 386 A; *Theatetus*, 152.

94   Cf. Plato, *Laws* IV (716 D).

95   Cf. Aristotle, *Nicomachean Ethics* X, 7 (1077 B 31).

96   Literally: "The ethos to man (is his) daimon." Heraclitus, *Frag.* 119.

97   Cf. Gen 1:1, 26-27.

98   This could be said to be the theological justification of all humanisms of biblical origin.

99   Cf. John 1:14.

100   Cf. John 19:5.

101   Cf. the famous fourteen *avyakrtavastuni*, or unutterable things, to which Buddha refused any answer. Cf. the *vacchagotta samyuttam* (*Samyutta-nikāya* III, 33), *avyākata samyuttam* (*Samyutta-nikāya* IV, 44), *cūlamāluṅkya sutta* (*Majjhima-nikāya*, 63), the *aggivacchagotta sutta* (*Majjhima-nikāya*, 72). etc.

102   Cf., for instance, Buddha's refusal to elaborate on the nature of *karman* because the only thing that matters is to get rid of it. Cf. *Anguttara-nikāya* II, 80; *Dīgha-nikāya* III, 138; *Samyutta-nikāya* III, 103.

103   That Buddha "has no theories" (*Majjhima-nikāya* I, 486) is a constant idea in the Buddhist canon, converted later in the *Mādhyamika* into the central message of Buddhism.

104   *Rig Veda* X, 90, 2.

105   Cf. *Svetāśvatara Upanisad* III, 8 ff.; *et al.*

106   This reference to the Chinese world is meant to signify that no complete and valid discourse on humanization can take place today without including what is perhaps the most humane of all cultures, whose ideal has always been the perfect man. Cf. a single example, which may well be considered representative of more than one tradition: "Therefore the Perfect Man makes his spirit and mind penetrate the limitless and cannot be impeded by limits, pushes to the utmost the sight and hearing of eye and ear and cannot be constrained by sounds and forms — because he identifies with the self voidness of the myriad things. Thus, things cannot hinder his spirit-intelligence." Seng-Chao, *Emptiness of the Non-Absolute* (*Chao-lun* III; tr. R. H. Robinson).

107   There is no point in giving here any bibliographical list which would cover more pages than the entire paper.

108   Cf. the famous *splendida vitia* of Augustine for the "virtues" of those not reborn in baptism. And again, "Bene currunt, sed in via non currunt. Quanto plus currunt, plus errant, quia a via recedunt," *Sermo* 141, c. 4, nr. 4 (*PL* 38, 778). Or again, "maius opus est ut ex impio iustus fiat, quam creare caelum et terram," *In Ioh.* tr. 72, nr. 3 (*PL* 35, 1823), which is commented upon by Thomas, "Bonum gratiae unius maius est quam bonus naturae totius universi" (*Sum. theol.* I-II, q. 113, a. 9, c. et ad 2), and again developed in his own way be Meister Eckhart in his *Serm. lat.* II, 2 (*Lateinische Werke*, IV, 16, n. 10); *et al.*

109   Cf. the etymological hint: *saeculum* is certainly not the *kosmos*, but rather the *aion*, the life-span (cf. the Sanskrit *ayus*), i.e., the temporal aspect of the world.

110 We say one-sided, because it cannot be denied that the heretofore traditional answers attempting a solution have, in point of fact, not taken into account the whole of the human horizon, as it becomes imperative to do in our kairological moment.

111 Needless to say, we can make only some general indications here as to how fundamental research on this problem could be started.

112 In point of fact, *karuna* and *sunyata* are the two pillars of the whole Mahayana Buddhism, and many texts link them together.

113 Cf. the well-known "tu autem eras interior intimo meo et superior summo meo" of Augustine (*Confessions* III, 6, 11). Cf. also Thomas, *Sum. theol.* I, q. 8, a. 1; I, q. 105, a. 5; Calvin, *Institutiones christianae religionis*, II, 7; not to quote the mystics.

114 Cf. Acts 17:28.

115 Cf. John 17:22-26; *et al.*

116 Cf. 2 Cor 5:17; Gal 6:15; Eph 4:24; Col 3:10; *et al.*

117 Interestingly enough, the Buddhist intuition of the *nairātmyavāda* tallies with the Christian doctrine of the *perichōrēsis* (*circumincessio*) in an astounding way.

118 Cf. Thomas, *Sum. theol.* I, q. 1, a. 8, ad 2; I, 1. 2, ad 1; although Aquinas does not have the literal words of the later famous principle.

119 Any humanism entails an affirmation of man transcending the "man" who makes the actual affirmation.

120 A recurrent theme of the teachings of the Buddha is that they do not have authority of their own, but only inasmuch as the hearer experiences them as conveying a real message of liberation. Cf. the Buddhist tradition: "Those who fantasize about the Buddha, who is beyond fancies and imperishable, are all slain by fancy and do not see the *Tathāgata*" (Chandrakirti, *Prasannapadā* XXII, 15 [ed. La Vallee Poussin, p. 448; tr. R. H. Robinson]).

121 This goes to the extreme of Lin Chin, *Taishō* 45, 500, b: "Kill the Buddha if you happen to meet him!"

122 Cf. Mark 2:27.

123 Cf. Rom 8:21; *et al.*

124 Cf. John 8:32.

HUMANITY AND APOCALYPSE:

CONFRONTING THE HOLOCAUST

Albert H. Friedlander

> *"Wer bin ich? Einsames Fragen treibt*
> *mit mir Spott.*
> *Wer ich auch bin, Du kennst mich.*
> *Dein bin ich, o Gott."*
> D. Bonhoeffer (*Widerstand und Ergebung*)

Self-definition is a lonely personal quest. Who am I? A rabbi, a teacher, brought into your midst to tell you what cannot be told, to remind you of what our age cannot ignore but has suppressed. George Steiner, the brilliant Socratic gadfly of our times, has noted in *Language and Silence* that the Word was there at the beginning but not necessarily at the end. And he cites Karl Wolfskehl:

> Und ob ihr tausend Worte habt:
> Das Wort, das Wort ist tot.

I also have no words to bring you into the darkness. I do not even have the silence which might accomplish this. There *are* those who could lead you into the innermost circle of the Inferno: Elie Wiesel. Eugene Heimler. Primo Levi. The witnesses; the survivors. And the word has not completely died. It lives with the poets. Theodor Adorno once said that no peoms could be written after Auschwitz. Then came Paul Celan, arguably the greatest German poet of postwar times; and Adorno retracted that saying. Sylvia Plath sang the song of Lady Lazarus; and Nelly Sachs wept for the children. But Nelly Sachs lived in the twilight zone and died alone. And Paul Celan and Sylvia Plath rushed into death because it seemed brighter than life. Already Hoelderlin had noted

Better to sleep, than to be without comrades.
And I do not know how to wait, what to do and
what to say
And why to be poet in a time of want.

Who wants to be a poet at a time like this? But we need them: they are today's prophets, remembrancers who give us our awareness of the night — and who may also let us know when dawn is breaking. We also need the remnants of language which have been preserved through them. Commenting on the Peasants' War, Friedrich Engels noted that "in a religious epoch, even revolutionary ideas have to be expressed in a religious rhetoric." In apocalyptic times, religious ideas have to be communicated in that anguished stammering which is all that remains when the darkness closes in. And at that time, our religious differences almost disappear. We are united in terms of *whatever remains* of our humaneness, and through our glimpses of the Infinite entering the finite. And so we will now join together and share our perplexities, our anguish, and the small spark of hope left to us. We will attempt to confront the Holocaust.

I

The organizers of this Congress set a specific task for our endeavors with which we can commence. The initial prospectus contained the following paragraph:

> *The humanizing of man in an apocalyptic world:* The civilized world with which this century began has become the apocalyptic world with which it moves towards its end. Item: the Holocaust! The historical circumstances which made it possible for this impossibility to happen have at least in part to do with the history of the religions of the Western world. The problem of the role of religion in the humanizing of man cannot ignore the inhumanity of modern times.

Much of this is accepted by all of us here at this Congress. We recognize the twentieth century as the Age of Brutality. Hindsight enables us to note a steady progression into darkness commencing most clearly in the trenches of World War I. It was von Falkenheym and Haig who first used the concept of the body count in modern warfare, who saw the trenches as blood pumps and who played the numbers game. Vietnam is only the last remake of that movie. But there are enough historians and histories who can and do chart the course of the unfolding evil before us. The origins of totalitarianism are clear to us. I trust that we have not forgotten that the Nazi state pioneered a number of innovations in our time which are directly related to the Holocaust: *It was the first openly criminal state in which inhuman acts were applauded and made the norm; land it managed to win over the minds of its citizens.* We hear much today of those who spoke out at the very beginning and at the very end. The time has not yet come that we can forget the reverberating silence which sent millions to their death.

Let us take a frank look at the suppositions underlying the statement that the Holocaust "has at least in part to do with the history of the religions of the Western world." Basically, we are here talking about Christianity. I know all about the Judaeo-Christian heritage which is Western Civilization. I like it. And I accept full responsibilities for the evils of our society as I have accepted its blessings. Almost three thousand years ago, Judaism taught the doctrine of communal responsibility and, to this day, our penitential prayers on the Day of Atonement take us into the recognition that the sins of our society are our own sins. But while the act of evil links aggressor and victim into a fratricidal pattern, the distinction between them endures. *In the beginning,* Cain held Abel responsible for being a victim. *In our own time,* here in America, the black community is castigated for having been brutalized by a system which promised equality but proved to be color-blind. *And yesterday,* as Jews entered the death camps, there were those who criticized them for not fighting against machineguns with their bare hands, or who indicated, really, that the "Jews had brought it on themselves!" Surely, the brutality of our time does not only consist of napalm and bombs: it is found in words and thoughts.

Christianity's involvement with the Holocaust. Perhaps it were better for a Christian to state this than for a Jew. Yet I remember long afternoons in an East Hampton garden spent in the company of Paul Johannes Tillich; and much of what I say and teach comes from him. Wilhelm Pauck at Union taught me to appreciate Martin Luther — I still feel that "Concerning the Jews and their Lies" was more than a pamphlet written by Luther in a moment of weakness. And if I link Luther with the German madness and see a relationship to the Holocaust, I do so because I want to understand Christianity, through its great men whose failings reflect the failings of Christianity. We cannot judge on the basis of weak men who claimed to be God's deputy but who surrendered to dictators. We can judge attitudes which recur again and again within the faith. Leo Baeck's classic essay on Christianity as the romantic faith underscores the emotionalism which blurs the sharp ethic of the Christian call for social justice. Yet this romanticism was endemic in fascism as well. Carl Schmitt, a lover of Streicher and Hitler (now back in business in West Germany), had defined political romanticism as "subjectivated occasionalism" in which everything can become romanticised and nothing matters. In 1919, he admitted that "the core of political romanticism is that the romantic... wants to be productive without becoming active ... without [assuming] responsibility ... " Religious romanticism faces the same dangers; and a concordat between religion and the state unites common emotions within both structures which evade ethical controls and find their own existence sufficient self-justification. Fascist actions were often condemned by Christianity; but they were carried out by professing Christians or by those who felt their Christianity to be a subservient but substantive part of the State which commanded its individual members to act in this inhuman fashion.

Religion's task of humanizing man is curtailed when secular and religious authority become intertwined — perhaps that is one lesson for the history of religion rising out of our exploration of the Holocaust. I fear that it is not the only lesson. Religion on its own can also misdirect human emotions and separate man from fellow man. It can stress human guilt — in an effort to promote repentance — to the point where everyone is totally guilty and where guilt therefore ceases to have meaning. It can stress the Divine to the point where the human is lost. It can accept the Holocaust as part of God's plan — but only by substituting human vision for the Divine. Christianity has made all of these mistakes; and Judaism has made some of them.

II

The loftiest vision of Christianity is that of the Cross. Non-Christians can only view it with the deepest of respect, and marvel at the self-sacrifice, at the devotion and service to fellow-man kindled among those whose spirits are truly at Calvary. And yet there is a danger in that vision. One Jew was crucified on that hill. Six million Jews died in the gas chambers of Europe. There are those who would say that Auschwitz and Golgotha are the same. They are not the same. They can never be the same. Six million sacrifices as a vicarious atonement? It is blasphemy to think so. It is even wrong to put these deaths into a framework where one begins to think of six million martyrs testifying of their faith to the world. They were not martyrs. They were victims. Their skins became lamp shades, their fat became soap, their golden dentures became loot, and their prayers were not heard. Their death was tragedy, not testimony. They died as human beings and nothing more. Their murderers survived, less than human, still part of our contemporary society.

Christianity can only come to terms with Auschwitz under the sign of the Cross. Is man still redeemable after this ultimate collapse of his humanity? Does Golgotha still illuminate the human situation? Juergen Moltmann's most recent book addresses itself to this problem:

> In the New Testament the question "Who is man?" points towards the one man, Jesus of Nazareth . . . concerning whom (deserted by God and man) it is stated: *Ecce Homo!* But at the same time God's answer is given: "I will be with you!" . . . Faith unites the recognition of God and self-recognition within the recognition of the Christ. The Crucified One is the "mirror," says Calvin, in whom we recognize God and ourselves. For in his cross there is revealed, together with the misery of human forsakenness, the love of God which accepts man in his state of misery.[1]

In his book *A Theology of Auschwitz*, the Christian scholar Simon makes the same point:

> By holding the mirrow of Auschwitz before Golgotha we remove the veil of unreality from the latter; by contrasting Golgotha with Auschwitz we bring the latter into a wider morality and give spiritual meaning to the meaningless.[2]

Gruenewald's altar piece of the tortured face and mangled body comes to replace Raphael's serene vision of the crucified Jew. It may well be that the contemporary Christian gains a deeper understanding of his God by pouring the full measure of human suffering, now known to man, into that moment of history which was Golgotha. But if there were aspects of Auschwitz and Golgotha, the non-Christian will still challenge the notion that Golgotha gives morality and meaning to Auschwitz. For Moltmann, *Ecce Homo* and *Ecce Deus* are *one word* written upon the Cross at Golgotha. Those standing outside that mystery who look at Auschwitz can only say *Ecce Homo*. The Christian sees the suffering of one person at Golgotha and finds it encompassing all human suffering, including Auschwitz. In the core of the suffering upon the Cross he discovers the love which will assuage all pain. Man is both impotent and heroic, the protagonist of a tragedy resolved *outside* the arena of its performance. For the Jew, the process is reversed. He starts with the six million victims of Auschwitz, and moves from there to the single man who must confront his own Auschwitz. In the words of Rabbi Ignaz Maybaum:

91

The Cross, as the poetic symbol of suffering, hides the truth. Auschwitż . . . is the truth mankind must face. The Irish who perished in their great famine perished in their Auschwitz. The yound boys who died in 1914 in the mud of Passchendaele died in their Auschwitz. The soldiers who died at the Somme and at Verdun . . . the soldiers, airmen and sailors of the second world war, the Russian prisoners who were starved to death in Germany, the Russian peasants who were destroyed like useless cattle by Stalin, the men, women and children who died in the air raids, the victims of Hiroshima and of the air raid on Dresden, they all died in their Auschwitz; they died because what happened was a monstrosity (and not a poetic tragedy) . . . [3]

Auschwitz — can never be Golgotha. Golgotha is the attempt to bring man, through the limits of human weakness, into the confrontation with God. Auschwitz demands that man must confront his own monstrosity and take full responsibility for it. Those who ask: "Why was God silent?" are influenced by the Christian tradition. The Jew still wants to know: "Why was man silent?"

It is passing strange that at the moment of asserting human culpability for the monstrosities of life Judaism also asserts its hope that man can survive and regain his humanity. Every human being is a new hope, an individuality in which aspects of the Divine are revealed. He cannot be defined: *individuum est ineffabile*. Man is made in God's image; as the Talmud interprets this, the Divine imprint does not create men like identical coins: each is unique, each is in God's image. A reconciliation between Judaism and Christianity can take place at this point: the discovery of man leads to the awareness of God, just as the awareness of God must lead the Christian to the awareness of man. And the mystery of individuality leads to respect between differing faiths. Differences remain. There is an ancillary insight here for those of us who teach comparative religion courses: one must learn to listen to nuances. Confronting Auschwitz, one could select Jewish and Christian statements which would give the impression that there is absolute agreement between these religions as they confront the ultimates of human suffering. We are *not* agreed. But we respect each other's grief and walk our own way. At the end of time, the roads converge and become one.

III

Meanwhile, how shall we live with each other under the shadow of Auschwitz? *Can* we confront the past and present monstrosities out of the resources of our religious traditions? Or are these to be abandoned? Can we still talk of the resources of our democratic

92

tradition? Or is this to be abandoned? Are we still brothers?

In the realm of human relationships, the problem of theodicy becomes the quest for the *Mitmensch*, the fellow human being. Some years ago, a Public Letter was published in which a Jew addressed a fellow human being on the problems of life after Auschwitz. The author of this letter was Guenther Anders. He entitled it "We Sons of Eichmann" and addressed it to Klaus Eichmann, the son of Adolf. The text evidences a deep concern for a young man living under the shadow of the past. It dealt with our generation in our monstrous time.

Anders also emphasizes the horror of Auschwitz which has made itself at home in all areas of our apocalyptic age. He summarizes the specific *monstrosity* of Auschwitz:

> What is monstrous?
> 1. That there was an institutional and factory-like extermination of human beings: of millions.
> 2. That there were leaders and assistants for these actions, namely — *slavish* Eichmanns (men who accepted these tasks like any others and excused themselves on the basis of commands and loyalty); *dishonorable* Eichmanns (men who fought to obtain these posts); *stubborn* Eichmanns (ready to surrender all of their humanity in order to enjoy total power); *greedy* Eichmanns (men who did the monstrous precisely *because* it was unbearable to them — and they had no other way of proving to themselves that nothing could shake them); *cowardly* Eichmanns (men who were delighted for once to do the infamous with a good conscience, that is, as not just something no longer prohibited, but as something which was commanded).
> 3. That millions were brought and kept within a condition in which they did not know of this. And they did not know of it because they did not want to know of it; and they did not want to know of this, because they were not supposed to know of this — that is, millions of *passive* Eichmanns.

Once more, Auschwitz is here used as a mirror. It is not Golgotha which is reflected, but our own home and that of our neighbor. Anders is aware of this: he recalls the immediate past to avert the immediate future.

One of the causes of Auschwitz was — technology. Anders cries out that

> our world, despite the fact that we discovered it and built it, has become so enormous that is has ceased to be "our"

93

world in a psychologically verifiable sense. It has become "too much" for us.

Our actions now have effects which are beyond our awareness. This conflict between man and his technology has been noted earlier; the concept of "alienation" has been assimilated into modern life. Yet Anders sees a new dimension here, a growing darkness. In the last century, man suffered from lack of knowledge. In our time, man suffers from too much knowledge, from intentionally produced false knowledge. And if our intellect is insufficient or misdirected, this also applies to our feelings. All of us know this. The death of an infant moves us; the death of six million simply stuns our senses.

There is a sense in which Anders' words apply to all of us: we are "Eichmann's sons," removed from the consequences of our actions, inheritors of a dark past, actors in new monstrosities which poison the continents and destroy our immediate neighbors. We are also victims. While we distinguish between those who killed and those who were killed, we recognize that the monstrosities which were perpetrated in those days have etched themselves into the structure of our corporate existence. The fine edge of our sensibilities has been worn away by the monstrosities of our age. The six o'clock news is the most brutal program on television — and we do not even turn it off. Each day, murder and destruction flicker across the screen as part of our home life. Is it any wonder that we have learned to live comfortably with the knowledge of the death of the Six Million? We can keep a body count of our own, right in the privacy of our living room.

Which came first? Did the new monstrosities wipe out our knowledge of Auschwitz? Or was it our inadequacy of dealing with the Holocaust which gave the new monstrosities, the Belsens of today, their place within our society? The inheritors of Freud remind us that the encapsulated traumas of our childhood must be confronted at some stage of our growing up period. How else can we become more humane? Our various religious disciplines may be of help at this point — confession is a way of self-confrontation. Nor can history be ignored: the passive, greedy, cowardly Eichmanns who staffed the camps are still among us — where they have not been replaced by new recruits. Which machine are they serving — and how many of us serve the same establishment? The complexities of modern existence make it difficult to discover the answers. Yet there are moments in every life when we break out of the structure, when we are no longer controlled but, suddenly, in control. And then we can be human beings. We can be humane. We can reach out towards our fellow-man. And our shared suffering and our shame can be a bridge and can cease to be a barrier. Auschwitz — remembered within the community of human fellowship — can then become a question addressed to God. Then. But not until then.

IV

When Dante left the Inferno, he once more looked up at the stars. And I am a witness for the Jewish tradition which will not end a prophetic reading on a note of despair, but will continue in the text until words of hope have been expressed. We may query the initial announcement of this congress which noted that "nothing seems so irrelevant in the modern world as religion." The presence in our midst of Father Berrigan and Dorothee Sölle is a welcome reminder of the relevance of religion in our time. In Europe, we find a biblical concern with human needs in the "theology of revolution" which combines Moltmann's theology of hope with radical change:

> [the theology of revolution means that] the qualitative new future of God has united with those who are now oppressed, set aside, and persecuted; that, therefore, this future does not begin on top, at the peaks of "progressive society," but at the bottom, with its victims . . . [4]

And our exploration of myth and symbols assures us that not only theology but also the sanctuary is open to the struggle for the rehumanization of man.

Jews do not often "do" theology — we have no word for it in the Hebrew language. But our experience of the Holocaust, our rediscovery of the land of Israel, and our involvement in the open society have led to a verbalization of our religious thinking. The outer structure of it parallels Christian thought; and I am pleased rather than embarrassed that I can thus pay tribute to my old teacher Paul Tillich and my new friend Heinrich Ott (mind you, reconciling these two becomes a problem). Sometimes, this involvement brings rabbis beyond the boundary as they move through death-of-God-theology into the Dionysian fields of Brown and Kean. Even then, Jewish thought finds itself stimulated by its rebels and will not let them go — whether their names be Elisha ben Abuya, Spinoza, Freud, Marx, or Bloch.

Our neighbors teach us. But the foundation of our thinking is still the Bible and the rabbinic interpretation, a *shalshelet ha-kabbalah* (a chain of transmission) which has lived through all the generations of Jewish life and speaks through us in testimony of the encounter with God. The Jew has lived with the problem of theodicy since Abraham pleaded for the inhabitants of Sodom and Gemorrah: "Should not the Judge of all the earth do what is just?" The Book of Job expresses it most clearly — but I am afraid that Job has been

95

grossly misused in our time. It is a work utilized to achieve instant recall of all dimensions of the problem: human suffering, the distant God, and the encounter. Its misuse has created the illusion that one has controlled the situation because one can discuss it! Even Job's friends had more sense: they waited for seven days and seven nights. Those who entered the inner circle of hell can find themselves expressed in this book. But while all of us are survivors, we are more inheritors: we are the next generation. Our book is the Book of Ezekiel. More than constantly reliving the anguish, we have to relieve the pain, we have to bind up the wounds, we have to start again. We have seen new life. Our function, and our self-understanding, rises out of a prophetic text which is unmistakably priestly and pastoral. These are the functions which we presently query in religion. The prophet, after the Churban (Destruction) of 586 B.C., could see then in life; I commend him to your attention.

The Second Churban took place in A.D. 70. At that time, the rabbis began to stress a new aspect of God, whose suffering, involved presence — the Shechinah — went into exile with the people. The dialogue between man and God continued — the personal God of the Bible and the questioning figures of the Abrahams and Jobs of rabbinic times. It has changed little in modern times. The modern Jewish thinkers who have expressed themselves most clearly on the subject of Auschwitz are those who have remained within the rabbinic tradition and who formulate the experience of the last two thousand years within the pattern of rabbinic logic: Emil Fackenheim and Leo Baeck.

Leo Baeck is already considered one of the classic Jewish teachers of modern times. He died in 1956, and his 100th anniversary will be observed next year. His importance to a theology of the Holocaust rests not only in his teachings but in his life. His last major work *This People Israel* was partly written in the concentration camp. Within the innermost circle of hell, he remained a teacher: and he taught the human dimension where God is encountered. What is man? And where is God? Man is defined in the interrelationship with fellow-man, with the *Mitmensch*; and God is encountered at that point.

Different traditions within contemporary religion use the concept of the *Mitmensch*. Baeck drew its modern formulation out of the teachings of Hermann Cohen, the founder of the new-Kantian Marburg school who was also the great teacher of Martin Buber and Franz Rosenzweig. The outer structure of Baeck's teachings was thus related to the language of Kant and his successors. In some ways, this has proved a barrier to his thoughts — we all know colleagues who empty their shelves every five years in order to remain fully contemporary! Kant! (Dare I even mention Hegel's influence on Fackenheim?) Our inheritance from Leo Baeck does

contain a stress upon duty and an ethical rigorism — but this is
derived from the rabbis of the first century and not from German
idealism. Out of the concentration camp, there came a teaching
concerning man whose inner tensions bring him to the knowledge of
God. Man encounters the mystery — and it brings him to the ethical
commandment. Man acts in an ethical manner — and finds himself
before the mystery. The near and the far God are part of the
polarities of existence. It was Buber and not Baeck who tried to
explain some aspects of the Holocaust by stressing the far God, the
God who has hidden His face for a moment. But when Martin Buber
asked himself, "Can one still call to God after Auschwitz" he shared
Baeck's thought by answering in a positive manner:

> Do we stand overcome before the hidden face of God . . . ?
> No, rather even now we contend, we too, with God, even
> with Him . . . We await his voice, whether it come out of the
> storm or out of a stillness . . . we shall recognize again our
> cruel and merciful Lord.[5]

God is far and will be near. He is near, and He will be distant. But in
the darkness, and after the darkness, He can be found within the
area of human interrelationships, in the I-and-Thou encounter, in
the actualities of social existence.

Heinrich Ott notes that God is found within *Mitmenschlichkeit*:

> It is in this sphere that the question of God must be
> articulated and worked out for theology. It is here that the
> concept "God" must be explained and defended. It is here
> that one thing must be shown: within the human stance,
> within the interrelationship between men, i.e.: in the
> *Mitmenschlichkeit* there is a noticeable, understandable
> and meaningful, an expressable difference when God is
> accounted to be a reality. That which is named "God" must
> here make its appearance. And it is here that we must be
> responsible for God to man.[6]

Theology too often makes a concordat with philosophy. A
common language is discovered, and one can then discuss God as a
Process, or a limited God (Hans Jonas' Ingersoll Lecture on
Immortality always almost convinces me). But Leo Baeck teaches
the God of the rabbis: "God is the place of the world, but the world
is not His place"; that is the distant God. But God is also the near
God, the personal God. The constant experience in the realm of
human interrelationship is a testimony which cannot be ignored.

Nor would I have you ignore the Jew who has walked through the
darkness and still reaches out towards his fellow man in love and
hope. As Emil Fackenheim has noted, he has learned a special lesson
at Auschwitz: his right to survive. It is not a new statement: Hobbes,
Spinoza, and Freud have all stressed the universal and ineradicable

tendency of human beings to preserve themselves, to think of themselves first and foremost.[7] But there is a different sound in Fackenheim's statement:

> Jews are forbidden to hand Hitler posthumous victories. They are commanded to survive as Jews, lest the Jewish people perish . . . Jewish life is more sacred than Jewish death . . . The Voice of Auschwitz commands the religious Jew after Auschwitz to continue to wrestle with his God in however revolutionary ways; and it forbids the secularist Jew (who has already, and on other grounds, lost Him) to use Auschwitz as an additional weapon wherewith to deny Him . . . The Voice of Auschwitz commands Jews not to go mad. It commands them to accept their singled-out condition, face up to its contradictions and endure them . . . The Jew after Auschwitz is a witness to endurance . . . "*mir zeinen do:*" we are here, exist, survive, endure, witnesses to God and man even if abandoned by God and man.[8]

"*Mir zeinen do*" — we are here. Let us close with a story told by Elie Wiesel. There was a madman who burst into a synagogue in Eastern Europe, in Nazi territory. The Jews were assembled for prayer in the synagogue; and he screamed at them: "Shhh; not so loud. God will hear you. Then he will know that there are still Jews left in Europe!" But on another occasion, years later, Elie had a different ending: "They continued to pray. Each day, the shammes commenced the service by striking upon the pulpit and exclaiming: *Gott, mir zeinen do!* When he was the last one, he still cried out: God, I am still here!"
And we are still here.
All of us.

NOTES

1   *Mensch*, 1971, p. 35.

2   Ulrich Simon, *A Theology of Auschwitz*, 1967.

3   I. Maybaum, *The Face of God After Auschwitz*, 1965, p. 48.

4   *Internationale Dialog Zeitschrift*, 1971, p. 13.

5   Martin Buber, *At the Turning*, 1952, p. 62.

6   Heinrich Ott, "Gott in Mitmenschlichkeit," *Wort und Wahrheit: Zeitschrift für Religion und Kultur* (Jan/Feb, 1971), 20.

7   Cf. R. S. Peters, *Reason, Morality and Religion*, The Swarthmore Lecture, 1972.

8   Emil Fackenheim, *God's Presence in History*, 1970.

THE AMERICAN NATIONAL FAITH:

HUMANE, YET ALL TOO HUMAN

Sydney E. Ahlstrom

All nations are exceptional. Germany, France, and England each in its way celebrates the uniqueness of its history, yet surely none of these can challenge the uniqueness of Ethiopia or Cambodia. Americans, however, have steadily proclaimed — or at the very least have been accused of claiming — that the United States of America was especially exceptional. And even Europeans contributed to this legend by ascribing very grand purposes to their early colonial ventures. So it shall be my purpose here to pursue this theme of American exceptionality and, above all, to trace the development of those conceptions of destiny which European founders projected and which the Americans wholeheartedly appropriated, and in terms of which they have continued to understand their mission as a nation. There is probably no better road to an appreciation of the inner spirit, the formal church life, or the external behavior of the country.[1]

This theme was announced in 1609 by William Symonds, the first minister chosen by the Virginia Company to address the stockholders of the first permanent British colony in the New World. Jamestown was then not two years old and in a very precarious condition, but this did not prevent the preacher (who was a noted commentator on the New Testament Apocalypse) from boldly taking God's promise to Abram as his text:

"Now the Lord had said unto Abram, Get thee out of thy Countree and from thy kindred, and from thy father's house, unto the land that I will shew thee. And I will make of thee a great nation, and will blesse thee, and make thy name great, and thou shalt be a blessing. I will blesse them also that blesse thee, and curse him that curse thee, and in thee shall all families of earth be blessed" (Gen. 12:1-3).

Virginia, however, did not at first bear out these hopes. The earliest settlers sought wealth and mostly died; and those who prospered in later years depended on the labor of black slaves who had been dragged out of Africa. Indeed, by one of America's most ironic conjunctions, the single year 1619 gained remembrance not only for the meeting of the first elective legislative assembly in the New World, but also for the introduction of tobacco culture and the first importation of Negro labor.

So it was not Virginia which became the great symbol of American origins, but rather the little band of Pilgrims who made their famous Compact in 1620 and then landed on New England's "stern and rockbound coast." It was this expressly Puritan commonwealth that America took to its heart and celebrated on successive Thanksgiving Days. And it is the Puritan sense of purpose which provides the foundations for the prevailing view of American nationhood. For this reason there has always been a vital religious dimension to the American's understanding of his country's nature and mission. The country's "civil religion" and its "patriotic piety," moreover, have for the same reason always stood in close reciprocal relations to the traditional religion of the churches. A kind of reverence and sense of moral commitment entered into the understanding of national loyalty. And in the 20th century these developments have come to be recognized as essential ingredients of modern nationalism.

A few years ago one of this country's wisest historians, the late David M. Potter, in an essay on "The Historian's Use of Nationalism and Vice Versa," posited "the rise of nationalism" as the "major political development of modern times." He also made clear that he was not using the term only in its demographic and juridical sense by insisting that, in the secular world of the 20th century, nationalism was one of the faiths "which have replaced the religions of an earlier age."[2] Events in Ulster and the Indian sub-continent, not to mention the United States, would suggest that "the religions of an earlier age" retain enormous potency even today, but few would deny the insistence of C. J. H. Hayes that nationalism is a religion. Beyond these general assertions, moreover, one may note that the religious dimensions of nationalism have not only been unusually strong in the United States, but that in this "nation with the soul of a church" (to use G. K. Chesterton's phrase) the interrelationships of patriotic piety and institutionalized "positive" religion have been so close that they are together intrinsic to the development of American culture and politics. Because of the pioneering role of this country during the age of democratic revolutions, moreover, this "first new nation" has the dubious distinction of being an important factor in the rise of Western nationalism.

Given the role that millennial ideas will play in this account of the American tradition, it is perhaps appropriate to take an organizing concept from the apocalyptic literature that has provided so many themes and images. We have heard of the seven-headed beast that rose from the sea, of the seven trumpets, of the seven seals, and of the seven angels who pour the seven vials of wrath: and now despite the abhorrence of America's evangelical leaders for the theater and the stage, I shall speak of the seven *acts* in the drama of the American's developing national faith. Support for this device comes from one of the most thoughtful of the country's founding fathers, Dr. Benjamin Rush of Philadelphia. "The American war is over," he said in 1787, "but this is far from being the case with the American revolution. On the contrary nothing but the first act of the great drama is closed."[3] The American faith, like the social order itself, changes through time. In the historical drama here depicted, however, the separate acts tend to interpenetrate each other: one begins before its predecessor ends. Thus John Adams saw the American Revolution beginning long before 1776 and Benjamin Rush saw it continuing long after 1787. Indeed none of the acts really terminates, for all of them persist to some degree in the present day. For this reason we are unable to say if the ending is happy or tragic. History has no future.

It is well to begin where the authors of the Declaration of Independence bade all Americans to begin, with Old Israel. When they were asked to design a great seal for the new nation, both John Adams and Jefferson proposed that the national seal depict "the cloud by day and the pillar by night" which led the children of Israel in the wilderness, while Franklin proposed the depiction of the Red Sea being divided as Moses lifted his hand. Thomas Jefferson in his Second Inaugural (1805) spoke of "that Being in whose hands we are, who led our forefathers, as Israel of old, from their native land and planted them in a country flowing with all the necessaries and comforts of life, who has covered our infancy with His providence and our riper years with His wisdom and power." The experience of Israel provides the chief inspiration for America's national faith and its model of dedicated nationhood. And over and over again through the years Americans would be applying to this broad land the words spoken to Moses out of the burning bush in Horeb: " . . . Put off thy shoes from off thy feet, for the place whereon thou standest is holy ground" (Exod. 3:1-5).

In the Hebrew Scriptures as nowhere else lies the paradigm of Western (and perhaps in a later day even Eastern) conceptions of a holy people, a holy land, and a holy destiny, just as they convey to the entire biblical tradition (including the Christian and Islamic) a single linear conception of history, with the Creation at one end and the messianic Kingdom at the other. It is only with the age of

Renaissance and Reformation, however, that Western civilization experiences the rise of national self-consciousness in something like its modern form, and this is particularly true of England after the papal excommunication of Queen Elizabeth in 1570, and the concomitant rise in that realm of a prophetic movement for the root and branch purification of English church life. The gradual intensification of these efforts led in turn to the Puritan Revolution and the Cromwellian commonwealth (1640-60), and then after the flight of James II in 1688, the "Glorious Revolution." Well before this, however, the forefathers to whom Jefferson referred had become disillusioned about the potentialities for establishing the Puritan counter-culture in England and had been moving to the New World. This great swarming of the Puritans began just about a decade after the Mayflower Compact with the arrival in Boston of the great expedition of 1630 which was led by Governor John Winthrop. Even while aboard the *Arbella*, Winthrop made clear what this new commonwealth was to be, and his words have become almost as familiar to American students as the great utterances of the Revolutionary period:

Thus stands the cause between God and us: we are entered into covenant with Him for this work; we have taken out a commission, the Lord hath given us leave to draw our own articles . . . So shall we keep the unity of the spirit in the bond of peace, the Lord will be our God and delight to dwell among us, as His own people, and will command a blessing upon us in all our ways, so that we shall see much more of His wisdom, power, goodness and truth than formerly we have been acquainted with. We shall find that the God of Israel is among us, when ten of us shall be able to resist a thousand of our enemies, when He shall make us a praise and glory, that men shall say of succeeding plantations: "The Lord make it like that of New England." For we must consider that we shall be as a city upon a hill, the eyes of all people are upon us. So that if we shall deal falsely with our God in this work we have undertaken, and so cause Him to withdraw His present help from us, we shall be made a story and a by-word through the world . . .[4]

Before the decade was out, this and two other Holy Commonwealths would have joined Plymouth colony in New England, and in each of them representative assemblies elected through the widest franchise in the world were ordering civil and ecclesiastical affairs according to their understanding of God's Word and the rights of Englishmen. In 1639 in Connecticut they drew up what has with some justice been called the first written constitution.

In addition, various groups of Puritan radicals whose views proved incompatible with those of Winthrop and Bradford had erected still another Puritan commonwealth in Rhode Island under the leadership of Roger Williams. In this little republic the implications of Puritan views on conscience, the Church, and "soul liberty" were legally implemented. The Baptists, who later became the country's most numerous bearers of the Puritan spirit, also made Rhode Island their earliest center of influence. Later in the century came the Holy Experiment of William Penn, who represented the Quaker left wing of the Puritan impulse. In Pennsylvania more than any other colony did the idea of America as an asylum for the oppressed of all creeds and nations become an active principle, with the result that the Keystone State became the great anticipatory laboratory of American pluralism. Here, too, Penn found opportunity to implement his unusual conviction that government could and should transcend its original mandate "to terrify evil doers." He believed it was "as capable of kindness, goodness, and charity as a more private society."

Due in part to these and other experiments in Puritan statecraft, several extremely important attitudes and convictions became very widespread — even in those colonies which were originally founded with very different intentions or with only mercenary ends in mind. Undoubtedly primary among these was the idea of a covenanted community, solemnly dedicated to carry out the Lord's purposes and to make all institutions and all the laws of men subordinate to the will of a just God. Closely allied with this covenant obligation was the belief (firmly rooted even among latter-day rationalists such as Adams, Jefferson, and the historian George Bancroft) that the Lord would favor a community and its posterity if it remained true to this sacred trust. Hardly less fundamental was the corollary that even those of little faith rarely doubted: that sinful man is always tempted by this-worldly gain and in danger of falling into corruption, and therefore that churches of God were essential to the public welfare and that they should be shown a certain solicitude or deference even when church and state were separate.

The extensions of the Puritan logic advanced by Baptists and Quakers, as well as the more conservative types of church reform framed by Presbyterians and evangelical Anglicans, were by no means greeted with favor in Massachusetts and Connecticut; yet even the radical doctrine of church-state separation did win increasing approval as the pluralism of colonial society became more marked and as the advantages of voluntaryism were discovered by church leaders. In due course, therefore, the principles of religious freedom became part of the colonial ideological heritage, though never in their anti-clerical form. This large consolidation of outlook, moreover, rested on three other more general factors, to which brief allusion must be made here.

First are the revolutionary innovations in evangelical piety which Anglo-American Puritanism introduced into the thought and church-order of Christendom — above all, its unprecedented emphasis on the contrite searching of the heart and the experience of regeneration. Puritanism, in other words, must be understood as a revival movement; and nothing revealed its consequences for America so well as the community-wide revivals that began to appear in the late days of the 17th century and then with more force in the "great and general revival" which swept through the colonies in the 18th century. It is in this tumultuous Awakening that evangelical Protestantism developed revival preaching as the major mode of church extension and at the same time discovered itself to be a culture-shaping power of *national* significance. The revivals, indeed, were a major means for breaking down intercolonial barriers and laying bare an *American* self-consciousness.

A second factor is the apocalyptic emphasis that convinced devoted Puritans that they must found and maintain a godly commonwealth that would be acceptable to the Lord in the fast-approaching Last Days. This eschatological concern, however, also underwent a vital transformation during the Great Awakening — for then it was that a new and far more exciting interpretation of the millennium began to gain acceptance — with the revival's greatest theologian, Jonathan Edwards, playing a major role. In this new departure the New Testament Apocalypse was given a "post-millennial" interpretation. The Kingdom of God was being realized in history — and what was most exciting of all, men became convinced (in Edwards' words) "that the latter day glory is to begin in America." Now more than ever before it could be believed that America would be a "city upon a hill and a beacon to the world." One can wonder, indeed, if any idea has worked with greater animating power in American history than this millennial sense of purpose. It took the inspirational content of the idea of progress as it had been formulated in the Enlightenment and clothed it in the garments of evangelical eschatology.

The third great force accentuated by the Puritan impulse has to do with those practical effects of piety: the dynamic new sense of vocation and individual responsibility which Max Weber and his many critics and defenders have done so much to illuminate. Perhaps nothing did more to distinguish the character of American colonial life than the attitudes and behavioral norms that issue from, or are associated with, the Puritan Ethic. Long before the War for Independence, moreover, the steady effect of this moral stance was alienating Americans from the corruption, profligacy, indolence, arbitrariness, and inequities of Baroque-Rococo civilization. Faithfulness to one's calling in each order of Creation (family, state, market-place, school, and church) was one's primary mode of serving one's neighbor and the ground for public esteem. Its effect was to heighten a person's sense of responsibility, industriousness, and self-respect, but it also gave a broad egalitarian tone to the social order. John Cotton, who had left behind a prestigious ministry at St. Botolphs in old Boston to become the minister of the First Church in Boston, Massachusetts, clarified this new "American" scale of values in a polite letter written to a "gentleman" who had inquired about a possible move to the New World:

Thus standeth our case: . . . Where God Blesseth any branch of any noble or generous family with a spirit and gifts fit for government, it would be a taking of God's name in vain to put such talent under a bushel, and a sin against the honour of magistracy to neglect such people in our public elections. But if God should not delight to furnish some of their posterity with gifts fit for magistracy, we should expose them rather to reproach and prejudice, and the commonwealth with them, than exalt them to honour, if we should call them forth, when God doth not, to public authority.[5]

With seemingly unlimited land and natural resources at their disposal, Americans carried out the economic implications of the social revolution which the English civil war had effected. Long before Adam Smith had added to the significance of the year 1776 with his systematic statement of *laissez faire* principles, Americans believed that in a free society the Unseen Hand would regulate economic affairs to the greatest benefit of all. Few ideas have had a longer and stronger life in America than this.

Thus it was that a new kind of society came into existence in America — one that was Western, yet not European. Moreover, this society was imbued with an ideology that Bernard Bailyn, after extensive researches, found to have reached virtually its full revolutionary character already in the 1730s. It gained dramatic statement in 1749 when Jonathan Mayhew observed the centennial of the execution of King Charles I with his celebrated sermon on *Unlimited Submission*: "they that did NOT resist (one unreasonable, ambitious and cruel man) . . . would receive to themselves damnation." Wesley Frank Craven also states that "it would be difficult to find anything fundamental that has been added to the legend of the founding fathers since Adams wrote his 'Dissertation on the Cannon and the Feudal Law,' in 1765."[6] As this same John Adams would later insist, the real American Revolution — the change in human attitudes and affections — was accomplished long before it was confirmed by the march of military and political events.

II

The Puritan Revolution, carried out impermanently in England but permanently in America, was a decisive break with the old order. Yet its full implications became fully manifest only in the American Revolution — which became overt in the Stamp Act crisis of 1765 and reached its nationalistic completion only with General Jackson's military victory at New Orleans in 1815, when James Madison (the "father of the Constitution") was president. It was during this period that the American faith was stamped with its essential form. After two wars with England, a "Quasi-War" with France, and five presidential elections, the Federal Union had become the world's climactic embodiment of the bourgeois revolution, while the baton of revolution in France was being handed from the Emperor Napoleon I to the restored Bourbon monarch, Louis XVIII.

In the Declaration of Independence and the Constitution, the democratic implications of Puritanism as restated in the public and rational categories of the Enlightenment received classic form. America's second set of founding fathers, moreover, had inwardly appropriated the conviction of their forefathers that God favored these undertakings, and that a new order of the ages had come into being: "E PLURIBUS UNUM . . . MDCCLXXVI . . . ANNUIT COEPTIS . . . NOVUS ORDO SECLORUM" (see reverse, Great Seal of the U. S. A., on a dollar bill). After 1803 the sheer geographical immensity of the nation added other signs of divine favor and inspired hopes of even greater glory. In 1811 John Quincy Adams had dreamed of one nation, speaking one language, stretching to the Pacific; and in 1819 it was his privilege to negotiate the treaty which not only added Florida to the Union, but defined a boundary that did span the continent.

Yet there can be no question but what the climax of Act II consists of those fifteen exciting years between the First Continental Congress (1774) and the inauguration of President Washington (1789). During these years a slowly forming democratic tradition was transformed into a full-scale sovereign republic — the world's first, and in 1972 one can still say, the world's oldest. In 1776 this nascent nation was provided with a statement of principles and in 1787 with a federal constitution by a group of men, mostly very young, who embodied the excellences of the Enlightenment to a most remarkable degree. Between these events lay the trying years of war, when an army of military amateurs (with decisive aid from Louis XV of France) taught Great Britain what the United States is now painfully learning in Vietnam.

And what came out of this long experience of national parturition was a body of egalitarian and libertarian principle, an heroic myth, and a new kind of civil theology in which the Union was understood as a transcendent reality, a proper object of reverence and loyalty, an enduring, possibly eternal, source of moral inspiration, and surely something that was far greater than the individuals or the states of which it was composed. Its makers stood in awe of their handiwork and often ascribed its real authorship to a benevolent Deity. And even such strict Calvinists among them as Roger Sherman or John Witherspoon regarded these convictions as neither wayward nor idolatrous.

III

During the early decades of the 19th century the growth of the American republic and the optimistic patriotism of its people were at once a wonder and an enigma of the world. And part of the marvel was that in the midst of a great resurgence of evangelical Protestantism there flourished an ideal of nationhood that had been formulated in the courts of rationalism, infidelity, and freemasonry by men who were often castigated as participants in a worldwide anti-Christian conspiracy. The working out of a remarkable ideological compromise, therefore, is the central action of the third act in the long-term American revolution.

The dominant phenomenon is the Second Great Awakening itself. Political upheaval and military disruption had made the last half of the 18th century a time of religious depression in America; yet, by a remarkable irony, the tide had turned during Jefferson's first administration with the unexpected appearance of revivals in every part of the country. In the west there were tumultuous camp-meetings and a veritable explosion of church membership. In the older states, both north and south, there was more decorum — but yet a compensatory rise of well organized interdenominational campaigns in which newly chartered voluntary associations advanced the causes of foreign and domestic missions, Sabbath-keeping, Bible and tract distribution, Sunday schools, seminaries, temperance, moral reform, and a wide gamut of humanitarian causes — all of which were directed to the larger aim of giving the world a model of a Protestant Republic. Lyman Beecher and others went so far as to see no other parallel to this ideal than the "republic of Moses." In seeking to attain this objective the "evangelical united front" became so powerful a force in American ante-bellum culture that the term "quasi-establishment" is warranted. And as usual, establishment (even if extra-legal) brought oppression to many minorities. Roman Catholics who were immigrating in vast numbers became the object of an especially ugly "crusade"; but several other deviant groups (such as the Mormons, infidels, and freemasons) were also treated as subversive.

Yet as one considers the popular and sermonic outpourings occasioned by the death of Washington in 1799, the triumphal return of Lafayette in 1824-25, and the simultaneous deaths of Adams and Jefferson on the 50th Fourth of July (none of whom were evangelical Protestants), it becomes apparent that an extremely important reconciliation had been accomplished. This joining of traditions, however, injected a dialectical element into the American faith at two distinct levels — both of which have been too little appreciated, and neither of which has been squarely faced or fully resolved.

At one level was the contradiction between the universal claims of self-evident principle and the particularistic spirit of nationalism. The Declaration of Independence was addressed to "a candid world," and the "secular mysticism" with which it invested the ideals of liberty, equality, and felicity became an inspiration to oppressed peoples everywhere, and continued to do so for over a century. The Constitution added concrete governmental proposals which gave added force to these waves of idealism. Yet American patriotism compromised this cosmopolitan impulse in ways that accorded with its Puritan heritage — by understanding itself not simply as a sovereign state with a loyal citizenry, but rather as God's chosen People with a saving mission in the world. Americans have thus wavered and disagreed about their loyalty: was it directed to a universal republican model always seeking to perfect itself or to an Elect Nation with a providential purpose.

Related to the aforementioned problem, but proceeding at a deeper level, was another long dialogue between Puritan, or more generally Christian, theology and the rationalist tradition. This conflict was given a new and more urgent turn by Isaac Newton and John Locke. Both Cotton Mather and Jonathan Edwards were profoundly concerned with the resultant tension. The Great Awakening in fact had riven the old standing order of New England over this issue; and by 1815 the Unitarian establishment of Boston and the planter aristocracy of Virginia had taken their stand with the Enlightenment in opposition to the rising tide of revivalistic evangelicalism. Yet there had also been efforts at rapprochement. The Founders of '76, for example, invoked the example of Israel and made the national seal itself a proclamation that America was a creature of divine providence.

More spectacular, however, was the process by which optimistic doctrines of natural rights and human progress were woven into "orthodox" Protestant theologies. This came about by means of two gradual modifications of Reformed doctrine. The first of these was achieved by a subtle but steady modification of strict predestinarianism, especially with regard for man's freedom and his natural moral powers. Corresponding to this, and equally appealing to an expansive young democracy, was a new and more "progressive" departure in eschatology. The origins of this impulse can be traced at least to the Eternal Gospel of Joachim of Flora (1145-1202) and his announcement of a new age of Holy Spirit. But it was the Reformation which naturally produced many exegetes who found divine support for Protestant revolt in the biblical view of history. In England especially, and often among Conformists, an historical reading of the apocalyptic texts replaced Augustine's allegorical rendering as well as the notions of an imminent Second Advent favored by many early Puritans. Even in specific victories of English armies during the great imperial wars of the 18th century, Jonathan Edwards had found evidence that the Antichrist was being subdued; and in the Great Awakening he saw clear signs that the Kingdom of God might first be experienced in America. After the furor of Independence Edwards' cautious exegesis yielded to more confident assertions; and in the many writings of his grandson, Timothy Dwight, this form of "American millennialism," coupled with enlarged views of human moral ability, became almost an article of belief. Even in 1777, when the military issue was still very much in doubt, Dwight provided his country with a national anthem in which nearly all of the standard post-millennial interpretations appear.

> Columbia, Columbia, to glory arise,
> The queen of the world, and child of the skies:
> Thy reign is the last, and the noblest of time,
> Most fruitful thy soil, most inviting thy clime;
> Let the crimes of the east n'er encrimson thy name
> Be freedom, and science, and virtue thy fame.
>
> As the day spring unbounded, thy splendour shall flow
> And earth's little kingdoms before thee shall bow;
> While the ensigns of union, in triumph unfurl'd
> Hush the tumult of war, and give peace to the world.

When Dwight became president of Yale in 1795, he placed these millennial notions in the context of a full theological system in which Westminster doctrines of predestination were modified and a rationale for revivalism was provided. He also led the attack on infidelity and worked to extend the evangelical united front. He thus almost personifies the ways in which a fervent patriotic tradition became an integral part of 19th-century Protestant evangelicalism. It was his admiring protegé Lyman Beecher, however, who became the chief propagandist for this form of "New School" piety as well as its linkage to the nation's providential role in world history. In antebellum America, moreover, evangelical enthusiasm drew support from parallel developments in the socio-political realm — for this was also the heyday of "Jacksonian democracy" and "the age of the common man." The churches in turn did much to unleash the individualistic self-assurance that led to this democratization of society.

In this ethos of optimism patriotic enthusiasm reached such heights that even Roman Catholics and Jews found it contagious, despite condescension and overt persecution. Thus Isaac Mayer Wise, whose rabbinic education had begun in the Orthodox Judaic context of central Europe, exchanged the messianic hope of his forefathers for that of the United States. Washington, D. C., not Jerusalem, became his holy city. Nor was he isolated from other Jews by this *volte face*, for he became by far the most influential spokesman for the American Jewish community. He also became the chief architect of the famous Pittsburgh platform published by the Reform rabbis in 1885. "We deem it our duty," concluded this statement, "to participate in the great task of modern times, to solve on the basis of justice and righteousness the problems presented by the contrasts and evils of the present organization of society."

And Roman Catholics, even from the days when John Carroll became the first American bishop, entertained a similar vision. Increasingly convinced of the benefits to their church of religious freedom and church-state separation, they developed a strong tradition of "Americanism." In this spirit Isaac Hecker, a convert, founded the congregation of Paulists to advance an American apostolate. And just a year before the Pittsburgh declaration just quoted, Archbishop John Ireland of St. Paul, Minnesota, the leader of the Americanist movement in the hierarchy, addressed the Third Plenary Council of the American church on the subject. Although he had felt the intolerance and contumely that Catholics still had to face, America, for him too, was a city upon a hill.

There is no conflict between the Catholic Church and America. I could not utter one syllable that would belie however remotely, either the Church or the Republic, and when I assert, as I now solemnly do, that the principles of the Church are in thorough harmony with the interests of the Republic, I know in the depths of my soul that I speak the truth . . .

Republic of America, receive from me the tribute of my love and loyalty . . . *Esto perpetua.* Thou bearest in thy hands the hopes of the human race, thy mission from God is to show to nations that men are capable of the highest civil and political liberty . . . Believe me, no hearts love thee more ardently than Catholic hearts, . . . and no hands will be lifted up stronger and more willing to defend, in war and peace, thy laws and thy institutions than Catholic hands. *Esto perpetua.*[7]

IV

These forward glances into the Gilded Age show how ante-bellum forms of patriotic faith not only persisted but became more inclusive. But such facts can not obscure the cruciality of the *Volkskrieg* that was visited upon this proud and confident nation during the intervening years. The fourth act in the history of the country's self-knowledge, with slavery and expiation as its sombre theme, is probably the most important of all. It was in the Civil War that the terrible anomaly of institutionalized chattel bondage in the "land of the free" exacted its awful price. Yet it also brought forth on this continent a new republic dedicated not to the preservation of slavery but to liberty and equality.

The origins of this tragedy, of course, were anything but recent. In fact the underlying racism may be as old as mankind. As for Christendom's reversal of its historic opposition to slavery, it goes back to Europe's almost simultaneous discovery of both black Africa and the New World. Without thought of either the Great Commandment or the Great Commission the major imperial powers — Spain and Portugal first, but fiercely rivalled by Britain, France and Holland — made slavery an instrument of exploitation. In America there were occasional early attacks on the institution and countless admonitions to evangelize the blacks, but neither counsel was much heeded. Slavery simply became the chief shaping influence in the emerging southern culture. Henry Melchior Muhlenberg, who viewed the horrors of slavery on his arrival in Charleston in 1842, was one of the first to look into the future and predict that this monstrous business would "entail a severe judgement" on the nation. About this time, however, the Great Awakening did arouse a new concern for the souls of the slaves; and during the era of the Revolution there was understandably an increase of moral discomfort over the institution itself. In fact, slavery was barred from the Northwest Territory and put on the way to extinction in the northern states. But the anti-slavery impulse during succeeding decades was weak and innocuous.

Then almost suddenly in the 1830s came a revival of protest that coincided with the surge of revivalism inspired by Charles G. Finney and which did not subside until Emancipation was proclaimed and the Constitution amended. Inexorably, with rising intensity of thought and action, the ordeal of the Union unfolded. On January 1, 1831, William Lloyd Garrison published the first issue of the *Liberator* while the nullification controversy between President Jackson and the state of South Carolina moved toward its critical stage. On December 20, 1860, not long after Abraham Lincoln's election victory, a South Carolina convention voted unanimously for secession from the Union, and in February Jefferson Davis became president of the Confederate States of America. On April 12, 1861, the shore batteries in Charleston harbor opened fire on Fort Sumter and war came. On April 7, 1865, General Lee surrendered his Army at Appomattox Courthouse, Virginia. A few days later, on Good Friday, Lincoln was assassinated, whereupon the Congress moved ahead with a program for Radical Reconstruction. On April 10, 1877, in partial fulfillment of the bargain by which he had become president, Rutherford B. Hayes signalized the end of Reconstruction by ordering the removal of Federal troops from South Carolina and soon after from other states, whereupon the ex-slaves were subjected to almost a century of extra-legal white supremacy. To telescope thus the narrative of the nation's central experience may seem both blasphemous and absurd. But it is not likely that a few additional paragraphs could do much more to convey the intensity of thought and feeling that went into those forty-six years of conflict, carnage, and inner turmoil. As for the intense convictions, nowhere do they gain more concentrated expression than in the lines that came to Julia Ward Howe one night shortly before the army encamped around the nation's capital went into its first action. Few national hymns have equaled the concentrated force of its biblical imagery.

Mine eyes have seen the glory of the coming of the Lord:
He is trampling out the vintage where the grapes of wrath are stored;
He hath loosed the fateful lightning of his terrible swift sword:
His truth is marching on.

I have seen Him in the watch-fires of a hundred circling camps;
They have builded Him an altar in the evening dews and damps;
I can read His righteous sentence by the dim and flaring lamps:
His day is marching on.

I have read a fiery gospel writ in burnished rows of steel:
As ye deal with me contemners, so with you my grace shall deal;
Let the Hero, born of woman, crush the serpent with his heel:
Since God is marching on.

He has sounded forth the trumpet that shall never call retreat;
He is sifting out the hearts of men before his judgment seat:
Oh, be swift, my soul, to answer him! be jubilant, my feet!
Our God is marching on.

In the beauty of the lilies Christ was born across the sea,
With a glory in his bosom that transfigures you and me:
As he died to make men holy, let us die to make men free,
While God is marching on.

One must ask, however, what this double holy war — or rather this total ordeal — meant for the faith of the nation as a whole. Most important perhaps is the simple fact that because of the war's outcome the Union was preserved. Just as it had always been one in its complicity in slavery, so now the nation would remain one in its halting efforts to overcome human limitations and bring the blessings of life, liberty, and the pursuit of happiness equally to *all* Americans. The commitment was made; and in establishing the indivisibility of the Union the war gave new grounds for Lincoln's hope that "the unfinished work" begun by those who died, would be done. And in Lincoln, who stands as the veritable founder of "the new nation" which emerged from the war's myriad sacrifices, the United States gained an incomparable source of idealistic inspiration. His words could temper the arrogance of the victors and assuage the defeated. Because Lincoln seemed to be so autochthonously American, and a man of both the South and the North, his thought and deeds and character lived on in the country's memory with peculiar force: he could make Americans less sure that they had "seen the glory of the coming of the Lord" and more committed to "the unfinished work." Lincoln is the great theologian of this "almost chosen people," but he became so only because he lived at the center of the nation's greatest agony and by his death symbolized the war's expiatory meaning.

V

In 1876 the United States entered the second century of its history with jubilant observances in every locality — and with the country's first great international exposition in Philadelphia. This was also the year of the disputed presidential election that would bring Hayes to the White House and deliver the Solid South to the Redeemers. Since these events mark the end of Reconstruction, the year also marks the advent of the Gilded Age — which derives its name from the novel (and play) written by Mark Twain and Charles Dudley Warner (1873-74) as a critique of the nation's unbridled acquisitiveness; though if human acquisitiveness were the mark of an age, it should probably be seen as beginning in Eden and ending on the battlefields of Armageddon. In actual fact, America's large-scale expansion in the economic sphere began in last pre-war decades, was much stimulated by the war, made sensational advances in the later 19th century, and probably should be seen as reaching its apogee just before the Crash of 1929. For present purposes in any event, Act Five shall be seen as the half-century heyday of *laissez faire* which, aside from obvious overlapping, stretched from the Compromise of 1877 to the Great Depression. Almost every segment of this long period has had a bad press, and to most Americans it is still an odoriferous time of corruption, exploitation, and bigotry. Even the revisionist emphasis on the positive achievements of the Robber Barons seems less convincing in our own time, when opposition to unchecked industrial growth and fears of environmental disaster loom large in popular thinking. Because this period is remembered for the rise of economic royalism, dollar diplomacy, militant Anglo-Saxonism, and outright military imperialism, people of conscience have always viewed it with disfavor. Even the reform efforts of "the best men" of the time seem to be primarily concerned with the maintenance of their own status in society. Ideologically speaking, the entire period was a time of degeneration and catastrophe, a time when the country's dominant economic attitude ranged from "The farmers be damned" of the railroad kings to President Coolidge's pronouncement that "America's business is business." It was a time when the Bloody Shirt replaced Lincoln's Second Inaugural; a time when the Supreme Court took the teeth out of the Civil Rights Act, diverted the 14th Amendment to the protection of business, and validated segregated public education; a time when the government prosecuted continuous Indian wars in the West, implemented plans for the dissolution of Indian culture, and delayed the statehood of non-Anglo-Saxon territories of the far South-West; a time when fears about immigration and the urban vote brought northern racial attitudes in line with the Ku Klux Klan, and when the old evangelical tradition lost its morale and turned to increasingly inglorious crusades; a time when the nation, including the churches, gave unrestrained support to the War of 1898 "for our little brown brethren for whom Christ also died" (President McKinley's words), and to the war of 1914-18 against the "Huns"; a time when "Manifest Destiny" was taken from its ante-bellum context as an agressive slogan for continental expansion and given a global meaning, and when the head of the Evangelical Alliance bade America to put on the mantle of Rome and Britannia and "Anglo-Saxonize mankind"; or when others, who were more attuned than Josiah Strong to millennial exegesis, saw the westward course of empire coming full circle: as American influence advanced in the Far East, it would return to the point of origin of the Caucasian race in the central steppes of Asia. It was a time, moreover, when the countervailing voices, despite their considerable numbers, were no match for the mediocrities who were in a position to influence popular attitudes.

The chief presidential exceptions to the prevailing temper of the times were Cleveland, Theodore Roosevelt, Taft, and Wilson, though even these had a very muted impact — except Roosevelt who spoke out for economic and military imperialism, celebrated the winning of the west, and objected to "hyphenated Americanism." Yet the Progressive interlude between 1898 and 1916 deserves a more favorable estimate. Labor legislation, conservationism, food and drug laws, "trust-busting," the democratization of political processes, and above all, the recognition of the problems and complexities of government in a large industrial nation, are signs of a genuinely broadened conception of the Union and a serious effort to realize the promise of American life in modern post-agrarian terms. The Progressives provided many guidelines for future reform that have almost never been regarded as anachronistic or oppressive.

Even harsh judgments of this long period as a whole would be irresponsible, if unaccompanied by some account of the extenuating circumstances — for these were times of extraordinarily difficult social and intellectual transition. A rapidly expanding nation — flooded by immigration and moving cityward in droves amid vast institutional changes — was making adjustments such as have rarely been expected of any people. Beneath the brashness and national arrogance, therefore, lay a desperate search for social order. And beneath this problem lay a profound spiritual crisis which stemmed from the collapse of the great evangelical consensus that had underlain the Protestant campaigns of the ante-bellum period. Thomas C. Cochrane wisely refers to this "loss of the historic certainties" as the age's "inner revolution." Among the efforts to allay the age's uneasiness and to face the questions raised by scientific advances, biblical criticism, and new philosophical trends, a rising group of liberal theologians was probably the most creative and influential. The Social Gospel movement, in turn, was the response made by many of these liberal church leaders to the urban and industrial problems. Yet nothing better reveals the emergence of an almost fatuous kind of self-confidence and optimism than the millennial vision with which Walter Rauschenbusch, the toughest and most celebrated of these social prophets, concluded his most influential book, *Christianity and the Social Crisis* (1907):

If the twentieth century could do for us in the control of social forces what the nineteenth did for us in the control of natural forces, our grandchildren would live in a society that would be justified in regarding our present social life as semi-barbarous. Since the Reformation began to free the mind and to direct the force of religion toward morality, there has been a perceptible increase of speed. Humanity is gaining in elasticity and capacity for change, and every gain in general intelligence, in organizing capacity, in physical and moral soundness, and especially in responsiveness to ideal motives, again increases the ability to advance without disastrous reactions. The swiftness of evolution in our own country

117

proves the immense latent perfectibility in human nature.

Last May a miracle happened. At the beginning of the week the fruit trees bore brown and greenish buds. At the end of the week they were robed in bridal garments of blossom. But for weeks and months the sap had been rising and distending the cells and maturing the tissues which were half ready in the fall before. The swift unfolding was the culmination of a long process. Perhaps these nineteen centuries of Christian influence have been a long preliminary stage of growth, and now the flower and fruit are almost here. If at this juncture we can rally sufficient religious faith and moral strength to snap the bonds of evil and turn the present unparalleled economic and intellectual resources of humanity to the harmonious development of a true social life, the generations yet unborn will mark this as that great day of the Lord for which the ages waited, and count us blessed for sharing in the apostolate that proclaimed it.

Glorious though this vision may be, it was precisely the kind of unrestrained thinking that led conservatives to despair for both the churches and the nation, especially since such extravagant heresy was accompanied by a widespread breakdown of traditional forms of piety and behavior. They, therefore, responded with a fundamentalist stand on biblical interpretation and an otherworldly eschatology in which a pre-millennial judgment was the most important event in the future of both America and the world. The central revivalistic tradition, meanwhile, with men like Dwight L. Moody and Billy Sunday as its most noted leaders, went ahead as though not much had changed. Yet the old evangelical accent on making the United States a world model of humanitarian concern yielded to a concentration on personal conversions, temperance reform, and missions, often with nativistic overtones and seldom with a concern for modern social and intellectual problems. During the 1920s, especially, fundamentalism, revivalism, and pre-millennialism began to become significant components of a new type of extreme political conservatism which drew much of its support from one of the country's least understood sub-cultures.

Despite social stress and nationalistic superficiality, however, the period from 1876 to 1932 was a time of artistic and intellectual triumph — not gilded but golden. In philosophy, scholarship, science, technology, architecture, poetry, fiction, music, and painting it was one of America's richly productive periods. Even in the area of radical social criticism and on the meaning and purpose of America some of the nation's finest writing and thinking was done. What was lacking was the kind of political leadership which could mediate this greatness and deepen the popular understanding of the country's civic faith. So we have the anomaly of a great cultural flowering time during which the public concern for the nation's nature and purpose is largely given over to outsized patriotic weeds.

VI

The sixth stage in the history of the American faith began resoundingly with the great economic crash of 1929, but it is defined for the most part by the international upheaval that followed in the wake of World War I: the aftermath of the Russian Revolution and the fascist response to the collapse of world economic order in the 1920s. At the period's center is World War II, and then after it comes the long Cold (and not so cold) War. One could argue as to when this period came to an end, but the assassination of President John F. Kennedy in November, 1963, perhaps serves best to signalize a fairly drastic shift of national sentiment and a growing disenchantment with traditional ideological formulations that, by 1966, had in any case become apparent to almost everyone.

For the United States World War I was an exhilarating experience, "over there," not a tragedy. In Europe its devastating effects were more directly felt and men spoke of the end of Western civilization as an organized and coherent reality. But among Americans during the Twenties only a relatively small group of intellectuals drew attention to signs of cultural crisis. For most other Americans it took the Crash and fifteen million unemployed to bring home the fact that all was not well at home and that the great crusade in Europe had by no means made the world safe for democracy. Yet the country did not panic or turn to extravagant departures from the national faith. Extremist political leaders did, of course, appear; but their followings were notably small. Most remarkable in fact was a widespread awakening of the people to the importance of the federal government. With Adam Smith's Unseen Hand performing so badly, rugged individualism lost much of its appeal. Widespread agricultural distress also brought the South to a deeper commitment to the Union. Group effort of all kinds became more meaningful and a sense of common involvement in a national disaster became widespread. Even individuals and groups that had long regarded the government with hostility or indifference now looked to it for leadership and succor. President Roosevelt, moreover, responded to this feeling of disorientation with a kind of decisiveness that inspired hope, and with a view of the state as a humane benefactor that reminds one of William Penn's famous claim. His "fireside chats," meanwhile, brought assurance and confidence into the nation's households.

Contrary to the frequently made observation that the New Deal was a pragmatic hodge-podge, Roosevelt was himself actively interested in the rejuvenation of America's liberal tradition. To this end he applied himself and encouraged others to a search for a "usable past." And one of his most notable efforts was to reach back over the decades to Lincoln and to a reaffirmation of *his* hope for a new birth of freedom and *his* plea for government "of the people, by the people, and for the people." For many reasons, therefore, one must agree with Heinz Eulau's assertion that the New Deal's impression on the American experience can in the long run "only be compared with the birth of the nation itself and the fratricidal blood-letting of the Civil War."[8]

Beyond the efforts of Roosevelt and his many friends and aides, the rise of totalitarianism abroad served these same ideological ends, with the result that scholars and publicists turned in great numbers to similar tasks — sometimes with an uncritical celebrationism that seemed almost cloying to a later generation, but equally often with strong revisionist aims, and with no intention of suppressing evidences of dissent and radical criticism in the American past. After 1936, moreover, the president himself provided genuinely new and important dimensions to the long neglected egalitarian theme — and not only by pronouncements such as that on the Four Freedoms, but by giving the New Deal a more clearly reformist direction.

In the strictly religious realm this period also experienced important changes. During the 1920s the mainstream denominations, which had founded the National Council of Churches in 1908 and supported World War I with such uncritical enthusiasm, continued their largely symbiotic relationship with the American social order — though their more conservative members participated heavily in various reactionary campaigns of the day against Jews, Catholics, and Negroes, as well as jazz, ballroom dancing, Sunday golf, and the teaching of evolution in the public schools. For almost all Protestants support for liquor-law enforcement was a major preoccupation — almost a surrogate for the social gospel.

After 1932, however, the Protestant churches began to receive much internal criticism for their complacent acceptance of the prevailing cultural values. The unduly optimistic views of liberals on man and history were also undermined by a new realistic movement in theology. These "Neo-Orthodox" critics were much influenced by postwar European theologians, but they also drew heavily upon the whole range of Western thinking from Augustine and the Reformers to Kierkegaard, Marx and Nietzsche, as well as from the older American traditions of prophetic religion. Very notable in this latter respect is the much higher evaluation and close study that was given during these years to the Puritans, Edwards, and the great writers of the American renaissance. With Paul Tillich and the two Niebuhrs (Reinhold and H. Richard) in very prominent positions of influence, they engaged (each in his way) in a broad critique of the churches' absorption in American culture and of the culture itself. Neo-Orthodoxy, in America especially, was also a revival of the social gospel, and its advocates and adherents brought strong support to the New Deal, though they tended toward more radical positions on social and economic issues than either Roosevelt or the Congress.

In matters of theology, Neo-Orthodox thinkers, despite their sobriquet, carried forward the scholarly interests of liberalism, though with far less confidence in man's natural religious consciousness and a strong emphasis on secular, as against sacral, values. The demythologizing interest, so prominent in Rudolf Bultmann, also had a strong place in their thinking — and in every case these tendencies were brought to bear on traditional forms of the American national faith. The spurious excesses of the Gilded Age were their easiest target, but notions of elect nationhood and manifest destiny were also criticized. In the long run it seems probable that their persistent emphasis on realism, irony, and pragmatism, as well as their exaggerated fear of idolatry, tended to weaken the force of American idealism. Yet their awareness of human finitude and selfishness, and their opposition to a *theologia glorie*, whether in churches or nations, did much to restrain American arrogance and intolerance. American loyalty naturally deepened after Pearl Harbor brought the United States into the war, but the Neo-Orthodox thinkers are at least partly accountable for the fact that the excesses of 1916-1918 were not duplicated.

Unlike World War I, which was followed by two decades of American isolationism, World War II yielded almost immediately to the polarized world of the Cold War. And the domestic scene as well soon became equally polarized. Irrational fears of communism attained their greatest destructive power during the years of Senator Joseph McCarthy's ascendancy (1950-54), though the fear of subversion and allegations of communistic influences became a dominant characteristic of almost two decades of American history. In this atmosphere the national faith suffered incalculable damage, as flag-waving and patrioteering became instruments for maintaining the status quo and silencing critics. Especially during the Eisenhower years (1953-61), moreover, extraordinary measures were taken, even by the president himself, to tighten the connections between loyalty and religion. Congress declared "In God we trust" to be the national motto, and added the phrase "under God" to the Pledge of Allegiance, perhaps not realizing that they thereby strengthened "higher law" doctrine which would place conscience above the laws of men, just as anti-slavery leaders had done before the Civil War. Formal religious affiliation itself (whether Protestant, Catholic, or Judaic) became a way of expressing one's support of "the American way of life." The wider revival of religion that featured these cold-war years no doubt gave additional strength to traditional aspects of the American sense of destiny, though the religious interest of this period was for the most part a break with tradition. In retrospect it can be seen as an anticipation of the more radical changes which lay ahead both in theology and ideology.

President John F. Kennedy, however, in his inaugural address and through subsequent efforts sought to revive the American faith by linking it with concrete objectives so that it would once again resonate with a concern for liberty, equality and social justice. And for a time the memory of his assassination made it possible for President Johnson to implement these hopes to a remarkable degree, though during these years it was the civil rights movement which provided the chief incentives. And in Martin Luther King this movement found a leader who for one remarkable decade (1956-66) gave goals to the national faith such as it had not had since anti-slavery days. By the time of his assassination in 1968, however, the national temper had undergone such a drastic transformation that one must deal with it as a distinct period in American history.

VII

The final stage in the development (or degeneration) of the American faith — the act in which we all are playing — began at the dawn of history. The present situation (its race consciousness, for example) is a product of the whole past. Moreover, we could not possibly know the significance of this or any decade without knowledge of the whole future as well. If St. John the Divine or Jonathan Edwards were bold enough to assign a special historical place to their own times, it was because they believed that Scripture had given them signs, from the Alpha to the Omega. And if the post-millenial tradition changed the spirit of this view (leaving matters of historical development more open-ended), it at least took the letter very seriously. Even Rauschenbusch's view of the kingdom made broad appeals to the older eschatalogical exegesis — though in fact his evolutionary adaptation of apocalyptic language reveals the mind of a modern historian. And so it is with the "acts" that I have delineated; they belong to a realm of discourse very different from the "vials" of the Apocalypse. They are heuristic approximations that become, alas, less susceptible to plausible explanation as they approach the present.

Yet granting all this, let me suggest that in the troubled years following the election and the assassination of our first Roman Catholic president, America began to experience a new post-Protestant, post-Puritan, and, indeed, a post-Christian state of affairs. In other words, a major ideological advance was made. Even the Supreme Court underlined this transition with its controversial ruling of 1963 against sectarian religious ceremonies in the public schools. In the realms of race relations, censorship standards, sexual relations, drug usage, marriage, divorce, abortion and birth-control legislation, women's rights, and many others, there could be seen a sharp rupture with traditions that were once supported by strict religious sanctions. The concepts of liberty and equality have also been substantially enlarged. More sociological in character, though similar in its effect, has been the near disappearance of the Melting Pot as a symbol of Americanization, and with it the declining power of the Protestant Establishment and the rising self-consciousness of many different minorities. Even the "vanishing" Indian has returned to goad the American conscience. And soon the WASPs will be forming an anti-defamation league!

The landing of men on the moon, massive use of automation, and the coming of age of the television generation betoken the immense degree to which applied science has produced a new popular *Weltanschauung*. Perhaps the most striking effect of the resultant change of world-view was the radical turn in theology which made news in the 1960s — and this was seen not only in the much reported "death-of-God," but in the marked downward trend in church affiliation and monetary support of religion, heavy losses of parish clergy through demissions and vocational transfers, and, among Roman Catholics, the decline in monastic vocations. One could also note the shift in aesthetic standards, ubiquitously in poster art, but more significantly in the growing dissatisfaction among clergy and laity alike with traditional forms of worship. In the most conservative communions a new generation of Jesus People was forcing many revisions of old attitudes toward worship, evangelism, personal appearance, morals, and life-styles. Most stirring of all was the awakening of counter-cultural moral concern among the youth of college age. Accompanying these changes was a rising concern for consumers' rights which challenged many time-honored methods of advertising, merchandizing, and manufacturing. Raising much more fundamental questions about the American economic system was a great environmental awakening, with both scientific and religious origins, in which, among other things, the claims of posterity of the country's beauty and bounty were acknowledged.

The dating of the various elements in this fermenting situation is next to impossible; but there is little doubt that an important revolution in American attitudinal structures had taken place, and that it had for the most part become manifest during the 1960s. The question as to why it should have happened just then is intrinsically unanswerable — especially since global consciousness and international parallels are part of the *explicandum*. In the United States, however, one may locate the proximate sources of catalysis in three interrelated phenomena: (1) the attainment of a critical stage in the fiscal, educational, social, and ecological predicament of most large cities; (2) the accompanying attainment of a critical stage (usually with an urban setting) in American race relations; and (3) most important by far, the escalation of the war in Southeast Asia and the continuance of that war regardless of its consequences for other domestic needs and despite the visible deterioration of the nation's moral cohesion, to a degree — and for a length of time — without parallel in American history.[9]

When one speaks of the American faith in 1972, therefore, it must be in a very muted and tentative way. In the form in which it commanded the respect and adherence of nearly all Americans, including many severe critics of the social order throughout the 19th century, and even as recently as 1945, or 1960, it simply no longer exists. According to opinion polls carefully taken in 1971, half of the adult population feared that the country was heading for a "breakdown." In that same year the "Average American," as statistically defined, believed — not that his country was a beacon to the world with the Kingdom of God just around the corner — but that the overall situation of his country was worse now than it was five years ago, and that it would be still worse after another five.[10] The traditional symbols of loyalty and national reverence are everywhere in a state of decay and disuse. Congress itself has transformed the great holy-days of the nation into long (or lost) weekends. The Pledge of Allegiance is widely used in the schools as a kind of discriminatory discipline. Patrioteering has become so marked a proclivity of conservatives, law-and-order people, and racists, that blacks in search of rooms for rent avoid districts where flags are fluttering at the doorsteps. The martial themes of "The Star Spangled Banner" have lost their allure, while the threat of pollution has made "America the Beautiful" only a sad reminder of past glories. "The Battle Hymn of the Republic" is often sung as a kind of crusader's chant — but certainly not with Julia Ward Howe's confidence that God, with the Federal Union as his instrument, *is* trampling out the vintage where the grapes of wrath are stored.

More concrete and more unfortunate than these signs of changing sentiment, rising fears, frustrated hopes, and withdrawn affection, is the fact that "domestic tranquility" and social justice have become opposing aims of different elements in the population.

The events of these years, however, cannot be viewed with neutral passivity, for they have made great and productive contributions to America's understanding of itself — both by things done and by things revealed. As in so many other times when powerful voices of dissent have been raised, genuine and enduring benefits to the country's ideological tradition have accrued.[11] It may be, therefore, that Little Rock, Selma, and Kent State will be remembered like Shiloh and Gettysburg — or Harper's Ferry — and for similar reasons.

We can agree, moreover, with Jean Francois Revell that the modern revolution must occur, in fact, only could occur, in America — and "without Jesus or Marx." Perhaps only a nation of immigrants on the make, with a richly endowed continent before them and no feudal heritage to hold them back, could chart so many paths and innovate so boldly. And there are benefits in this revelation, too, for oddly enough, this new country has become, in a sense, the Old World — scarred, ugly, and over-exploited, a living example of those forms of profligacy that only the Puritan ethic can inspire, and ironically a kind of negative example to the world. Perhaps the United States needs this knowledge.

Yet serious dangers remain. And they stem from the fact that a very young nation such as this, without ancient ties of blood and place, composed of people from many different racial, ethnic, and religious backgrounds, situated in widely varied status relationships, differing in their degree of assimilation — such a nation stands in especially great need of a common sense of purpose and of common commitments. This commitment, moreover, must be to those ideals which were and are literally constitutive of this "first new nation."

This constituting process has continued now for over three and a half centuries, if we go back no further than the earliest plantings. The foundations were laid in the colonial period, both with regard to a lively sense of divinely guided destiny and to the achievement of a free and democratic socio-economic order. During the 18th-century Enlightenment these results of the Puritan Revolution were reformulated and enlarged in the rational categories of natural law and self-evident principle — and then ratified by the American Revolutionary experience. Thereafter followed the great achievements of the early 19th century: the rapid occupation of the continent — "from sea to sea" — just as the old royal charters had said; the ideological amalgamation of the double Puritan-Enlightened legacies under the aegis of the evangelical united front;

and the belated dealing with slavery, which to that time had blighted and corrupted American civilization. The Brothers War of 1860-1865 became, therefore, not only a war of liberation for four million slaves but for the very principle of freedom itself. Then, after this ordeal of the Union had come to its incomplete resolution in 1877, there followed a troubled half-century of incredibly rapid growth during which the country assumed its modern form, but during which the expansionist concept of Manifest Destiny was given a more aggressive international interpretation while the purposes and full meaning of the Civil War were being obscured, denied, or forgotten. The next great phase in the development of the American faith began with the Great Depression and the New Deal but continued on through World War II and the "Cold War" which followed. These times, from Franklin D. Roosevelt to John F. Kennedy, were by no means given over to undeviating development of the grounds for American loyalty, above all because there was no escape from the worldwide polarization of ideologies; but they were nevertheless marked by a constant enlargement of the function of the government in the implementation of equality. Despite seasons of witch-hunting, moreover, it was also a time when personal liberty and civil rights gained far more cognizance as American principles. One may even say that the potentiality of the state-as-benefactor emerged in theory, if not always in practice.

It may thus be truly said that the American Union has, "by good fortune" (to use a neutral expression) come into possession of a profound and viable ideology. One may even say that it has been endowed in ever-deepening ways with a transcendent purpose of great ethical significance. It is a purpose, moreover, that no longer need arouse the anathemas of any church or sect, and which in its unobscured essence no longer makes any revealed or special "theological" claim on the citizen, although American history, admittedly, is replete with examples of those who saw an absolute divine purpose being fulfilled in American history; and there are still others who have tried to concoct a Christian or a Judaeo-Christian "creed" for the country. It may also be admitted that there are philosophical problems in the idea of "self-evident" principle as it is set forth in the Declaration of Independence, just as there are inescapable tensions between the practical achievement of liberty *and* equality. The idea of the Union itself involves ontological problems. All of which is to say that the times call for serious thought on the question as to what is transient and what is permanent in the nation's ideological heritage. Given the degree to which the United States has actually functioned over the centuries as a model republic, it might even be said that this would be a problem of world-wide significance even if the United States were not a major world power.

126

In any event, it has been the purpose of this paper to provide some slight additional provocation to the players in Act Seven, that they may, as Benjamin Rush in 1787 hoped, play a constructive role in the on-going American Revolution.

NOTES

1   Given the vastness of this subject, running bibliographical annotation is utterly impracticable in an essay of this size. Only the sources of especially relevant quotations not identified in the text will be cited, though many readers will recognize my very specific indebtedness to dozens of other works which deal profoundly with the many subjects which I treat. The following recent works provide an excellent introduction and bibliographies to the subject as a whole: Yehoshua Arieli, *Individualism and Nationalism in American Thought*, 1964; Conrad Cherry, ed., *God's New Israel: Religious Interpretations of American Destiny*, 1971; Robert T. Handy, *A Christian America: Protestant Hopes and Historical Realities*, 1971; Winthrop S. Hudson, ed., *Nationalism and Religion in America: Concepts of American Identity and Mission*, 1970; Paul C. Nagel, *One and Indivisible: The Union in American Thought, 1776-1861*, 1964; *idem, This Sacred Trust: American Nationality, 1798-1898*, 1971; Edwyn A. Smith, ed., *The Religion of the Republic*, 1971; Ernest Lee Tuveson, *Redeemer Nation: The Idea of America's Millennial Role*, 1968. On the general historical background see John M. Blum, ed., *The National Experience: A History of the United States*, 2nd ed., 1968, in which six eminent authors provide unusually thoughtful accounts of each succeeding period, with valuable and up-to-date bibliographies for each chapter. See also my own forthcoming *A Religious History of the American People*, 1972, which contains a fairly substantial bibliography.

2   David M. Potter, *The South and the Sectional Conflict*, 1968, pp. 34-35.

3   Quoted in Edmund S. Morgan, ed., *The American Revolution: Two Centuries of Interpretation*, 1965, p. 5.

4   Perry Miller, ed., *The American Puritans: Their Prose and Poetry*, 1956, pp. 82-83.

5   Quoted from Hutchinson's *History of Massachusetts* in Barrett Wendell, *Liberty, Union and Democracy: The National Ideals of America*, 1906, pp. 27-29.

6   Bernard Bailyn, *The Ideological Origins of the American Revolution*, 1967, p. xi; Charles W. Akers, *Called Unto Liberty: A Life of Jonathan Mayhew*, 1964, p.86; Wesley Frank Craven, *The Legend of the Founding Fathers*, 1956, p. 31.

7   Quoted in James H. Moynihan, *The Life of Archbishop John Ireland*, 1953, pp. 33-34.

8   Heinz Eulau, "Neither Ideology nor Utopia: The New Deal in Retrospect," in *The New Deal: Doctrines and Democracy*, Bernard Sternsher, ed., 1966, pp. 198-200.

9   I have dealt at greater length with the problems of interpreting recent religious history in "The Radical Turn in Theology and Ethics: Why it Occurred in the 1960's," in *The Sixties: Radical Change in American Religion, The Annals of the American Academy of Political and Social Science*, Vol. 387 (January, 1970).

10   The presence and recurrence of dissent, doubt, and faltering hope is the major sub-theme in the history of the American Faith, with perhaps the Lamentations of Jeremiah as its source: "The crown is fallen from our heads: woe to us that we have sinned." Indeed the Puritan jeremiads mark the national origin of this theme and each subsequent generation heard from those who worried about the avarice, the love of mammon, the inhumanity, and the overt cruelty that might keep the Union from its high calling. Fred Somkin in *Unquiet Eagle: Memory and Desire in the Idea of American Freedom, 1815-1860*, 1967, and Nagel in his two above-cited works underline this minor key, while David B. Davis, ed., *The Fear of Conspiracy: Images of UnAmerican Subversion from the Revolution to the Present*, 1971, illustrates one major kind of response that such fears provoked. In this brief essay the expounders of these often profound misgivings have been slighted.

THE ROLE OF POLITICAL THEOLOGY

IN RELATION TO THE LIBERATION OF MEN

Dorothee Sölle

The Gospel is wonderful. It speaks about my life in the way in which I want my life to be talked about: without any contempt. It speaks with a seriousness that does not permit even a single day of my life to be despised; it speaks of a hope that does not permit even a single person to be omitted. It speaks of a sorrow which does not allow itself to grow blind, and of a joy that is contagious. The Gospel speaks without any contempt about the life of all human beings: every hour counts, every hunger means the right to eat, all the tears will be collected, nobody is talked out of his fear, nobody is counted out.

The Gospel is beautiful because it abolishes all cynicism, all self-contempt, and all contempt for other people. It does not allow me to accept life only partially — so long as it is young or healthy or fit; it confounds those who only love their life to a certain extent or under certain conditions. The Gospel expresses an infinite affirmation of life. It deals with a man who has lived this infinite affirmation. He was a worker who wandered about with a group of friends. They shared what they owned, they helped the sick. He told stories which dealt with liberation. Competition and fear were excluded, money and power played no role. "As you know," he said, "the rulers of the people oppress their people, and whoever holds power uses it recklessly. But this is not the way it shall be with you" (Mt.20:25f.) He came into conflict with those who held power. Clerical circles and civil authorities collaborated; he was put on trial. He was sentenced to death. But the reason for his speaking and acting remained in the memory of the people. He himself, the murdered one, remained with them; his stories passed from mouth to mouth. He could not be put to death. "Why should one still be a Christian?" many ask today. I shall attempt to render a simple answer: because we still need liberation.

The Gospel stands in the cause of freedom for all human beings; or more precisely, in view of the reality of oppression, the Gospel's business is the liberation of all human beings. Its concern rests with the oppressed, the poor, the crying. This interest, this bias, is not just an inference. The Bible demands that we participate in this concern for the liberation of all, or rather that we understand it as our very own interest. Only the liberation of all can really mean the liberation of the individual; only the happiness of all human beings deserves the unambiguous affirmation which the word "faith" involves and which transcends the present level of realization. Having faith, we put our wager on the liberation of all people. In the activity of having faith all our powers — thinking, feeling, working, anticipating — are concentrated on this liberation. We recall the liberation which has been experienced in earlier times, and we plan for the coming liberation.

Theology, as a reflection on faith, has to comprehend the social situation of those who are injured and expose the social causes of their injury. Theology has to become political theology.

Theology cannot afford to say out of hand to a man: "God loves you." Since every fact of reality is substantial, established by social processes, such a sentence has to be actualized politically. It will only have meaning if it initiates the movement of change in the status quo. Imagine that this sentence is said to a person who has lived fifteen years in our urban slums. The hatred he has experienced renders such a sentence unbelievable for him. It gives him no reason to trust in the love of God. He has experienced that he cannot get work because he comes from a slum, that his children are sent to special schools for slow learners, though they are as talented as others. The society which did not accept him made itself his enemy through the experiences of his life. Thus such a situation cannot be glossed over by a mere word. The capacity to love and to trust somebody is determined by the history and experience in which someone has participated. Therefore the socially determined situation can make it impossible for someone to decide whether he will trust or distrust. The decision has been taken away from him. He cannot start to have faith, to hope, or to love; he has to be made healthy first.

In the Gospel of John a story is told about the sick at the pool of Bethesda, who wait for an angel to come and move the water. Then whoever is first to enter the water will be cured. Jesus talks to one of the sick who has been waiting for years. He is not able to get down to the water, and says to Jesus: "Lord, I do not have anybody who will take me to the pool when the water is moved" (Jn.5:7). As long as he has to say this, as long as he is alone and therefore without help, he is condemned to sickness. Without other persons he does not have a chance. His sickness, whether physical or social (within the view of the New Testament these are much closer to each other than in our thought, which tends to divide the two fields) — this sickness is not his private affair which he has to manage all by himself. Rather, it becomes social and turns into a question for other people. Jesus abolishes the situation in which one has to say "I don't have anybody," the isolation which is the consequence of despair and at the same time the cause of new despair. Within the perspective of this story, to be cured means that nobody has to say any more: "I don't have anybody."

The Gospel places sickness and cure in their original context. It makes the sickness of the ill the sickness of Jesus through which he ultimately dies, and binds his own healing to the healing of the other. Therefore the language of the Gospel, being the language of liberation, must at the same time maintain a critical function. Today we need a political theology which is conceivable only on the basis of a critical analysis. Without "Law" the Gospel cannot be understood. The critical tradition of the Bible has to be taken up and realized as a critique of religion, of power structures, and of society within the context of our own social situation. However, to this day there is still lacking a theology which systematically reflects upon the relationship between faith and politics.

There stems from the history of the Constantinian age the legacy of a certain distrust and insecurity, because of the fact that the Church has agreed with and joined politics: indeed the Church itself took over state-supporting and state-forming positions and accommodated itself to those in power (frequently by subverting or suppressing its own message). Therefore many Christians today plead for neutrality. From embarrassing experience they draw the conclusion that the Church should remain politically neutral and stand above partisanship. At most the individual Christian — so they think — could or should himself engage in political matters. From the very beginning a political theology is confronted with rejection. One fears that the Gospel will be dissolved into a socialistic strategy, that Christians will let themselves become "useful idiots" who tend to undercut the democratic structure of a capitalistic society. One is afraid of a new totalitarian consciousness within which politics is no longer endowed with its own rationale, but is subordinated to an ideology that claims an insight into the entirety of history — an insight which thinks only monolithically in matters of value, and therefore proceeds to the accomplishment of this singlemindedness in a totalitarian manner. However, political theology is not the same as politics based on theology. Nor does it mean a factual political program developed from Christian faith. There are no specific

Christian solutions to the problems of this world for which a "political theology" would have to develop a theoretical framework. Rather, "political theology" means the interpretation of the Gospel in which "politics" is understood as the comprehensive and crucial field in which Christian truth has to be actualized.

We understand the Gospel in its seriousness only when we keep in mind the political horizon of our life; that means, when we are aware of the winning and losing of our life as being dependent on social presuppositions. From the Gospel we receive the unmediated promise, as well as the demand, of peace, freedom, and justice for all. Theology will assume the task — within the actual society — of presenting critique and design. The truth which is meant by Christian thought cannot tolerate abstraction — that is, neither mere theory, nor pure doctrine. The truth of Christ exists only as concrete truth. Theological concepts convey truth only to the extent that they help to realize the change of reality. "Reality" in this context is not simply to be understood in the sense of given power structures, and "to change" not only in the sense of just doing something for its own sake. The sentence "your sins are forgiven you," for instance, can overcome the real situation of an individual — that is, the situation as it had been determined by the past. However, it can have this power of changing reality only if the person who makes this statement participates in the change — that is, only if he himself starts to restructure the past, along with the one who bears the onus, and only if he dismisses the magical use of religious slogans. The sentence "you are called to freedom" does not become true for wage-earners simply by its being proclaimed to them; rather, it becomes truth through social realization: you are called to self-determination, to cooperation, and to organizing your own work yourselves. The reality of those persons will be changed if they acquire a different awareness of themselves. The sentence "you shall be my people" becomes truth if it also concerns the users, producers and sellers of napalm, that is, if it opens the eyes of those who are co-responsible for the destruction of the life which has been promised to all men. Political theology starts with the question of how an authentic life is possible for all men. That does not mean, however, that the question of individual life should be silenced or should be put aside as being unnecessary. Nevertheless, even this question can only be answered with respect to the social conditions and within the context of social hopes. No one can save himself alone. The individual does not believe and understand things just for himself; rather, he believes in the indivisible salvation of the whole world. An understanding to be considered valid must be adopted and mediated politically, relevant to the lives of all human beings within the society. In saying this we start with the idea of the basic transparency of political conditions and thus with the potential changeability of those conditions. Social change renders the change of men. Behavior patterns such as competition, for instance, or the stress of having to be successful, or the relation to present status-symbols, can be overcome if the society no longer requires such behavior.

Even if we turn away from the older, individualistic-oriented hopes of mankind that pointed to conversion, it still is not correct to think that institutions "create" the man — that is to say, that a change in the social structures will produce the new man just by itself. Critical thinking can only deny such a thesis. Nonetheless, under certain social conditions a liberated and liberating life style is almost impossible. There are lodgings which systematically destroy the relationship between mother and child. There are organizational patterns of work which define the relationship between the strong and the weak in Darwinian terms and so exterminate the humane capacities, such as the ability to help. Compassion and fairness stand as being undesirable for the process of production. If conditions are changed, if housing becomes humane, and the forms of organization become cooperative, then the conditions for the possibility of another life style will be present — nothing more and nothing less.

This consciousness of the changeability of society is today as indispensable as the critical non-mythological understanding of natural scientific contexts has been for Rudolf Bultmann. The theologian Bultmann was not ready to use the electric light and at the same time take over a three-storeyed mythological theory of life with regard to faith. But is it true that the world view, the metaphysic which presents to us wars, hunger, and the neurotic state of our world is any less mythological? Can we admit we advocate birth control, and yet at the same time leave unquestioned the social mythology that certain classes must necessarily suffer, or the mythology that work must necessarily be alienating? Because this presupposition of "social fate" is no longer the conceptualization of our present world, the critique of ideologies assumes for us the place held by "demythologizing."

The awareness of the possibility of change cannot and does not need to be justified in terms of biblical thought. It is completely lacking in meaning to ask whether Jesus directly worked for the change of social conditions. We know that for him publicans were just that — publicans — and harlots just harlots, without his asking who had made them publicans or harlots. He could not ask this question because — to speak in terms of Marxist philosophy — the powers of production had not yet reached the evolutionary stage at which social reconstruction could actually become a possibility. Thus to ask this question over against the New Testament as an

135

ancient document is unhistorical and likewise pre-Marxist. It makes no difference if this question is posed as a criticism, as it is by Joachim Kahl, or whether it is posed in a positive sense by biblical theologians in order to affirm their own evaluation of the New Testament. The bases for change, in the comprehensive sense current today, did not exist at that time. Given the state of affairs now, we cannot back away from the questions which arise out of it. We cannot permit ourselves to ignore why chemists work within the military industrial complex, or why young men prefer the army to the peace corps. The current intellectual predisposition to the idea of the changeability of structures is now confronted by the Gospel; that means, it is criticized, modified, and liberated through a hermeneutical process. By no means, though, is it dismissed out of hand. Within this hermeneutical process the question concerning Jesus' relationship to the changing of this world is modified. It is to be denied that Jesus effected such structural change in the direct sense in which the dialectic of an individual and society is viewed on the basis of social structures. However one cannot overlook that, in an indirect sense, the way in which Jesus thought and behaved broke open and changed the social structures of the world in which he lived. Familial bonds and limits lose their old and natural rank through the new brotherhood (Mk.3:31-35), and there begins the historicizing of human relationships. Jesus asks: "Who is my mother, who is my brother?" The attachment to social orders such as the family, as well as to behavior such as piety, is suspended within the life of Jesus — for example, "Let the dead bury their dead" (Mt.8:22). Likewise the socially important division of people by means of education into those who are literate and informed about religious matters on the one side, and those who belong to social classes without this expertise, is divested of its dignity and importance: "You shall not let yourselves be called Rabbi. Do not call anyone on earth your father . . . You shall not let yourselves be called teachers." The authority is suspended: patriarchal society is replaced by one that is fraternal. This quotation from Mt.23:8-10 expresses the continuation of Jesus' starting point by the congregation. Above all, Jesus' suspension of the then valid horizon of the society religiously defined, and yet achievement oriented, naturally had its consequences. For the blind and the lame who had no access to the temple, to be cured meant at the same time to be religiously re-integrated into society. Jesus associated with women — that is to say, with declassified persons in regard to social status and religion. Jesus associated with the outcasts. With Jesus' proclamation begins an exodus out of familiar, traditional, cognitive, and success oriented power structures. It was to this proclamation that those who needed an exodus into liberation have harkened. "You know that the Princes

136

of the Gentiles exercise dominion over them . . . But it shall not be so among you" (Mt.20:25f.). The religious liberation which this sentence expresses in a pre-scientific way can now be defined at least partly in a scientific way. Today we have the means for formulating in a more precise way the conditions under which power structures can be made transparent, controlled, and finally suspended. No longer can we consider the conditions of life such as class, race, hereditary factors, sex, talent, or accident to be the fated texture out of which faith saves: such faith necessarily goes together with other-worldliness ("Entweltlichung") because the only possible realm of freedom that can be imagined under such presuppositions can only lie outside of any concrete conditions, and at a distance from them. The understanding of faith as other-worldliness ("Entweltlichung") is oriented towards the predisposition that there is a fated character to every reality and order

A theology which understands itself as being non-political will attempt to describe the Gospel outside of this horizon of change which for us is vital. Such a theology demands as downpayment the surrender of our social and political reasoning and thereby the surrender of that reasoning which considers the world to be changeable. Such a theology considers history as a process which has come to an end, and interprets salvation as other-worldliness ("Entweltlichung").

Certainly there is a difference if as in the Gospel of John Jesus, at the end of a life full of attempts, doubts, and fears, says "It is finished," and if this "It is finished" is systematized into a sentence which can always be said without costing anything, a sentence which includes the surrender of our predispositions about the possibility of change because it no longer maintains the necessity of change.

I should like to quote a few sentences from a widely popular book for religious teaching in high schools (in Germany). "If we ask about the future of mankind, the Bible points to this center . . . He said on the cross 'It is finished' (Jn.19:30). Now nothing new and exciting can happen ever again on earth. Whatever occurs or happens is of no importance for the world and mankind. Sickness and war, hunger and misery, luck and fortune, success and progress can strike us. But these events can change neither the world nor man."[1] Even these seemingly pure theological sentences carry massive political implications. The verbal manipulation of certain circumstances stands in the way of concrete change. The sensibility for suffering is suffocated — which means that a concealed brutalizing of the world takes place with the help of theology. The consciousness of a possible failure of life — that is, the sense of the tragic — is destroyed, and the consequence is a loss of humanity. The incorrect religious statement — that "Neither the world nor man can change"

— destroys the liberating character of the Gospel. It also destroys the distinct consciousness of sin which belongs to a political theology, since it interprets events as being fated and denies that we ourselves are the ones who produce hunger and wars. Today we cannot understand sin in a private way as something which happens between two individuals or within a family. Sin to us is eminently a political, a social term: the sins of which Jesus reminds me and which he puts before my eyes are the sins of my own people, of my own white race, of my own bourgeois and propertied class.

I live in a country where certain medicines and methods of healing are reserved for only the members of some particular social strata. When I eat a piece of chocolate I cheat some peasant in Ghana — who, by the way, has not done anything to me — of about 20 cents. If I eat a banana, I help the United Fruit Company in exploiting Latin American slave-workers. Next to me stand people who live under the stress of a success oriented society, and people who get and keep ulcers, or who become neurotic because they no longer can bear it. And I myself continue to stand next to them and just carry on. In the Federal Republic of Germany children head the lists of traffic casualties, but there is no cheap public transportation — yet the production of cars rises and rises. Are we to blame for all that? What do we have to do with this? Did I want this? These are our questions. But Christ does not allow us to get away with it that easily. Sin — this is what he has taught us, even if we tend to forget it — is the state of affairs in our world which accuses us. The dead in the slums of Brazil are ours because we feed from them and because we live well at their expense. Such things are not natural catastrophes or obscure laws of economics; rather, these are what the Christian tradition means by the term "original sin." That is to say, we are living within a context of incompetence and weakness, of hopelessness and wickedness, which we have not created ourselves but nonetheless support and preserve. We are the collaborators of sin.

Jesus Christ asks us what we have done "unto one of the least" of our brothers or what we have not done for one of them. In view of this question we discover the relation of incompleteness and weakness, of hopelessness and blindness, which is so characteristic of the white race and of the bourgeois propertied classes. But how can this relation be abolished, and how is this late capitalistic experience of impotence to be overcome? Or, to ask this question theologically, how does forgiveness of sins appear today?

In order to experience forgiveness of sins we need a group of persons which enables us to start anew. That is, we need at least partners who accept us as we are, who believe in our regret, who give us credit for an about-face. In the early church this social place was the congregation, which criticized and absolved the individual person. But where do we today have comparable groups in the Christian Church? Persons who have become conscious of their sins during the time of the Nazi regime in our society scarcely have a chance for an about-face if they are alone. They cannot really be assured of the forgiveness that is proclaimed by the priest, since, for example, their consciousness of sin is much more weighty and serious than can be dealt with by the formulae of absolution in our present ecclesiastical life.

An about-face would be more than forgiveness because it includes the future. Our world and our life hinder the possibility of an about-face since they isolate people from one another, and because they maintain principles that make for the division of mankind into the less privileged and the more privileged. People today live as much as is possible in small familial units. They organize their work into senseless and unconnected pieces. They reduce their needs only to those of consumption. The stress of an achievement oriented society, the situation of competition, isolation, the deprivation of communication, and the adhesion to privilege are all typical of a society in which no one should make a mistake or, worse yet, admit a mistake. In such a society an about-face is excluded.

The power of the Gospel manifests itself in the fact that it crystallizes around itself groups who oppose and in fact abolish the above mentioned pressures, first among themselves, then vis-a-vis everyone else. The liberation of all, which is intended by the Gospel, abolishes the late capitalistic isolation. "Jesus wants us to be friends" — this is the first sentence in the catechism of Don Mazzi which he wrote for the congregation of Isolotto.[2] Thus within the groupings which the Gospel creates forgiveness will again be possible on a reciprocal basis. Out of the isolation and out of the success oriented thinking, it makes an about-face possible. The experiences which people have with the Gospel of liberation then become expressible.

Why still be a Christian? This is the question of many people today. We answer: for the sake of the liberation which we need. Some people, no doubt, will be dissatisfied with this answer, since it does not make an unmistakable distinction in regard to other groups which also work for a more humane society. But what kind of interest really stands behind such a desire for sharp distinctions? Is it not that of a truly misunderstood orthodoxy? I myself cannot understand the fear of some in the face of the fact that truth also appears in other places, or the fear that truth can use different languages. I suspect that it stems from a conception of competition which was totally unknown to Jesus. Nothing would have been more remote from him than the idea of separating the attempts to humanize the world which are done by non-Christians from those

139

which are done by Christians. Jesus, for instance, tells the story of a man who fell among thieves and about the one who helped him. The compassionate man in this story of Jesus was of a false religion. Today we should tell this story as a story about a compassionate Communist. Jesus tells this story without using the word God. But do we not have to say that the story still speaks of God? Does it not deal with the end of fear and the beginning of freedom, since we exist for other people?

The phrase "God loves us," and the assertion that he loves every single person, is a mere theological commonplace which becomes a lie if it is not translated. The translation of this phrase is the world-changing action itself. The phrase needs a certain concreteness without which it remains empty. At the same time, though, this phrase necessarily transcends every perspective and is never exhausted or done away with. Within this affirmation we have a still greater claim than is satisfied in a momentary partial fulfillment, and a deeper need than is satisfied. Thus this statement makes us aware that the actualization which our life represents, and the love of God which we are, has started but is not yet wholly present. The letter of Christ which we ourselves are (2 Cor.3:3) is still being written and received and read. There exists no other letter of Christ — for instance, not a letter from Paul to the Corinthians or Philippians — which could replace the letter of Christ, since we ourselves are it.

Liberation is only possible as the liberation of all men. Dostoyevsky tells a story in his book, *The Brothers Karamazov*, which places the subject of guilt and forgiveness into this — in its broadest sense — political connection:

> Once upon a time there was a peasant woman and a very wicked woman she was. And she died and did not leave a single good deed behind. The devils caught her and plunged her into the lake of fire. So her guardian angel stood and wondered what good deed of hers he could remember to tell to God. "She once pulled up an onion in her garden," said he, "and gave it to a beggar woman." And God answered: "You take that onion then, hold it out to her in the lake, and let her take hold and be pulled out. And if you can pull her out of the lake, let her come to paradise, but if the onion breaks, then the woman must stay where she is." The angel ran to the woman and held out the onion to her. "Come," said he, "catch hold and I'll pull you out." And he began cautiously pulling her out. He had just pulled her right out, when the other sinners in the lake, seeing how she was being drawn out, began catching hold of her so as to be pulled out with her. But she was a very

wicked woman and she began kicking them. "I'm to be pulled out, not you. It's my onion, not yours." As soon as she said that, the onion broke. And the woman fell into the lake and she is burning there to this day. So the angel wept and went away.

This story speaks about the fear which destroys life. The old woman lives without any interpersonal relationships. Only one tiny bit of her life has been opened to other people. Life for her was privacy and what she owned as an individual: "It is my onion, not yours." For her, possessing was the most important category. It is in owning something that people differ from one another. In owning things people find privilege. Even the possible forgiveness of sins for this woman becomes a matter of privilege, a privilege which she has to hold onto tightly and defend with all her might. She tries to come to terms with the God "above." But, still, the offered salvation does not pull her out of the rotation of her life, which consists of possessing things, being afraid, false security, holding tight, and kicking others. It is only consistent to move from possessing to kicking some one. Through such a sequence the concentration upon the one goal disappears — that is, the concentration upon salvation. The old woman "forgot" to look at the angel and to allow herself to be drawn up by him; she turned in the opposite direction and concentrated upon the privilege, upon the fearful and aggressive attempt to maintain it. Thus she herself broke the onion by holding it and at the same time kicking the others. Her will, her interest was split; she wanted forgiveness, but by wanting this only for herself she destroyed everything, which is typical with wickedness.

Everything we hold on to means death. Wherever life is founded on possessing things, on privileges over against those who have none, there it destroys itself. By clutching it, it perishes. There can be no forgiveness for only a single person; where it is sought in the individual's immediate experience of God — that is, behind the backs of other people and without the painful detour through the world, there it destroys itself: the onion breaks.

As long as life is founded upon the privileges of possession, and in the securing of those privileges, then life destroys itself. Life is only life if everybody belongs to it with the same right and share. Or in terms of the metaphor: the more people who catch hold of the old woman, the more unbreakable the weak onion becomes. If to hold something means death, then communicating means life. No one can save himself alone and nobody is forgiven only for himself — this is, if the words "forgiveness" and "salvation" are to maintain their seriousness, namely the seriousness of rebirth.

NOTES

1   *Die Gottesbotschaft: Ein biblisches Lese- und Arbeitsbuch*, ed. H. D. Bastian and H. Kremers, II, n.d., 194.

2   *Die Botschaft Jesu in Isolotto. Der Katechismus des Don Mazzi*, 1969, p. 41.

3   F. M. Dostoyevsky, *The Brothers Karamazov*, Book 7, Ch. 3.

THE RECOVERY OF THE HUMANIST'S

VOCATION: A PROPOSAL FOR

GRADUATE STUDY IN THE HUMANITIES

William F. May

I have taken the liberty of modifying the original topic proposed for me: "The Academic Study of Religion and the Humanizing Role of the Humanities." My reservations are over the word, "humanizing," which reappears in the overriding title for the International Congress, "Religion and the Humanizing of Man." If you want to humanize man, the first thing you need to do is get rid of phrases like that. Humanizing man sounds too much like finalizing agreements, sanitizing facilities, and sanforizing pants.

The phrase moreover is faintly tinged with a messianic pretension. Recent student alienation from other disciplines and the corresponding popularity of religion courses have tended to encourage this expansiveness. Students have lost a sense of connection between professional expertise and wisdom in human affairs. They are no longer convinced that the methods of the quantifiers will give them access to human experience in the round. They are drawn to a subject that promises to engage its experts in questions concerning human identity, authenticity, community, death, and destiny. This range of subject matter is not the unique privilege of professionals in the field of religion. Such problems should be the concerns of experts in literature, political science, sociology, history, philosophy, and other disciplines. But rightly or wrongly, students feel that they have been required only too often to divest themselves of these questions at the classroom door; and so, trained professionals in the field of religion — if they are lucky enough to have a job — are having their day.

Swollen enrollments, however, ought not to dilate academics with messianic ambitions. Before undertaking to humanize man, they had better remember the more dehumanizing features of their own university education. It included, first of all, those precious undergraduate years, squandered by most persons here present in over-achieving, cramming for exams, cadging for grades, cultivating letters of recommendation, and writing sublimely ambitious papers for courses. Nothing quite matches the feverish excitement with which one turned in that first creative effort — thrilled with the wonder of it, yet depleted, and half-fearful that it was a lucky achievement never to be repeated again. Then there were the rivalries of graduate school seminars, with a dozen or so students competing for the favor of the master. How difficult it was to be nourished rather than depressed by the work of an outstanding fellow student! His virtuosity seemed to establish him as belonging to the major leagues, while one's own efforts condemned one to a bush league of bad meals, overnight buses, and miserable batting averages. And then, the dissertation, that monomaniacal, wife-aborting exercise. In an attempt to cheer me up, in the course of the four indentured years I spent on my own thesis, Professor Harmon Holcombe of Rochester University told me the story of his surprise visit one Saturday morning to see a colleague, whose four year old daughter answered the door. "Is your father not at home?" asked Harmon Holcombe, "Oh yes, he's home," answered the little girl, "he's upstairs, working on the god-damned dissertation."

Captain Ahab, upstairs in his study . . . in pursuit of the white whale. His ambition, overweening, his project careening, and himself hopelessly snarled in a tangle of footnotes. The humanizers, dehumanized. E. B. White was closer to the way things are in the human muddle of things, when he confessed, "I arise in the morning torn between a desire to improve (or save) the world and to enjoy (or savor) the world. This makes it hard to plan the day." Much of the education that each of us has endured and imposed on others has been neither saving nor savoring. This much is clear in the cold light of day.

While foregoing the attempt to humanize man, I have tried to reflect on the vocation of the academic humanist. It has forced me to reconsider graduate education in the humanities and to offer a specific proposal for its structure with the field of religion in view. I offer this proposal, knowing that professionals in this relatively new field will be inclined to go one or two ways: either scrupulously conservative in order to legitimate themselves with colleagues in older, more established, disciplines; or bold and experimental, because professionals in this field, especially in the new departments, may be freer of those vested interests that ordinarily inhibit change. Since the universities at large have been troubled in our time and since the humanities in particular seem to have been sagging in their sense of mission, it seems foolish for the discipline of religion to imitate current practice without debating alternatives that may have some value as pilot projects within the university.

Increasingly the humanities in the United States (and those professions that have built on education in the humanities) have patterned their concept of education on the highly sequential training in the natural sciences. The resultant system is pervasively hierarchical, with non-professional groundlings at the bottom, pre-professionals at the middle levels, and Ph.D. professionals at the top. This development has occurred for at least the following reasons. First, the academic success of the sciences and their ability to attract outside support to the university has tended to make other disciplines reinterpret themselves in the reflected light of scientific education. Second, the highly sequential pattern of scientific training has its own apparent analogue in the maturation of an humanities scholar. Third, the jobs and the prestige in a highly technological culture have gone to the trained professional. Fourth, the United States has been too large a country to develop an educational system that relied, in the fashion of the British Isles, on a small, informal community of names, a society of sophisticated amateurs. We opted rather for the formal credentials of the German Ph.D. system as the only practical way of quickly spanning a continent with reliably trained people. Fifth, and finally, the United States has depended heavily on its educational system for the performing of non-academic services; along with the public school system at large, colleges and universities have been important in the socialization, democratization (and "bourgeoisification") of its culturally diverse people. These non-academic functions have swollen the numbers attending college and diluted (if one applies traditional standards of excellence) the undergraduate constituency, tempting, as a result, professional academics to locate serious education at another level in the hierarchy.

In consequence, most of the prestige in the universities has gravitated to those professors who, in their own right, produce Ph.D.'s. In academic life, turning out Ph.D.'s has become the functional equivalent of immortality: the reproduction of one's own kind. Any lesser occupation threatens with professional oblivion. Prestigious Ph.D.-granting institutions betray their low estimate of baccalaureate teaching when they make cynical arrangements for handling undergraduate instruction — whether through the un-monitored services of teaching associates, or the moonlighting of financially pressed faculty members who teach undergraduates for extra pay, or the use of a segregated group of undergraduate teachers who have a second-class academic citizenship as compared with their colleagues in the professional and graduate schools, or, last and most commonly, through the assignment of undergraduate teaching to junior, untenured faculty members, a ploy which permitted some senior faculty members to play the role of sky gods subject to all the religious and moral dubieties of a *deus otiosus.*

Graduate students have been critical of this system; but it should be noted that universities have been lavish in their expenditure of resources on graduate education, both in the provision of fellowships for study and in the proportional investment of faculty time. The ontological building block in graduate education has been the relatively expensive unit of the seminar. Most institutions have developed a complete superstructure of graduate seminars parallel to their undergraduate courses. To justify economically this huge expenditure of faculty time, universities have had to recruit hoards of graduate students to fill the seminars, with the unlovely result that the job market has been flooded with Ph.D.'s. It is difficult to achieve zero population growth in Ph.D.'s with a system that crowds eight to twenty students in a seminar. The results have been professionally demoralizing.

Three solutions to the problem of oversupply occur to mind. One is to reduce to a handful the number of cathedral institutions turning out Ph.D.'s. This solution has some merit, if it is accompanied by a renewed sense of the dignity of undergraduate teaching in the humanities. Its chief defect is the long-range conservative effect of concentrating graduate education in a few institutions, where, if past experience is any guide, undergraduates are most likely to be treated as stepchildren in the educational process. The second solution to the problem of oversupply is to ignore it. Some deans of graduate schools and tenured members of faculty have been heard to sing the praises of a Ph.D. degree, irrespective of job market, but I have yet to hear the wife of a graduate student talk on the subject like Marie Antoinette. Social conscience argues for a system of graduate education more responsive to the actual needs of the country and compassion demands it. The third solution is to move toward an apprenticeship system of graduate education more sensitive and flexible in response to need.

But all solutions to the problem of oversupply in the humanities will end up demoralizing if imposed by economic necessity alone and if unaccompanied by a renewal of the vocation of the humanist. This renewed sense of vocation, moreover, must be built into the very structure of graduate education itself. With all due respect to the current interest in the charismatics of teaching (including foundation support for symbolic teacher-of-the-century awards and "show and tell" sessions directed by gifted and innovative teachers) the problem of vocation is not simply a question of the descent of the

146

dove. It requires institutional, structural, and functional embodiment. With that interest in mind, I would like to turn to the three offices of the academic humanist as teacher, writer, and inquirer. These functions will be briefly reviewed in the current context of graduate education with most comments reserved for the discussion of the third.

1. The preparation of teachers. The seminar system makes no direct effort to prepare good teachers. The lack of standards and specific data about teaching ability shows up in letters of recommendation received on graduate students seeking jobs. Statements about a candidate in many respects are fairly straightforward, but comments about his potentialities as a teacher usually lapse from the indicative to the subjunctive: "I think he would make a good teacher" — which is to say — "he has no distracting ties, he speaks with some facility, and I like him as a person."

The usual efforts to overcome this lack of preparation for teaching are twofold: first, provision for some kind of teaching experience through the so-called "T. A." position; and, second, a program of teacher training. Teaching associate positions have been created to provide graduate students with sorely needed income to pay for their education (still carried on through seminars) and to give them additionally a little teaching experience. The basic defect of the program is the schizophrenia it imposes upon the student torn between his teaching assignment and his own courses. Some of the better students find themselves absolved in teaching, while their seminar courses — where their grades and future lie — suffer; meanwhile, the more ruthless student uses the teaching position for purposes of personal subsidy, while the undergraduates in his classrooms correspondingly suffer. Even when some balance is attained, something is amiss in a system that fails to integrate habits of research and teaching.

Programs for teacher training, on the other hand, usually consist of the establishment of a special departmental seminar on teaching, which is to solve the problem by segregating it, or by the requirement of weekly meetings for teaching associates in large courses, a procedure that has much to recommend it but that often deteriorates into a session on course management. The solution does not lie in "how to" courses imported from other divisions of the university but in honoring in the structure of graduate education itself the element of truth in the saying that if you want to learn a subject, teach it.

In response to the problem, some academic leaders have pressed for the creation of a new doctoral degree which emphasizes teaching, as opposed to the research-oriented Ph.D. In my estimate, this move is a mistake, not simply for the political reason that the prestige in the academic hierarchy is still likely to be vested in the Ph.D., but because the distinction between the two degrees will institutionalize a separation between research and teaching with destructive results for both.

2. The problem of writing. The development of a hierarchical, upward-oriented educational system in the humanities has not had a salutary effect on the quality of writing. Most writing in the humanities is excessively filial; that is, it presupposes the seminar where a dozen or so siblings compete for the attention of the professor. Students package their research in monographettes that rely on the technical shorthand of the discipline in order to impress their teachers — or their functional equivalents at meetings of learned societies. They rarely deign to write with the motive of teaching and nourishing *one another* in and through their writing. Thus in academic America we admit only two alternative social settings or directions for writing: either up (to the professor in the monograph) or down (to the non-professional in the textbook or the pot-boiler). The name for the latter kind of writing is popularization. In the first instance, academic community is reduced to the graduate school ghetto, with its impoverishment of language; and, in the second case, it is blighted by condescension, with its consequent destruction of community. No student is so tone-deaf to things of the spirit as to be unaware when another man is condescending to him.

We have not developed anything akin to the English essay tradition in which the student attempts to write neither *up* nor *down* but *over* to a wider audience of intelligent but less informed inquirers in the field. The latter social matrix for writing would force the student out of the abstract, limited, and univocal vocabulary of the discipline into richer veins of language and experience. (W. B. Yeats once complained about the scientific formula H_2O, "I like a little seaweed in my definition of water.") This enrichment and freshening of language, moreover, is more than a question of adornment. To write well is to see well and to know well; it is also to see afresh. Good writing forces one to see through the eyes of an outsider and retake one's subject by surprise.

3. The problem of critical inquiry. Complaints about teaching and writing have been heard before, but they constitute the form of which critical inquiry is the substance. The deeper vocational crisis for the academic humanist must be reckoned with at the level of research or learning, or what I would prefer to call critical inquiry. Of what human value is it? Why should a society support it? These are not idle questions since they are put by university trustees as they are about to reallocate funds.

Scholars in the humanities have not rushed to defend themselves. They proudly continue the ancient tradition of the liberal arts, that is, the pursuit of knowledge unfettered by immediate considerations of social utility; nevertheless, in expecting a society to support their research, they cannot ignore the question of social function and value, and, in facing this question, they may be helped to recover a sense of their distinctive vocation in the university community.

Clearly, as compared with the scientist, the humanities scholar faces several obvious disadvantages in justifying his enterprise to the community at large. First, the division of the humanities is at present the least coherent subdivision of the modern university. It draws together a rather disparate set of disciplines — in some cases, it seems nothing more than the accidental grouping of what is left over after the sciences have claimed their own. There are important cultural reasons for this incoherence. At one time, the *auctores*, read and studied by cultured people in the West, constituted a kind of secular canopy (an extended canon, if you will) under which civilization sheltered. This unity of tradition was lost, however, with the expansion of western culture in power and knowledge. The sciences experienced much of the exhilaration of this expansion; the humanities more acutely suffered its consequent loss of unity. In all their current disarray, the humanities are pitched out on a site over the deep places where a civilization hurts, but, by the same token, over the sources and problems from which its life may spring.

The humanities lack unity in their methods of research and standards of judgment not only across the division at large but also within a given discipline. Fierce internal debates over the proper methods and objects of inquiry compromise each discipline in the eyes of laymen who have already come to expect from the sciences results that are incremental and assured rather than contested. Many scholars in the humanities debase their choice of thesis topics when they mimic an incrementalist understanding of knowledge and strain for novel subjects. The whole procedure tends to force the young scholar out of the over-populated areas into the desert of the trivial. It can be a further mistake to aim for incontestable results. The apparent weakness of the humanities in this respect may be simultaneously their grandeur. Creative phases in the development of a discipline have often occurred at precisely those troubling moments when its own methods have undergone profound and contested revision. (The layman, of course, is not likely to be impressed by this bit of news unless he senses the intrinsic reasons for this paradoxical kind of progress and the social importance of its results. Otherwise the humanities will be left increasingly to their own private and underpaid disputations.) Finally, no obvious windfalls come to scholars in the humanities in the demonstration of their social utility such as are available to apologists for basic research in the sciences. The latter are able to point to the development of socially valuable techniques and products that are the unintended by-products of the enterprise. Consequently and oddly enough, the humanities which are the most non-utilitarian of the liberal arts, must offer a much more intrinsic justification of their social worth.

Despite earlier concessions to the diversity of disciplines within the humanities, it may be possible to generalize about them in such a way as to exhibit their indispensability to a society, if not to guarantee their inevitable social value. Professor Julian Hartt has argued that the humanities have as their distinctive purpose to interpret and criticize the acts of man, particularly the creative acts of man. Their concern for interpretation (of the significant and signifying past) establishes their natural affinity with the field of history — either as a distinctive department within the humanities or as a mode of inquiry that goes on within each of them. Their concern for criticism engages them in evaluative judgments with respect to the important and the trivial, the creative and the spurious in the acts of man. I shall argue that the activities of interpretation and criticism are the source of disputation within the humanities but also the basis for the contributions of the humanities to the social order.

Interpretation of the past perforce engages the scholar in all sorts of contestable decisions as to what is significant, humanly important, and worthy of investigation in the past and what that past signified also for its agents. These judgments, needless to say, suffer revision as changes occur in the value systems of the current age. (We need only remember the impact of black studies and environmental problems on the selection of course topics, research papers and guest lectures to recognize the degree to which historical studies reflect current value concerns.) Yet at the same time the historian is engaged in bringing to the attention of the present age cultural forms and value systems that either transcend the boundaries of current preoccupations or lie buried and unacknowledged within them. In this second respect, the historical component in humanities research performs the important social service of keeping the present generation open to the human past in all the diversity of its life. It need not be assumed, to justify its value, that this transmission of the past is inherently conservative or revolutionary in its effect on the social order. Rather it should have a civilizing effect on both parties in the controversies of our age. Openness to the whole of the human past may be important in contesting the narrow selectivities in the value systems of conservatives in the passing generation. At the same time, this openness to past values may have a sobering effect on a revolutionary generation, challenging it to a level of rejection that is knowledgeable rather than heedless, significant rather than trivial.

More than this, interpretation *qua* interpretation cannot do or ask, for the very word "tradition" means the act of handing on or handing over — into the freedom of others.

Like the work of interpretation, humanistic criticism cannot flourish without continuing revision in the standards by which judgments are made. In this respect, e.g., literary criticism differs intrinsically from the sciences. Revisions are forced upon literary criticism by the very nature of its object of inquiry. Its object is the creative works of man — works which perforce in some measure express and effect an alteration in human sensibility. Thus standards of literary criticism may simultaneously be valid in detecting the trivial and the spurious in art, and yet require constant alteration to offer adequate access to fresh expressions of human creativity. As R. P. Blackmur observed, greatness cannot be measured, it must be lived up to. (This process of "living up to" is both painful and celebrational — painful because any alteration of human sensibility includes its coefficient of tribulation [so Plato, in his Myth of the Cave, the ancient mystics, and any sensitive college freshman can tell us] and celebrational because few judgments about the worth can be made without some mode of participation in its life.) This painful need for constant revision does not dissipate the social value of criticism. The society at large has a vested interest in the clarification of its own culture, in the development of standards and language sensitive to the ordering of its consciousness, in the elaboration of those inferences for action and conduct which the logic of that consciousness may wittingly and unwittingly entail, and in remaining open prospectively to what that consciousness would currently ignore or demean.

In summary, the acts of interpretation and criticism are deeply immersed in the culture of the age that produces these acts; they are profoundly social acts. Research in the humanities, while affording its own private pleasures to its participants, should not be abstracted from the social matrix from which it emerges and to which it returns. This social matrix helps to energize, define, and continually to redefine the humanistic enterprise.

The consequences of this for graduate education are twofold. First, research in the humanities should not be separated from the inherently social acts of writing and teaching. The very phrase, "research in the humanities," is a concept more suitable to other divisions of the university since research in the humanities acquires its definition and reaches its fruition only as it issues in writing and nourishes teaching. Put another way, the content of research cannot be separated from its social form. This is why writing and teaching are always a more difficult, complicated, and rewarding business for the humanities than "reporting" on research may be for other disciplines. *Writing and teaching are heuristic acts in which the content of research is not simply packaged but discovered.* It would be a mistake then to make a proposal for graduate education in the humanities that seemed only to recommend certain improvements in packaging — i.e., in the quality of teaching and writing — without intending to benefit the substance of inquiry.

Second, and finally, research in the humanities stands to profit more from teaching at all levels than is the case for the social or natural sciences. Humanities scholars make a mistake when they structure education strictly in terms of non-professional, pre-professional, and professional constituencies. Only a few persons may be in a position to understand and appreciate the work of an advanced specialist in science since the sciences depend upon elaborate sequential training. There are analogous instances of sequential training in the humanities, but by and large the scholar in the humanities needs exposure not only to professionals in his own discipline, but also to the questions of professionals from other disciplines and to the raw, unformed, nonprofessional questions of the undergraduate classroom. The undergraduate reminds us, further, that education in the humanities — if its intent is the humanization of man — does not terminate in a gnostic elite, a special enclave of *illuminati.* The undergraduate is the functional equivalent in the educational process of the peasants and fishermen of Galilee. Although we should not sentimentalize the undergraduate and his sometimes only-too-breezy concerns, neither should graduate education be constructed in such a way as to pretend that the undergraduate does not exist or to treat him like the dumb patron of the arts whose money is readily accepted but whose company is to be earnestly avoided. For better or for worse, the scholar in the humanities needs the companionship of the amateur in the fruition of his professional life.

With the foregoing considerations in mind, I offer the following proposal for graduate education in the humanities, attempting to hyphenate the offices of teacher, writer, and inquirer and to open out all three to the wider constituencies of a university which the humanities need to serve in order to be themselves.

The Proposal. It is recommended that the total number of seminars taken in the course of a graduate education be drastically reduced with the substitution of the following: 1) a series of teaching assignments for graduate students in various aspects of the curriculum which would organize their basic program of readings; 2) further specialization for each student based on tutorial work in areas of developing interests; 3) the fruits of which would be presented in public colloquy before the fathered faculty, fellow graduate students, and appropriate undergraduate majors; 4) to be followed by a dissertation, the approach, style, and topic of which might be favorably affected by this new social matrix for graduate education.

Each of these items will be discussed in turn.

Instead of treating the teaching associate position as a way in which a graduate student earns money to *patronize* his research efforts, graduate schools should take advantage of the teaching assignment as an instrument for stimulating and organizing a portion of his or her research endeavor. Our own preliminary experiment at Indiana University centers in a graduate course open only to Master's degree students who have a teaching assignment as a discussion leader in one of the gateway undergraduate courses. In earning academic credit for this course, each graduate student is responsible for an additional set of readings coordinated with those required of undergraduates on each of the topics taken up in the basic course. He will prepare a paper or a series of work papers on problems of special interest related to his teaching. One of the purposes of his papers will be to instruct his fellow graduate students engaged in a collegial enterprise. It is to be hoped that this device will begin to establish a different social matrix and purpose for writing than presupposed in the traditional seminar. We want to establish a social context that is more collegial than filial, as students are called upon to share the results of their critical inquiry with their colleagues. Finally, graduate students will be evaluated on the effectiveness of their teaching performance and their control of course materials in the classroom. This evaluation will include personal observation by the director of the course as well as the use of student critiques. A student's final grade will be, in effect, a cluster grade including these various components of his work.

This course is not intended as a "teaching methods" course which is more properly the province of a school of education. Nor is it an opening gambit in an attempt to move the emphasis in graduate work away from research toward teaching as apparently is the intention of the advocates of the Doctor of Arts degree. Quite the contrary, we hope that the course will stimulate and improve the quality of research and writing just as much as it supports good teaching.

If teaching is part of the privilege of a humanistic scholar by virtue of which he partly discovers and possesses his subject, then an effort ought to be made to overcome the structural split we impose on future professionals, when we reduce the value of their teaching assignments to a device by which they earn their bread or acquire a low-grade skill. This course presupposes the view that the two enterprises are more integrally connected — as research nourishes and illumines teaching and teaching energizes and helps to define the research interests of the scholar.

Were we to proceed to a Ph.D. program after a period of successful experimentation with this course, it would be my recommendation that we develop an orderly series of teaching assignments in which a student would read in a specific area the fall semester, teach it the spring semester, and then take the functional equivalent of a qualifying examination over the material. In the spring semester, he would undertake a second program of reading in anticipation of another teaching assignment the following fall. Once again, on the principle that one learns through teaching, his work only then would terminate in an examination. At least three areas would be covered in this fashion as part of general preparation in the discipline. This program would dispense with the traditional convention of qualifying examinations, substituting instead the series of reading-teaching assignments and the resultant cluster grades. Undoubtedly this apprenticeship program for a graduate student resembles the training model of a junior executive in a corporation who in the early stages of his development is planted out for experience in various aspects of the enterprise.

One of the dangers of any such program would be the tendency to tie in the graduate student too closely to the pre-established patterns of undergraduate courses in which he teaches. This disadvantage might increase as the specialized interests of a graduate student matured. Three protections against this conservatism occur to mind: a) the maturing student should be permitted to clear out several weeks in each undergraduate course in which he is free to develop topics with his students that relate to special problems of interest to him; b) more experienced graduate students might be allowed increasingly to collaborate with the professor in the basic planning for the undergraduate course; and c) the most advanced students might be encouraged or required to design and teach their own courses or independent sections of courses.

None of these adjustments, however, will fully meet the need of every graduate student to pursue inquiry in an area of specialization that may not tie in conveniently with an undergraduate instructional program. Therefore the second component of this proposal for graduate education is a series of tutorials with appropriate professors in the area of his developing special interests. (I would predict that the current drastic reduction in the number of students admitted to graduate programs in any given field or its subdivisions will economically force departments to junk the seminar system in favor of the tutorial. When only two students are admitted in a single year in a major subdivision of a department it is hard to populate seminars.)

The difficulty with a tutorial system is that it is rather too private a relation to be fully satisfactory. The word "private," after all, is a variant of privative, and, in this case, with good reason. A faculty member rarely finds contact with a single student in tutorial session in the area of his specialization all that stimulating. It is also discouraging to write papers for the professor alone, whom the student (often mistakenly) supposes knows more than he and least needs to hear what he has to say.

There is need for public occasions in which the fruits of a student's labor in tutorial session can be shared with, discussed, and criticized by others; hence, the third proposal for a regular series of colloquia drawing together faculty members, fellow graduate students, and selected undergraduate majors. The main purpose of such sessions would be to encourage students, by virtue of social context, to write *out* to the intelligent inquirer instead of writing *up* to an audience of one. It is my conviction that this exercise would have a tonic effect on style, not simply in the technical sense of producing better writing, but also at the deeper levels at which style affects the apprehension and command of a subject.

I am not sure whether in the United States this particular proposal need even be urged. The requirements of fellowship alone will drive the gregarious American out of an eremitical tutorial system into the structure of the department-wide colloquy.

Finally, the dissertation — the white whale — with which this address began. Permission to proceed with a dissertation should depend upon regular, joint review of the student's research-teaching, research-writing performance. There is little point in proceeding with the thesis if an appraisal of the student's teaching and collected papers promises little by way of contribution to the profession. It is my further hope that the approach, style, scope, and topic of the dissertation will be influenced in positive ways by the proposed new social matrix for graduate education. I have little further to add to the discussion of this subject except to say that I am in sympathy with efforts across the last dozen years to cut the dissertation down to human size and to direct it toward publication of a kind that gives it a bona fide consummation in the public domain. To require publication at present, however, would be to encourage practices that would debase the meaning of that domain.

The problem of the dissertation, of course, really carries over into the question of the continuing research-writing career of the young scholar after he or she has joined the ranks of full-time teachers in the university. The teaching obligations of junior faculty members must be defined in such a way as to organize a legitimate fraction of their teaching loads around their vital and continuing research interests. Without such provision the young instructor finds himself in the old structural split between teaching and research-writing,

155

but newly defined. The cutting up of the great white whale into publishable chunks is something he worries about in his spare time. The institution makes no serious provision in the public domain of his teaching for the continuation of his research interests. It becomes his private careerist worry that looms as public crisis only when tenure and promotion decisions are made. Such provision will not likely be forthcoming until senior, tenured faculty members are willing to accept greater responsibility for the apprenticeship and maturation of the young scholar in the planning of teaching assignments.

But these are further issues beyond the immediate purview of this proposal. It is sobering enough for the speaker to concede that he has not delivered fully on his original title. The recovery of the humanist's vocation, after all, is not simply a question of the form and structure of graduate education in the humanities; it is also acutely a question of the content of that education, particularly at a time when the traditional civilizing function of the humanities has all but collapsed. I have barely touched on this crisis of content, and not at all as it affects the field of religion. This neglect results from respect for, rather than indifference to, the subject. The problem deserves its own extended treatment on another occasion. It has been enough to undertake here the more pedestrian job of examining the educational structure and social medium in the context of which that vocation has been most recently framed and perceived. A proposal for the reformation of that structure has been offered here in the conviction that professionals in the field of religion are freer than most to open up discussion and debate on the issue.

HUMANIZING MAN: DELPHI, PLATO, AND PAUL

Hans Dieter Betz

The theme of this congress, "Religion and the Humanizing of Man," is modern only in its formulation. The subject itself was a burning issue even in antiquity.

The use of ordinary language reveals that the necessity of humanizing man was already seen in antiquity.[1] In the chief European languages the word "human" first means the "merely-human," the human in its frailty, as expressed in the proverb "To err is human." Then, the term "human" refers to the attitudes of kindness, forgiveness, and tolerance as adequate reactions to the "merely-human." Finally, the terms "man," "humaneness," "human dignity," "human rights," etc., call attention to goals man has set for himself. This use of language reflects the anthropological fact that man considers himself, on the one hand, as a given being and, on the other, as a being still incomplete; further, that man is conscious of the possibility of ruining what is given, and of falling short of that which is to be achieved. When, therefore, we speak of man, we do not speak of a definitely established species, but of a being which moves back and forth between the factors given in his existence and his possibilities. Our use of language also indicates an implicit agreement that man is obliged to avert his own "dehumanization" and to attain his "true humanity." The many designs for living provided by ancient religions and philosophies are, in fact, precipitations of concepts of humanization, showing how ancient man tried to understand the matter in application to the particularities of his life.

Antiquity was also always aware of the fact that religion and the humanizing of man belong together. The Greeks, however, were the first to see that this arrangement has its problems.[2] They recognized that man's religion, like man himself, must be humanized. "Popular religion," in many ways, thwarts the humanization of man and society, and for that reason must be stripped of its power, transformed, or even abolished. The attempts to humanize religion made by the Greeks were, however, nothing but manifestations of certain other concepts of religion. Although there was no lack of acumen and courage among the Greeks, they shied away from a total abolition of religion. They had a profound fear that man, once he has completely thrown off religion, will tumble into "hybris," pose vaingloriously as "superman," come into conflict with the realities of life, and thus pave the way to his own downfall. By innumerable examples, Greek literature illustrates this danger, and teaches man to avert it. For this reason, the humanization of man without some form of religion remained inconceivable in antiquity. Rather, the controversial question was only which of the multitude of religious and philosophical systems would really be capable of humanizing man?

In what follows, three ancient programs for the humanization of man will be discussed. We can say of all of them that they very deeply influenced the ancient world, and that as fundamental concepts they are accepted as valid even today, in spite of all the changes which have taken place in history, and in spite of all the objections which can undoubtedly be raised against them. We should add, however, that their present advocates are often unaware of the background which these programs have in the history of religions. Therefore, it is the task of the historian of religion to shed light upon this background and to dissolve uncritical illusions and false hopes, which often enough were already recognized as such in antiquity, in order to make possible an encounter with the subject matter itself.

I. DELPHI

It is the merit of W. Schadewaldt's essay,[3] "Der Gott von Delphi und die Humanitatsidee," to have rescued from obscurity the old Delphic "idea of humanity." "Idea of humanity" sounds somewhat abstract, but we shall see that Schadewaldt means by this nothing less than a program of humanization comprehensive in both theory and practice. This becomes clear from certain sayings of the poet Menander,[4] which are to be connected with the Delphic religion:

"How charming a thing is man when he is man"[5]

"You are man, this know and remember always"[6]

In these sayings the poet calls attention to that which we call "human." This "humanness" signifies, first of all, man in his givenness, that is, the "merely-human," human frailty and perishability, man's lot of transitoriness and fragility. But then Menander addresses man as the being who is constantly in danger of losing sight of these fundamental conditions of his life, and who must be continually reminded of them and called back to them. If man does not listen to the poet's words, sooner or later Tyche, Chance, will see to it that he experiences, and indeed suffers, his humanity. Through exhortation and experience man is called to learn to bear his human lot "humanely." Here the term "humanely" signifies the attitude of the man who has learned to confront the dispensations of Fate with composure and dignity and to look at human weakness with understanding and tolerance. This use of language moves us back and forth between the meanings of "merely-human," "all-too-human," and "appropriate to the human." In this movement we are supposed to come to grips with the fundamentals of our existence, and thus to become "humanized."

In his essay, Schadewaldt has shown that this doctrine points back to the "Delphic theology." In his opinion the great power which the Delphic Apollo exuded into all of Greece was "a comprehensive education to — humanity." "The humane," as it is called later, is implicit in the commandment of the Delphic Apollo, "in a harsher and sterner way, primarily in terms of mortality — the mortal being in his mortality."[7] This theology expresses itself especially in the "Delphic maxims," the most famous of which were inscribed at the temple of Apollo at Delphi. In antiquity the most important of them all was the maxim "Know thyself"(γνῶϑι σαυτόν).According to its older interpretation the saying means: "Realize that you are mortal."[8] Plutarch, who himself served as a priest at Delphi in the First Century A.D., preserved this old interpretation. In his treatise "De E apud Delphos" he contrasts the maxim "Know thyself" with the "Thou art," as he interprets the meaning of the "E." When one enters the temple with awe and reverence, one addresses the god as "Thou art." The god admonishes the worshipper by the corresponding "Know thyself": "a reminder to mortal man of his own nature and the weakness that besets him."[9]

The question, when and how the Delphic sayings were first connected with the cult of Apollo, is still unanswered. In any case, their connection with the temple as inscriptions seems to be a development of a secondary order.[10] The origin of the sayings was disputed even among the ancients. Some attributed them to Apollo, others to the "Seven Sages"; Plutarch himself names the amphictyons. Most probably, the attribution of the sayings to the god happened in conjunction with the development of the figure of Apollo himself.[11] In regard to humanization, one can say that the sayings address individuals who are humanized through an inner appropriation of the practical wisdom which the sayings contain, and which is, in addition, authorized by the Delphic god. In the course of this development, the god himself was humanized as well, because the attribution of the wisdom sayings to Apollo presupposes that the god has changed from a god concerned with fertility and purification, which he originally was, to the god of the arts and the intellect, of measure and order.[12]

In the latter part of the 20th century the old Delphic doctrine seems to have regained new relevance. Incomparably more than in ancient Greece, contemporary man sees himself confronted with his own limitations. Not only is it considered necessary that individual human beings recognize their own limits, but mankind as a whole has reached an impassible limit of possibilities. Nowhere and never was the danger of extravagance and chaos greater than it is today. When today ecologists and other sensible scientists call upon man to recognize his own limits and to conduct himself accordingly, they in fact reiterate, even if often unknowingly, the Delphic maxim in its older interpretation.

In view of such appeals it should, however, be realized that even ancient man recognized how difficult it is to move man towards self-recognition, and to make him draw from it conclusions that apply to his moral conduct. Plato's Socrates once remarks that he has no time to spend with other questions, because he had not yet succeeded in obeying the Delphic maxim.[13] At the end of antiquity Augustine came to the conclusion that it is impossible for man to know himself completely.[14] If this failure to obey the Delphic maxim was recognized even by the ancients, one must raise the question, what reason there is to hope that man today is willing and able to take the saying seriously. Whatever answer one may give to such a question, we will have to affirm today also that humanization depends upon the condition that the human individual is led to the recognition of his possibilities and limitations, and that he is motivated to draw ethical consequences from it.

II. PLATO

The Platonic idea of humanization also seems to have begun with the Delphic religion. However, in Plato we find for the first time another interpretation of the Delphic maxim "Know yourself" (γνῶθι σαυτόν).

In the discussion about "self-control" (σωφροσύνη) in the Char-mides, Critias interprets the Delphic maxim as Apollo's address to those who enter the temple. Instead of greeting with the usual "χαῖρε," the god admonishes those who enter to exercise "self-control"; thus "self-recognition" is nothing but "self-control."[15] In the Charmides, this discussion about "self-control" must be seen in connection with the psychagogic goal of the dialog. The interrogation of Charmides

160

is intended to reveal whether he, about whose well-formed body there is no difference of opinion, possesses a well-formed soul as well. For it must be assumed that Charmides can be called a perfect man only if his beautiful body houses a soul equally well-constituted. This is what Plato puts upon Socrates' lips.[16] Similarly, Aristotle claims that Socrates was inspired by the Delphic maxim to undertake his inquiries.[17] In the *Alcibiades I* Socrates formulates, in explicit reference to the Delphic maxim, what the "Know yourself" means in this new interpretation: "He who enjoins a knowledge of oneself bids us become acquainted with the soul."[18] This kind of self-recognition is then defined as "self-control" ($\sigma\omega\phi\rho\sigma\sigma\acute{\nu}\nu\eta$).[19] Therefore, man in the strict sense of the word is nothing but his soul.[20]

It is on this basis that Plato develops his doctrine of the soul. Many-sided as this doctrine is, its intention can hardly be missed.[21] Plato's main concern is to grasp fully and scientifically what the Delphic maxim commands. If it commands the recognition of the soul as the human self, Plato seeks to take into account all of the different aspects of this knowledge. This is the goal of his doctrine of the soul, with its division into the "reasoning" part ($\lambda o\gamma\iota\sigma\tau\iota\kappa\acute{o}\nu$), the "passionate" part ($\vartheta\upsilon\mu o\epsilon\iota\delta\acute{\epsilon}\varsigma$), and the "desirous" part ($\dot{\epsilon}\pi\iota\vartheta\upsilon\mu\eta\tau\iota\kappa\acute{o}\nu$).[22] Plato correlates this trichotomy with his epistemology in such a way that the parts of the soul correspond to the notions of "knowledge" ($\gamma\nu\tilde{\omega}\sigma\iota\varsigma$), "opinion" ($\delta\acute{o}\xi\alpha$), and "ignorance" ($\dot{\alpha}\gamma\nu\omega\sigma\acute{\iota}\alpha$).[23] Ontologically they correspond to the gradation of "Being," "Appearance," and "Non-being."[24] The significance of such investigations becomes clear again and again during the discussions: Plato wants to find the conditions under which the soul may obtain "virtue" ($\dot{\alpha}\rho\epsilon\tau\acute{\eta}$) and "righteousness" ($\delta\iota\kappa\alpha\iota o\sigma\acute{\upsilon}\nu\eta$), in order then to lead the soul "to doing its own."[25]

Plato has also seen that this cannot happen unless the individual soul is harmoniously related to the society in which it finds itself. For this purpose he has designed his "model" of a perfect state, which corresponds to the structure of the soul as well as to the structure of Being as a whole.[26] The lowest, "desirous" part of the soul corresponds to the social class of the workers, the "passionate" part of the soul corresponds to the class of the defenders of the state (the "guards"), while the "knowing" part of the soul is related to the class of the "philosophers," who "really know" — that is, whose knowledge is constantly nurtured by their contemplation of Being. The soul obtains "virtue" ($\dot{\alpha}\rho\epsilon\tau\acute{\eta}$) by letting its highest part rule over the lower parts, as within society the "philosophers" rule over the other social classes. Depending on whether "knowledge" "opinion" ($\delta\acute{o}\xi\alpha$), or "ignorance" ($\dot{\alpha}\gamma\nuo\iota\alpha$), respectively "$\lambda o\gamma\iota\sigma\tau\iota\kappa\acute{o}\nu$," "$\vartheta\upsilon\mu o\epsilon\iota\delta\acute{\epsilon}\varsigma$," or "$\dot{\epsilon}\pi\iota\vartheta\upsilon\mu\eta\tau\iota\kappa\acute{o}\nu$" predominate in the soul, a person possesses "wisdom" (σοφία), "courage" (ἀνδρεία) or "self-control" (σωφροσύνη), and belongs to the class of the philosophers, guards, or working-men.[27]

Looking at Plato's philosophy from our own perspective, we can very well regard and present his doctrines as a "program of humanization." The particular significance of these doctrines must be seen in the fact that Plato was the first to understand man's humanization as a problem that encompasses all aspects of his existence at once. In addition, Plato attempted to attack the problem in a scientific way. He tried to coordinate ontology, epistemology, doctrine of the soul, doctrine of the society, and ethics in one comprehensive system. Plato also decisively clarified the relationship between humanization and religion. It is not only significant to recognize that Plato's philosophy is eminently "religious." Of primary interest to us is the fact that for him, the humanization of man includes the humanization of religion. He rejects the so-called "popular religion" as unfit for the education of man. But Plato's own religion is identical with his philosophical thinking.[28] In this transformation, religion is by no means replaced by something else, but it is changed by means of its own resources, together with Plato's philosophical thinking.

Admittedly, many objections can be raised today against Plato's conceptions, but one should also recognize that many of his insights are valid even today. At least in theory it is agreed that the humanization of man can be brought about only through scientific thinking and method, whereas antiscientific ideologies and resentments have dehumanizing effects upon man. In theory it is beyond dispute that the humanization of man cannot be achieved through individual branches of the scientific enterprise alone, but that the cooperation of all the sciences is required. However, the practical situation in the universities and other scientific institutions directly contradicts those theoretical agreements. Since there is no longer any concept providing a common ground for all the sciences, the individual branches make themselves more and more independent, and produce a similar kind of specialist whose tendency is to isolate himself through ideology and bureaucracy. In this way, the sciences become obstacles to the humanization of the individual as well as of the society. Plato himself learned through experience that the political side of his program was far more difficult to realize than he had first assumed. His political experiments in Sicily, which we must mention in particular, made him aware of the fundamental difficulty which characterizes the attempts to relate philosophical thinking and political action.[29]

Finally, even today we must agree with Plato that the "popular religions" — and these include most of what passes as Christianity,

Buddhism, Islam, etc. — hinder rather than help man's humanization. This does not mean that modern man must completely give up the religious dimension. All past attempts to abolish religion altogether have failed. The humanization of man under the banner of atheism is as inconceivable to the whole human race today as it was in antiquity. We can neither abolish religion nor dispense with it. Rather it must be included in the humanization of man in such a way that the humanizing powers inherent in religion are encouraged to develop.

III. PAUL

The apostle Paul was the first Christian theologian who developed and presented a well-conceived anthropology.[30] This fact justifies the assumption that, in his anthropology, he must have taken into consideration the problem of humanization. However, anyone who attempts to lift Paul's anthropological ideas out of his letters finds himself confronted by serious difficulties. Paul's lack of terminological systematization and his excessive intricacies appear overwhelming. Therefore, it is not surprising that a presentation of Paul's anthropology which includes all aspects has not yet been written.[31]

Apparently, conceptional systematization was not the goal of Paul's anthropology. To be sure, Plato also can vary his concepts and may adjust them to new insights, but there is no doubt that his basic intention remains the interpretation of the phenomena with the help of a lucid system of concepts. In contrast to this, Paul always presents his anthropological ideas only in the application of them to the concrete problems with which his congregations were wrestling. In so doing he attempts, like Plato, but in a completely different way, to do justice to the complexity and the continual changes of these problems.[32]

Paul's doctrine of the humanization of man is embedded in his doctrine of salvation through Christ.[33] This doctrine is universal in scope, but is related specifically to a concrete and historical community, the Christian churches to which Paul wrote. If one looks over the Pauline ideas as a whole, three aspects strike the eye as being of particular concern to Paul: man's historically given potentialities to be human, the correspondence between the individual man and the societal unit, and the processes of transformation and change which man undergoes as an individual and as a societal unit.

Of primary significance for Paul's anthropology is the fact that he envisions man as a historical being. Although it remains true of mankind, as well as of individual man, that man always was and remains man, the way to be human is variable, depending upon the factors which constitute it and which are operative in it. Therefore, in the history of mankind "being human" was not the same thing at all times, and for present man there is more than one possible way to be man.

Paul has quite a peculiar understanding of man's "development," as he makes clear especially in Romans, chapter 5, verses 12ff.[34] Of course, "development" does not mean for Paul the gradual unfolding of biological predispositions, as we understand it today. Rather, in his view mankind has "developed" through sudden mythic-historical changes. First Paul shows man in his primordial phase: Adam, as he was created by God. His humanity was free from "sin" and "death." But Adam, through an act of disobedience against God, introduced a new element, "sin," into his humanity; this new element fundamentally and universally changed his humanity. For Paul "sin" is a superhuman and demonic power which, in turn, draws in a further demonic power, "death." Henceforth, both powers contribute to man's human nature as constituent elements: they represent the "dehumanizing potentials" inherent in human existence. However, "present man" in Paul's view is not simply man dominated by "sin" and "death." For meanwhile another sudden change has occurred in mankind. In his christology Paul describes the redeemer-figure, Christ, as a "heavenly man" (ἄνθρωπος ἐξ οὐρανοῦ), as a divine being who descends from heaven, through transformation becomes an earthly man in Jesus, and who through his death on the cross, resurrection, and installation as "cosmocrator" brings about redemption. In regard to the concept of humanization, two elements of this doctrine of redemption call for special attention. First of all, the Redeemer-Anthropos descending from heaven is not a being totally alien to the "Sinful-Adam," but is his "type": they are united by a relationship of correspondence. Although the Redeemer-Anthropos appears out of heaven, he is in fact a form of humanity, as his designation "Second-Adam" reveals; this form of humanity is able to merge with the humanity of the "Sinful-Adam." The merger of the two humanities was accomplished in Jesus' birth and it resulted in a new "humanity" antitypically contrasted with that of the "Sinful-Adam."

Furthermore, Paul's doctrine of Jesus' resurrection and exaltation means that this new humanity was not extinguished when Jesus died, but continued to be available as a possibility of being human even after his death. Consequently, "present" man, according to Paul, has two fundamental options in being human: the humanity of the "Sinful-Adam" or that of the "Redeemer-Adam."

This shows that Paul in principle has seen that humanity is "pluralistic" in nature. In his opinion, all men have certain given elements in common, while apart from those their humanity is open for possibilities of existence which can be taken up or rejected. Therefore to a certain degree, man has the possibility of changing his humanity; for Paul, this "certain degree" was a matter of ultimate importance.

With this anthropological view Paul has described the christological and soteriological foundations of his doctrine of humanization. Humanization itself, however, requires that the human individual appropriate this new way of being human, which was made possible through the Redeemer-Anthropos. As he explains especially in Romans, chapters 6-8, he regards this process of appropriation as extremely complicated.

With regard to the question of how man is to be brought into connection with the Christ event, Paul answers first by reference to ritual. He is in substantial agreement with all of antiquity that some form of "conversion" is indispensable.[35] Therefore, the Christian undergoes the ritual of baptism. It is characteristic for Paul, however, that he is less interested in the traditional rituals and concepts than in demonstrating, through the interpretation of those rituals and concepts, what it is that occurs — and must occur — to man, if he is to be made part of the Christ event.[36] To begin with, the rituals show that the individual person enters into a relationship with a historical and societal unit, the Christian church, which understands itself as the "Body of Christ." On the one hand, the new humanity must be *appropriated by the human individual*; but, on the other hand, this can only happen through a *transformation of that individual*, together with his acceptance into the Christian community. In this act, the transformation is not identical with the ritual, nor is the acceptance into the congregation the same as the appropriation of the new humanity. Rather, the rituals are symbolic *initiations* into far-reaching processes occurring to man and within man; only these processes themselves lead to the appropriation of the new humanity. It is characteristic of Paul that his concern is focused upon these processes of change which accompany man's transition from the "old" to the "new" humanity.

Generally, this transition from the "old" to the "new" way of being human consists in man's liberation from the "dehumanizing potentials" which have been constitutive elements in man's existence since Adam's fall.[37] However, for Paul the new way of being human is much more than merely the restitution of the humanity of the primordial Adam before his fall.[38] In Paul's view, the corruption of the "old" man was so complete that Paul is able to describe man's participation in the Christ event only in terms of "re-creation."[39]

165

Furthermore, it is noteworthy that Paul avoids a concept which was all too readily available in his time: the concept of deification. Undoubtedly the "heavenly man" Christ is a divine being, but he does not open up for man the possibility of deifying his existence in this world. Rather, Christ's divine power manifests itself primarily by breaking the powerful grasp in which "sin" and "death" have held man in slavery; this means that participation in the Christ-event brings man "only" liberation from the *enslavement* by the "dehumanizing powers." Because during his earthly life man remains "in the flesh," he remains excluded from any form of constitutional "sinlessness," and deification, which Paul does not eliminate altogether, is deferred to the "eschaton."[40]

In addition, Christ's divine power manifests itself as "humanization." Liberated from enslavement by the dehumanizing powers of "sin" and "death," the Christian is enabled to participate in the new humanity. This is described by Paul as "love" (ἀγάπη), and as the fulfillment of true humanity.

It is important to observe Paul's tendency to make man's anthropological possibilities less dependent upon metaphysical givens than upon mythic-historical powers. This tendency led him with necessity into a collision with the categories of ancient anthropological thinking which were mostly metaphysical. Paul's lack of conceptual systematization may have been caused by an unwillingness to identify himself with any of the categorial systems of anthropology available to him. In any case, the main difficulty for Paul was to show just how the powers of "sin" and "death" can be broken in man, if this man continues to exist "in the flesh" — that is, under the very conditions which led to his enslavement by those powers. Paul's several solutions of this problem need not be discussed here. The important thing to see is that, in regard to humanization, Paul clearly focuses upon the human individual. Although he has no doubt that both man and the humanization process are inextricably bound up with history and society, he nevertheless emphatically ties humanization to the individual. It seems that Paul was exceptionally aware of the danger of "formalism" which threatens humanization. Without the full participation of the individual human being, humanization remains an empty phrase.

But what does it mean to say "full participation of the individual human being"? Paul understands this to be a complicated web of emotional, psychic, and intellectual processes which touch and change man at his deepest level, as well as a conscious reorientation of his ethical conduct. Of course, we are here referring to the traditional concept of "conversion," but Paul has by reflection deepened these traditional concepts so much that they are scarcely recognizable any longer. At any rate, we can say that man's liberation from the dehumanizing powers and his participation in the new humanity establish him as an individual; seen in this way, the process of humanization is a process of individualization.

This fact corresponds to the peculiar phenomenon that as a rule Paul does not issue concrete regulations for the reorientation of the Christian's ethical conduct. His exhortations are usually very general appeals and admonitions to exercise one's own ethical responsibility and critical control as a Christian. Even where he does offer concrete orders, he presupposes that the addressees will agree with him. This process of individualization is, interestingly enough, coupled with the integration of the individual into a concrete historical and societal unit, the Christian church. Participation in the new humanity is possible only in terms of membership in the "Body of Christ" and in terms of "being in Christ," which becomes manifest as "love"

In conclusion we can say: According to Paul, humanization occurs within a religious community, the Christian church, which believes itself to be constituted by a distinctive possibility of being human, which has newly appeared in history. Paul is primarily concerned with the individual who joins the Christian community. The converts' social, cultural, and religious origins do not matter. Everyone needs humanization and it is a possibility for anyone. Beyond this, Paul looks at the humanization of mankind as a whole. This happens through world mission, in the course of which Christian congregations are spread all over the inhabited world, presenting the new humanity to all men. However, we must add that, for the "apocalyptic skeptic" Paul, the complete humanization of all men remained inconceivable within the framework of "this world." Paul could not see the problems which would eventually arise from this skepticism, for he believed that the end of the world would come very soon.

Plato's demand that the humanization of man be carried out in conjunction with the humanization of religion, has been fulfilled by Paul. In his theology, humanization takes place *as a new religion*; not only are all of the old religions rejected without distinction in favor of the new religion, but it is claimed that the new religion is a totally new way of worshipping God. This new religion is thoroughly humanized by the fact that the entire process of salvation is nothing but a process of humanization.

In spite of the obvious fact that Paul's concepts are conditioned by the world-view of his time, many of those concepts have become common property of Western civilization. To list them here would not be very interesting. More important may be those points of view which have not, and, in part cannot, become common property.

167

Contemporary society overlooks too easily the fact that the humanization of this society cannot be achieved simply through the methods of science and technology. Undoubtedly humanization is a concern of science and technology! But what has been recognized by science as right and useful, fails with necessity in the practical field of society, if one does not succeed in fully involving the individual in the process of humanization. The institutionalizing of new modes of conduct must not be confused with issuing bureaucratic decrees. Too quickly and too often the individual is pushed aside, passed by, or suppressed for ideological reasons. Or his humanization is frustrated from the very beginning by the fact that his emotional, psychic and intellectual life is pressed into pseudo-scientific schemes, systems, and formalisms. Transformed into cliches and distributed by the mass media, humanization becomes an empty ritualism. Furthermore, a most serious problem arises from the fact that it is so difficult, in this day of the mass society, to integrate the individual into living communities, while any humanization of the individual, as well as of society, can be expected only through the medium of living communities within the society.

The main significance of the concepts of humanization we have discussed is not that they can, in one way or another, simply be commended as viable solutions for today's problems. Rather, they retain importance by liberating from their naivete those who reflect upon them critically. I mean the kind of naivete which as a burden hinders those who are working in science, technology, and society, and those who are in any way responsible for man's well-being. To lose one's naivete, however, means nothing but to be confronted with the subject matter of humanization itself in all its aspects.

NOTES

1   Cf. W. Schadewaldt, "Der Gott von Delphi und die Humanitatsidee," *Hellas und Hesperien* I, 2nd ed., 1970, 669-685. On the linguistic evidence, see p. 671.

2   Cf. E. R. Dodds, *The Greeks and the Irrational*, 1951, esp. Ch. 6, "Rationalism and Reaction in the Classical Age"; M. P. Nilsson, *Geschichte der griechischen Religion* I, 3rd ed., 1967, 767ff.; II, 2nd ed., 1961, 249ff.

3   See note 1 above; cf. also Nilsson, *Geschichte* I, 647ff.

4   Cf. Schadewaldt, "Der Gott von Delphi," pp. 673f., and the essay "Menander" reprinted in the same volume, pp. 549-558.

5   Fragm. 484, ed. Koerte: ὡς χαρίεν ἔστ' ἄνθρωπος, ἂν ἄνθρωπος ᾖ.

6   Fragm. 944: ἄνθρωπος ὤν, τοῦτ' ἴσθι καὶ μέμνησ' ἀεί.

7   Schadewaldt, "Der Gott von Delphi," p. 675.

8   I have dealt with this topic more extensively in my essay, "The Delphic Maxim ΓΝΩΘΙ ΣΑΥΤΟΝ in Hermetic Interpretation," *Harvard Theological Review* LXIII (1970), 465-484; reprinted as Number 2 of *Occasional Papers of the Institute for Antiquity and Christianity*.

9   *De E apud Delphos* 394C.

10   Cf. J. Defradas, *Les themes de la propagande delphique*, 1954, pp. 268ff.

11   Cf. Betz, "The Delphic Maxim," pp. 470ff.

12   Cf. Nilsson, *Geschichte* I, 529ff.

13   *Phaedrus* 229E-230A.

14   Augustine, *Confessions*, X,5,7; cf. P. Courcelle, *Recherches sur les Confessions de Saint Augustin*, 1968, p. 404.

15   *Charmides* 164D: σχεδὸν γάρ τι ἔγωγε αὐτὸ τοῦτό φημι εἶναι σωφροσύνην, τὸ γιγνώσκειν ἑαυτόν. Cf. B. Witte, *Die Wissenschaft vom Guten und Bosen* (Untersuchungen zur antiken Literatur und Geschichte 5), 1970, pp. 97f.

16   154D-E. Cf. Witte, *Die Wissenschaft*, p. 55.

17   Aristotle, Περὶ φιλοσοφίας, Fragm. 1 (Ross): καὶ τῶν ἐν Δελφοῖς γραμμάτων θειότατον ἐδόκει τὸ γνῶθι σαυτόν, ὃ δὴ καὶ Σωκράτει ⟨τῆς⟩ ἀπορίας καὶ ζητήσεως ταύτης ἀρχὴν ἐνέδωκεν.

18   Ψυχὴν ἄρα ἡμᾶς κελεύει γνωρίσαι ὁ ἐπιτάττων γνῶναι ἑαυτόν. *Alcibiades* I, 130 E.

19   131 B, 133 C.

NOTES

20 . . .μηδὲν ἄλλο τὸν ἄνθρωπον συμβαίνειν ἢ ψυχήν. 130 C. Cf. J. Pepin, "'Que l'homme n'est rien d'autre que son ame.' Observations sur la tradition de 'Premier Alcibiade'," *Revue des etudes grecques* LXXXII (1969), 56-70.

21 Cf. T. M. Robinson, *Plato's Psychology*, 1970, and the review by A. Graeser, *Gnomon* XLIII (1971), 342-346.

22 Cf. A. Graeser, *Probleme der platonischen Seelenteilungslehre* (Zetemata 47), 1969.

23 *Ibid.*, pp. 21f.

24 *Ibid.*

25 *Ibid.*, pp. 13f.

26 Cf. Schadewaldt, "Der Gott von Delphi," p. 618.

27 Cf. Graeser, *Seelenteilungslehre*, p. 40.

28 Cf. Dodds, *The Greeks and the Irrational*, pp. 207ff.; E. Des Places, *La religion grecque*, 1969, pp. 245ff.; D. Roloff, *Gottahnlichkeit, Vergottlichung und Erhohung zu seligem Leben* (Untersuchungen zur antiken Literatur und Geschichte 4), 1970.

29 Cf. K. von Fritz, *Platon in Sizilien und das Problem der Philosophenherrschaft*, 1968.

30 This has been correctly stated by E. Kasemann, "On Paul's Anthropology," *Perspectives on Paul*, translated by M. Kohl, 1971, p.10: "In the whole New Testament it is only Paul who expounds what we should call a thoroughly thought-out doctrine of man . . ."

31 The best work is still that of R. Bultmann, *Theology of the New Testament*, translated by K. Grobel, I, 1951, 190ff.

32 Cf. R. Jewett, *Paul's Anthropological Terms* (Arbeiten zur Geschichte des antiken Judentums und des Urchristentums 10), 1971.

33 The following ideas are based upon my book, *Der Apostel Paulus und die sokratische Tradition* (Beitrage zur historischen Theologie 45), 1972.

34 Cf. E. Brandenburger, *Adam und Christus* (Wissenschaftliche Monographien zum Alten und Neuen Testament 7), 1962; L. Schottroff, *Der Glaubende und die feindliche Welt* (WMANT 37), 1971, pp. 115ff.

35 This must be affirmed in spite of the fact that Paul only rarely uses the traditional terminology of conversion. Cf. R. Bultmann, *Theological Dictionary of the New Testament* VI, 208ff.; idem, *Theology of the New Testament* I, 292ff.; 314ff.

36 On this subject, see my book *Nachfolge und Nachahmung Jesu Christi im Neuen Testament* (Beitrage zur historischen Theologie 37) 1967, pp. 174f.

NOTES

37   Cf. Bultmann, *Theology of the New Testament* I, 330ff.

38   Cf. Rom 5:15-21.

39   Cf. Rom 6:4; 7:6; 12:2; 2 Cor 4:16; 5:17; Gal 6:15.

40   Cf. 1 Cor 15:49ff.; 2 Cor 3:18; 5:1-4; Rom 8:29f.; Phil 3:21.

BIBLICAL ANTHROPOMORPHISM AND
THE HUMANENESS OF GOD

John L. McKenzie

Feuerbach's witticism that man has made God in his image and likeness is overused and tired.[1] Feuerbach was in no position to compare the Yahweh of the Bible with the gods of the ancient Near East. We who can make the comparison can see that the aphorism is valid for the gods of Mesopotamia, Canaan and Egypt. Basically they were nature deities; I say this at the risk of a vast over-simplification. Beneath divine personalities there lie the forces of nature; for Mesopotamia Thorkild Jacobsen has described these as "a multitude of powerful individual wills, potentially divergent, potentially conflicting, fraught with a possibility of anarchy."[2] The gods were not simply personifications of the forces of nature. The ancients recognized the existence of cosmic forces which they could not control. It was inconceivable to them that these forces should be impersonal. Nature exhibited personal traits; it was unpredictable, even capricious, doing good and harm with an irrational indifference to the effects of its operations. Such behavior was possible only for personal beings who were free of any restraint except that which their personal disputes might impose upon them. The gods of the ancient world were supermen and superwomen who had the freedom to behave like children. Man did not make godlike conduct his moral ideal; he lived in the assurance that the gods denied man the amoral freedom which they enjoyed themselves.

The student of the Bible is always aware of the problem why Yahwism did not follow the pattern of development which can be seen in every ancient religion. Greek philosophers — and tragedians as well — finally proved to themselves that the Olympian deities were irrational, immoral, incredible, and unreal.[3] Greek philosophy as well as Greek religion ended in atheism and superstition. Zeus and Apollo never grew up. The philosophers who tried to find a *theos* who was worthy of man, as Zeus and Apollo were not, found no *theos* who was personal in any sense which corresponded to human experience. Evidently Plato's Idea of the Good and Aristotle's Prime Mover were not for those who sat in the three-obol seats. Epicurus was frankly if not formally atheistic, and Lucretius, his most brilliant disciple and apostle, was formally and aggressively atheistic. The Stoics were not clearly and surely theistic, and their god was impersonal. The god of the philosophers never got outside the lecture hall and the studies of philosophers and poets. The Greek genius never fastened on Zeus, educated him out of the Olympian sporting club, and raised him to the stature of *kalos kagathos*. Why did the Israelites stick with Yahweh?

It is dangerous to be dogmatic about early Yahwism, even more than for later Yahwism. The books of the Bible were written by later Yahwists, and it is their development which is of lasting interest, lasting enough to elicit an invitation to present it to a world congress of religious studies at Los Angeles in 1972. Nevertheless, there was an early Yahwism; and interpreters have sometimes hinted that the early Yahweh can hardly be distinguished from an uncouth El as ill-favored and ill-mannered as his believers. Some traces of the early Yahweh remain which the modern heir of the Judaeo-Christian tradition would prefer not to have brought out of the closet; it is something like publishing the fact that grandfather was a horse-thief. I am thinking of such episodes as the attempt of Yahweh to kill Moses (Ex.4:24-26). Brief as the passage is, it has suffered so much from the efforts of scribes to rationalize this irrational action that it is hardly possible to reconstruct the original anecdote.[4] I think also of poor Uzzah, struck dead for a hasty reaction to keep the ark from falling, perhaps on his foot (2 Sm.6:4-8).[5] Yahweh does not need the help of such as him to stand upright, and it is not for porters to touch the sacred throne of Yahweh. These are indeed few instances; but they disclose a deity who is seen as much like the kings and sheiks of the ancient world — supremely powerful in his own sphere, conscious of power, quick to anger at insult and opposition, and responsible to no one. Only slightly more refined is the image of the savior god who rises to smite his enemies as an armed man rouses himself from a drunken stupor (Ps.78:65).

Other examples of the anger of Yahweh have been given a higher moral quality, even though some modern scholars and readers would not find these interpretations much of an improvement.[6] Fortunately, we are able to compare the Israelite version of the deluge with the Mesopotamian versions.[7] The major theological difference in the two versions is the Israelite effort to make the total destruction of the human race, with the exception of one family, a rational and moral act. This is accomplished by the clear statement that it is a judgment executed according to the standards of justice in the society in which the myth was told. These standards of justice are not ours, although it is only quite recently that modern society has moved away from these standards. The Israelites could not tolerate the idea that the whole of mankind could perish because of the caprice of a god who acts like a spoiled child. The Mesopotamians could, and this tells us much about the two peoples and their religious beliefs.

Even greater refinement appears in the story of Sodom and Gomorrah (Gn.18:20 — 19:29). The destruction of the people concerned is total but less than cosmic. The dialogue between Yahweh and Abraham asks candidly whether such a destruction is a righteous act if there are even a few innocent people involved.[8] There is no dispute whether this would be righteous; it is conceded that it would not be. Since the destruction of Sodom was a datum of tradition, the scribe could do nothing with it unless it was assumed that no innocent were involved; and Lot and his family, innocent strangers, had to be snatched from perdition by heavenly messengers. Yahweh was once again saved from the charge of capricious anger or injustice; the death penalty was not then regarded as cruel and unusual. The justice of Yahweh has no clearer analogy than the story of David's execution of the man who confessed to killing Saul at Saul's own wish (2 Sm.1:1-16). Like Uzzah, the man had in all good will, according to his own story, laid hands upon the sacred. For this he dies, and only the fact need be established.[9]

In fact the Israelite scribes and storytellers who produced the stories of the deluge and Sodom were rationalizing not God but nature; I make this distinction with the conscious risk involved in putting ideas into their minds which were not there. But until some distinction is made between God and nature man cannot rise above the level of mythological polytheism. If nature is a person, it does not make a good presence. If it is a group of persons, it has all the order and decorum of a barroom brawl. The Israelites, we said, could not tolerate certain ideas which the Mesopotamians could tolerate. The Israelites could not tolerate them because a person with the ethical values exhibited in nature could not be admitted into a civilized community. There had to be more personal reality behind nature than nature itself reveals — or was revealed in the gods of the Gentiles.[10] The Israelites did not form an idea of nature as a unity, much less as a system; they had no word for it. But they did depersonalize "nature," and left its *disiecta membra* lying about as the tools of Yahweh's work. Philosophically this left a vacuum, but it enabled the Israelites to talk about God as a reality totally distinct from nature.

If George Mendenhall is right, early Yahwism saw Yahweh as a Feudal Lord.[11] The implications of this idea of God are as important for theology as they are for politics and sociology. It is not at all the same as the idea of Yahweh as Sheik or Kinsman, which has been more or less the prevailing theme most commentators have seen in

174

early Yahwism. We know something about these Bronze Age feudal lords, although we do not know them personally; inscriptions, whether treaties or recitals of victories, were not intended to make the feudal lord known personally to any one who read them. They are revelations of a powerful will which is fully able to execute its desires.[12] Lovable they are not, although "love" is a word used to designate the proper attitude of the vassal towards the overlord.[13] The conditions which the treaties impose upon the vassal demand everything from the vassal; they oblige the overlord to nothing. The vassal has to be faithful to the overlord because he has no hope in any other power. The overlord does not need the vassal, and in the ethics of the political world of the Bronze Age he can owe the vassal nothing. Anything he does for the vassal is done out of sheer goodness.

Yahweh's position as overlord is especially clear in Israel's understanding of its tenure of the land.[14] This is a deuteronomic theme, but it is not obscured by any other theme in the other sources. The land of Israel is held by the donation of the overlord. The theme of the holy war signifies that Israel need not do anything either to acquire the land or to defend it; Yahweh fights the battles.[15] The Israelites can lose the land only by infidelity to the overlord. And under this donation there are no subordinate lords who in turn let out the land to others. The land was given to Israel, not to its chiefs. Yahweh as overlord replaced the god-king-landlord system of the Canaanite city-states, and as such he has to be judged an improvement. It seems safe to say that the social democracy of pre-monarchic Israel was a product of faith in Yahweh the Overlord. When David and Solomon established a Canaanite kingship in Israel and Judah, there was a danger that Yahweh, who was now in covenant with David and not with Israel, would move into the god-king-landlord system which had a much longer history in the ancient Near East than the Israelite tribal league. For Yahweh as Overlord was a remote power figure; and the feudal system of the ancient Near East normally worked through vassal kings like David and Solomon. It may seem that I am unsympathetic to the messianic kingship of David and Solomon. I am indeed, but within the limits of this paper only to the messianic kingship as a distortion of the anthropomorphic image of Yahweh. The fairly constant invective of the prophets and of the deuteronomic historian that Yahweh had become a Baal was a response to the theopolitics of David and Solomon.

The biblical anthropomorphisms of eyes, ears, mouth, arms, hands, speech, hearing and so on are so obvious that there is no need to illustrate them by example.[16] They raise a question which lies deeper than these details: why, since Yahweh was described as a human figure, was it forbidden to represent him plastically as a

175

human figure? Several theological explanations of the Second Commandment can be and have been proposed.[17] I have myself long preferred that explanation which sees the commandment as theory implicit in practice; an image of Yahweh may not be made because he is like nothing which can be represented by an image. Thus the commandment serves as a corrective to the anthropomorphisms of language. Yahweh is described as a human being because he is personal, but he is really unlike man and unlike anything in the visible universe. I still think this explanation is superior; and since we have to explain a phenomenon without parallel in the religions of the ancient world, we ought to look for an explanation without parallel. That Yahweh could not have an image because he is totally unlike any other being is reasonable. At the same time, I now wonder whether the commandment should not be related to the absence of a temple in premonarchic Israel. Perhaps the refusal of a temple in 2 Sm.7:6-7 has been taken too casually by us interpreters, even by those who believe that the appended prediction that David's son will build a temple (2 Sm.7:13a) is secondary, as I do.[18] It is difficult to maintain that Yahweh lived in a tent simply because he was a nomadic god; the nomadic background of early Israel is open to serious doubt. It is more probable that Yahweh refused a temple because the temple was the palace in which the gods of the Canaanite city-states lived. The palace of the god was an adjunct to the palace of the king, and the god was the religious support of the Canaanite political and social system. The god was not merely present in his image in the temple, he was imprisoned there, bound to the service of the feudal land-owning system. No king, no temple, no image — it forms a pattern. It does not entirely remove anthropomorphism, but it was intended to remove one type of anthropomorphism, the type which saw Yahweh with the features of a Baal, the symbol and the representative of a ruling class.

What role, then, did Yahweh have in the Israelite structure? It is immediately apparent that if the criticisms some of my colleagues make of Canaanite kingship are well made, we can accept the role of Yahweh as king only with serious reservations.[19] The early Israelite rejection of kingship was religiously motivated in the sense that kingship was believed to be contrary to the will of Yahweh. We can, we think, show the social and political motivation of the rejection. We notice that if Yahweh was a feudal lord, he was by definition a remote figure of power. This is plainly not the dominant character of early Israelite belief, which saw in Yahweh a helper easy of access and ready to act. He was not a king, I believe, because king was a bad word; it had been made bad by its associations with the Canaanite theopolitical and social system. One might say that David could not become king until he had made Yahweh a king first. Until this happened, the figure of Yahweh the Feudal Overlord was modified by the figure of Yahweh the Great Kinsman, pledged to be easy of access and ready to help because of the kinship which was based not on blood but on covenant.

This is a tribal anthropomorphism, and it is not surprising that it should be found in a tribal society, even if that tribal society was in the process of dissolution. It is more surprising that modern Christians can so easily use the religious language of an ancient tribal society without choking on it. This language is far more natural in the Mafia than it is in the republic of the United States of America, in which Uncle Sam is no Godfather. Yahweh the Great Kinsman came nearer to his people at the cost of narrowed horizons. He was bound by kinship loyalty, *hesed w'emet*, to do things for Israel which he was absolutely not bound to do for anyone else, and indeed could hardly do for anyone else without betraying his kinship. When God draws near to one group, in their perspective he moves away from other groups. This is anthropomorphism approaching the limits of the tolerable.[20]

In their favor it must be said that the early Israelites were not going to let Yahweh become the private god of the landlords. They could not keep Solomon from making him such. A god of any description was a power figure, and all the power had been conferred upon Solomon, who was now the vicar and agent of the Great Kinsman. If the Great Kinsman still had any concern for the widow, the orphan, and the foreigner, he exercised it through Solomon. The real image of Yahweh, the one image which escaped the prohibition of the Second Commandment, was the figure of the king savior enthroned in his palace in Jerusalem, adjacent to the smaller palace which housed his god symbolized by the empty throne which stood in the Most Holy Place. The royal theology of Jerusalem had created a warm and breathing image which made an idol unnecessary.

In a way, the story of prophetism is the story of the effort to rescue Yahweh from the anthropomorphism of the King Savior, which became a dead end almost as soon as it was created. We must limit our discussion to the prophetic books, in spite of the fascination which most Old Testament students feel for Elijah and Elisha. We do not know them well enough to do much more than engage in romantic imagination, and my own belief that Elijah and Elisha created the anthropomorphism of Yahweh the Saintly Assassin may be no more than romantic imagination. It is certain that this anthropomorphism, however, has had a longer history in Jewish and Christian belief than other figures such as King Savior, Righteous Judge, and Loving Father. And it is with the Righteous Judge proclaimed by Amos that our discussion of the prophets must begin.

I choose the title Righteous Judge as a summary of the Yahweh figure of Amos, aware that it is not satisfactory; no other single phrase seems to be. Amos shows an interest in the position of other peoples before Yahweh which is no less than revolutionary, brief as the allusions are; he refers both to their moral evaluation and to a providence of Yahweh in their history. Thereby he shattered the narrow limits both of the Great Kinsman and of the King Savior. He shows no awareness of the Feudal Overlord or of covenant morality; these themes are not implied in his own theme of election. Righteous Judge is not original with Amos, not if we are to take Genesis, chapter 18, verse 25 as the work of J (or of Eissfeldt's L). For it declares: "Shall not the Judge of all the earth do right?" The *rib* or charge speech-form used by Amos is at home in the court of justice. It presupposes a law which can be cited against the offender. Yahweh does not appear as king of the whole world; kingship is not denied, but he is seen precisely as judge, one of the major functions of kingship. No previous relation of Israel to Yahweh allows a special position of Israel as defendant; it may not be merely romantic imagination to see in this theme a rejection of the partisanship which corrupted the Israelite system of justice.

All readers of Amos notice that Yahweh appears as unmoved by feeling, even by anger, much less by any softer emotions. Walther Eichrodt has well distinguished between anger and *Strafgerechtigkeit*, rendered by Eichrodt's translator, J. A. Baker, as "retributive justice."[21] Yahweh seems inhuman, particularly in contrast with the Yahweh of Hosea. In fact the earlier images of the Overlord or the King or the Kinsman did not lend themselves to a highly emotional picture. The Righteous Judge, as Amos presented him, could not allow himself to be swayed by feeling. It must be conceded that this reflected the personal experience of Amos; any idea of God reflects the personal experience of the one who forms it. I suppose one has to say that Amos saw no other idea of God by which one could move from the bankrupt ideas of the Great Kinsman and the King Savior — not that he explicitly weighed and rejected these figures, but that he asked himself who is Yahweh, and how do I respond to this thing which we Israelites now worship under the assumed name of Yahweh?

The Righteous Judge of Amos is not an amiable figure. If, as I believe with most interpreters, the last words of the book are: "look, the eyes of the Lord Yahweh are upon the sinful kingdom/ and I will destroy it off the face of the earth" (Amos 9:8a), the collection was not meant to leave an amiable impression. The Yahweh of Amos is not hostile or unlovely; he simply appears in a situation in which there is no longer any place for love. He does not need it, he does not need either to feel it or to experience it. When the capital sentence was still executed, it was felt that the judge and the hangman should do their work as impersonally as possible. Traditionally the hangman was masked to keep any personal involvement out of it. So has Amos

178

presented Yahweh. And if he presents a God who is too tired to love, it is an anthropomorphism of startling boldness.

It is also an anthropomorphism which is ultimately unsatisfactory. When God executes justice, must he be as impersonal and unfeeling as the hangman? We demanded this of the hangman, our representative, because we feared our own weakness. Yahweh should be above this weakness. The Righteous Judge is an aspect of God which seems to be demanded by human wickedness, and very few men have taken wickedness as seriously as Amos did. If he correctly assessed the seriousness with which God takes it, most of us are wrong most of the time, and much of what we call forgiveness and tolerance is moral flab. The fact remains that we expect God to be more than a Righteous Judge when he deals with human wickedness. There is not enough difference, if we deal with anthropomorphisms, between the Righteous Judge and the Great High Executioner.

It is all the more remarkable, then, that a contemporary of Amos should have created what most interpreters believe is the most impressive anthropomorphism of the Old Testament. With no introduction and no warning the book of Hosea introduces Yahweh as the Betrayed Lover. The feeling which is absent in Amos is present in Hosea in such abundance that it becomes embarrassing. At the risk of appearing irreverent, a risk which I am not afraid to run in such a perceptive company, I have told students that the Yahweh of Hosea is the Great Patsy; and this is surely the anthropomorphism to end all anthropomorphisms. He is the very picture of a strong man enthralled by his affection for a woman who has no heart and no character. To continue my own irreverent paraphrase, the Israel of Hosea is the Cosmic Tramp. How can there be love between two such? And when one asks the question, the answer comes clear; the love of Yahweh for Israel is inexplicable, which is to say it is irrational.[22] It defies analysis and rational discourse. It makes no sense; yet we deduce from most of the literature of premonarchic Israel that many of the Israelites thought it made excellent sense. Amos is more candid and cruel in letting Yahweh say to Israel that he does not need them. Hosea, possibly with more subtlety, implies that Yahweh ought not need Israel, but has some difficulty making up his mind to accept this. In a man an infatuation for a totally unworthy person is evidence of a weakness of character; Hosea was willing to accept the implications of this anthropomorphism in his desire to affirm the reality and the depth of Yahweh's love.

Some years ago I published an article in which I attempted to put some order into the final chapters of Hosea.[23] It was not a remarkably successful effort, perhaps even more deserving of the phrase which H. W. Wolff applied to another effort of mine on

Hosea, "etwas gezwungen."[24] I thought there might be a plan in the very lack of plan in these sayings, the lack of plan which all commentators have recognized. The plan without plan was to describe an emotional conflict in Yahweh himself, in which he goes back and forth, up and down, like a man faced with an inevitable decision which he hates to make. The plan without plan is probably my own contrived idea; the impression of wavering indecision does emerge from the text, and I must suppose that commentators do not notice it because they are afraid to remark upon it. It is an extremely bold anthropomorphism even for Hosea.

Now it is all the more impressive that the final solution of Hosea is the same as the final solution of Amos; but it is not the decision of the Great High Executioner. It is the decision of one who has chosen to act not from love but from hatred; I think this is not too strong for a comparison of Yahweh with a lion, a leopard, and a bear reft of her cubs (Hosea 13:7-8). The judgment of Hosea is delivered with feeling, as the judgment of Amos is not.[25] The continuation of tolerant and forgiving love towards an unworthy object would be immoral. But prophets recognize that there comes a time in the life of a man and of a people when a decision is made that will not be reversed. Israel has made such a decision. It is no excuse that Israel did not know it; people almost never know it. I find the resolution of the book of Hosea more terrifying than I find the resolution of the book of Amos, and it is difficult to explain why. When one moves against all his feelings to preserve a principle, it makes the principle terribly important.

Because Hosea saw judgment as an act which in his anthropomorphism is executed at great personal cost, I do not have the critical difficulty about the happy ending of the book which we all have with the book of Amos. Such love is not easily destroyed. It is not the promise of the forgiving love of Yahweh which is an obstacle to restoration, but the difficulty of seeing how a people so confirmed in malice can ever repent — of thinking of a way in which the Tramp can become a Lady.

This was thought of by another prophet known by the ungainly name of Second Isaiah (a kind of nickname for Deutero-Isaiah). In many ways this prophet rises above all earlier anthropomorphisms. Yahweh is not the King Savior or the Great Kinsman or the Feudal Overlord or the Righteous Judge or the Betrayed Lover, although the prophet makes use of the language of all these themes. But Yahweh has a new identity as Cosmic Lord — I do not imply that it was created by this prophet — which would seem to make him more remote than any earlier role. At the risk of making my personal religious sentiment the measure of all men, I have never found Creator an exciting title by which to invoke the Deity. On the contrary, the dominant theme of Second Isaiah is forgiving love with no echo of the Great Patsy. We asked how the relations of Yahweh and Israel could be restored. They are restored because Israel has a mission to proclaim Yahweh to the world; and if Israel proclaims a god whose dominant trait is something other than forgiving love, it is not Yahweh who is proclaimed. This love Israel knows by experience. Thus Second Isaiah shattered all the tribal and national framework of earlier anthropomorphisms. And while I have no intention of solving here the problem of the Servant of Yahweh, in any interpretation of the Servant the poems are a promise that Israel will fulfil its mission by suffering. Second Isaiah, however, does not escape the problem of earlier prophets; for he cannot affirm that Israel has now achieved lasting fidelity to its mission. If it turns unfaithful, some other prophet will have to find a new anthropomorphism for judgment — or repeat an old one.

It may be that the anthropomorphism of the Righteous Judge is the ultimate root of the problem of biblical anthropomorphism — that is, of biblical theology. Judgment is a moral success for society as a whole and a moral failure to deal with the individual who is judged. Judgment is a kind of self-mutilation of society. God, we think, should be able to do things better than the government; and we wonder whether this is much of a compliment to him. If the Righteous Judge is not a satisfactory picture, neither is the Great Overlord or the King Savior. Hosea sought for an anthropomorphism which would enable Yahweh to deal with human malice without destroying humanity. He did not find a way except in a hope that malice would change to virtue in a remote eschatological future. Apart from that, he was still on the theological level of Abraham trying to understand the Cities of the Plain. The theology of the New Testament expresses the Christian belief that the Word made flesh is the ultimate anthropomorphism and the figure which solves the problem of the prophets by identifying the saving act with the act of judgment — a genuine Hebrew interpretation of "judgment." But this, I take it, lies outside the area of this paper. As a belief which its adherents claim is a development of Old Testament beliefs it seems it ought to be mentioned.[26]

I have been unable to mention more than a few of the anthropomorphisms of the Bible, but I believe I have chosen significant examples. A few summary remarks will help us to formulate the topic in relation to the theme of this Congress, religion and the humanizing of man. It seems safe to generalize that the quality and the moral level — or, if one will permit the expression, the level of civilization — of the image of God is determined by the humanity of the people who worship the god.[27] This said with full recognition of the fact that we know nothing in the religion and culture of the Near East from which Yahweh could emerge. The Israelite could worship fertility gods; they have left us the literary

181

evidence that they did. This needs no explanation; why they worshipped Yahweh does demand an explanation.

That Yahweh is described in anthropomorphisms does not distinguish him from other gods. We have pointed out certain crudities which the Israelites, as far as we know, never admitted. We know other crudities which they did admit, and it is these which permit us to say that it was their own humanity which determined the quality of their god. At any given level man can reach God only at a given level. Maybe a fertility god is as high as some people can go. Our problem here is how man moves to another level where he can reach God at a higher level. H. M. Kuitert has said well that the God of the Bible is not anthropomorphic but hebraeomorphic.[28] A people who are vindictive — and just about everybody is — expect their god to be vindictive. If there is any religious development in the Bible, it lies in the realization that God is not vindictive. It seems the Israelites learned this lesson only by learning that God is just as vindictive to them as he is to any one else. Vindictiveness is sublimated into righteous judgment; and this insight was achieved in a language in which "righteous judgment" originally meant a judgment in my favor.

I do not mean to say or to imply that the humanity of God grows with the humanity of man. This would be in place if our theme were Man and the Humanizing of Religion. I mean simply that man is the sole obstacle to his own humanization. The biblical revelation — if I may use the word — is a revelation of human potentialities which are first seen as worthy of God, and then as demanded by the reality of God.[29] These potentialities are then seen as demanded by God of men, and ultimately as made possible by God; this is one of the meanings of grace. We simply do not believe in the Great Warrior who exterminated the Canaanites.[30] Some who shared our faith did. They also professed belief in Jesus Christ the Son of God who said that he who would save his life must lose it, and who implied that a good way to lose it quickly is to love those who hate you and pray for those who persecute you. How does one speak of a god who exhibits both these features? I am compelled to say simply that he does not exist, and that those who professed this monstrous faith worshipped an idol. That they were sincere touches me lightly; so, I suppose, were most of the worshippers of Baal and Anath, and most witch-burners. I have no doctrine to learn from any of them. If a group of people wish to burn witches, they are compelled to believe God is a witch-burner. They authorize their belief from Exodus, chapter 22, verse 17, the same context from which we derive the Ten Commandments. I have long known that sincere believers are much more dangerous than insincere believers. All of this suggests that it is still valid to say that the humanity of God is largely determined by the humanity of those who believe in him.

182

Conceding that the Savior God of Second Isaiah would have been gibberish to David, it remains true that the development of anthropomorphisms in the Bible is a history of steady growth in humanity; that God, to retain his position, must always move ahead of the human caravan, like the pillar of cloud and the pillar of fire. When he does not move ahead, like the gods of Mesopotamia and Canaan and Olympus, he loses not merely his divinity but his reality. As an anthropomorphic deity he does, however, remain within sight; and I wish to make this final point in dealing with the theomorphic god of the philosophers.

As a once diligent student of the theology of Thomas Aquinas I feel sufficiently acquainted with systematic theology in the proper sense to contrast it with biblical theology. The contrast has been made so often that I can hardly hope to add anything new. I summarize, perhaps unfairly, the deity of systematic theology by saying that he is formed according to what a philosopher thinks God must be; and this is not necessarily the reality which God is. A philosopher has no more direct experience of God than the unlearned; and it is possible that he may unconsciously think that God is the Great Philosopher. Only a philosopher, I take it, could ever locate supreme beatitude in knowledge. It makes more sense, but not much more, than it did to locate supreme beatitude in sex. In both schemes the fullness of life eludes analysis.

The Thomistic essence of God is a bundle of attributes which taken together deny all the reality of experience and raise the little that is left above the level of experience. The deity who emerges has attributes, but he is impersonal. This is the stumbling block of every philosophical approach to God — I suppose because we cannot think of a person without thinking of one who can be hurt. In protecting God from hurt we also protect him from reality. Epicurus succeeded best in protecting the gods from concern. The world meant nothing to them, and they meant nothing to the world. With consistency — more consistently than Thomas Aquinas — he affirmed that gods who cannot be touched by the world do not touch it. With all due respect to Thomas Aquinas and the late Paul Tillich, whose shoes I am not worthy to tie, no one was ever inclined to shout, "O Pure Act, come to my assistance; O Ground of Being, make haste to help me." You would not want to bother the Pure Act or the Ground of Being with your personal concerns. And since humanity is one of our concerns, why should a non-human being share this concern? Such a being takes wrongdoing less seriously than the Righteous Judge of Amos, and is altogether above the compassion expressed by the Betrayed Lover of Hosea.

God cannot be captured by the anthropomorphisms of the Bible; a biblical writer recognized this when he observed that God is not man (Hosea 11:9), and another writer says that the thoughts and ways of

God are incomparably above the thoughts and the ways of man (Is.55:8-9). The biblical writers never thought of capturing God, but only, to repeat the figure used already, of keeping him in sight, of moving forward to the fullness of life. Neither can God be captured by the anthropomorphisms of philosophy. Philosophical forms, if I may use the expression, are the idols of abstract art as opposed to the idols of realism. The constructions of the human mind are anthropomorphisms.[31] An early ecclesiastical document condemned the opinion attributed to Origen that the bodies of the righteous in the resurrection will be spheroid, on the ground that they will be perfect, and the sphere is the perfect figure.[32] That it may be, but not for a human body. So men reason that God must be Pure Act or Ground of Being because they can think of no higher form of reality. Then let us say simply that, but not say that there is no reality higher than the human mind can construct. Anselm went through all that nearly a thousand years ago. God appears in the Bible as one with whom man can communicate.[33] It implies that man rises to his full humanity when that communication is firmly and clearly established.

NOTES

1 Feuerbach was anticipated by Xenophanes, quoted in G. van der Leeuw, *Religion in Essence and Manifestation*, 1938, p. 174.

2 H. and H. A. Frankfort, eds., *Before Philosophy*, 1949, p. 139.

3 G. van der Leeuw, *Religion in Essence and Manifestation*, pp. 174-176; H. Kleinknecht, *Theological Dictionary of the New Testament* III, 65-79; K. Prümm, *Religionsgeschichtliches Handbuch*, 1954, pp. 105-212.

4 "Quite inexplicable" is Noth's summary of his own exegesis (*Exodus*, 1962, pp. 49-50).

5 H. W. Hertzberg, *I & II Samuel*, 1964, p. 279.

6 Th. C. Vriezen, *An Outline of Old Testament Theology*, 1966, pp. 157-159; J. Fichtner, *Theological Dictionary of the New Testament* V, 392-409.

7 A. Heidel, *The Gilgamesh Epic and the Old Testament*, 2nd ed., 1954; G. von Rad, *Genesis*, 1966, pp. 119-120; H. Gunkel, *Die Genesis*, 3rd ed., 1910, pp. 67-74.

8 Von Rad, *Genesis*, pp. 205-210; Gunkel, *Die Genesis*, pp. 203-205.

9 Hertzberg, *I & II Samuel*, pp. 236-238.

10 W. Eichrodt, *Theology of the Old Testament* I, 1961, 276.

11 G. Mendenhall, *Law and Covenant in Ancient Israel*, 1955; *idem*, "The Hebrew Conquest of Palestine," *Biblical Archaeologist* XXV (1962), 66-87.

12 See texts and discussion in D. McCarthy, *Treaty and Covenant*, 1963.

13 W. Moran, "The Ancient Near Eastern Background of the Love of God in Deuteronomy," *Catholic Biblical Quarterly* XXV (1963), 77-87.

14 Von Rad, *Old Testament Theology* I, 1962, 296-305.

15 *Idem, Studies in Deuteronomy*, 1953, pp. 45-59.

16 H. M. Kuitert, *Gott in Menschengestalt*, 1967, pp. 175-180.

17 Von Rad, *Old Testament Theology* I, 212-219; Eichrodt, *Theology of the Old Testament* I, 118f., 215; Vriezen, *Outline of Old Testament Theology*, pp. 130-131; Kaufmann-Greenberg, *The Religion of Israel*, 1960, pp. 17-20, 147-148, 236-237.

18 Hertzberg, *I & II Samuel*, p. 287.

19 G. Mendenhall, "The Hebrew Conquest of Palestine," pp. 75-79.

20 I do not believe that the theme of election can be defended in the terms proposed by Vriezen (*An Outline of Old Testament Theology*, p. 167), and perhaps it can be defended in no terms whatever.

NOTES

21   Eichrodt, *Theology of the Old Testament* I, 259.

22   *Ibid.*, pp. 252-253.

23   J. McKenzie, "Divine Passion in Osee," *Catholic Biblical Quarterly* XVII (1955), 167-179.

24   The same H. W. Wolff has also treated divine passion in Hosea in *Wegweisung*, 1965, pp. 151-164.

25   Eichrodt, *Theology of the Old Testament* I, 252.

26   Eichrodt, *Theology of the Old Testament* I, 212; Kuitert, *Gott in Menschengestalt*, pp. 52-53; 215-223; van der Leeuw, *Phänomenologie der Religion*, 2nd ed., 1956, pp. 190-191; Karl Barth, *God Here and Now*, 1964, pp. 1-10; *idem, The Humanity of God*, 1960, pp. 37-65.

27   The same point was made by Herder and Lessing, as quoted by Kuitert, *Gott in Menschengestalt*, pp. 145-146. I hope to go beyond their thesis.

28   *Gott in Menschengestalt*, p. 224.

29   *Ibid.*, pp. 224-228.

30   Eichrodt, *Theology of the Old Testament* I, 228-229.

31   Kuitert, *Gott in Menschengestalt*, pp. 74-75. The same author quotes Karl Barth to this effect, p.129.

32   The work is Justinian's *Liber Adversus Origenem* (543), confirmed by Vigilius, according to Cassiodorus (Denzinger-Bannwart-Umberg, *Enchiridion Symbolorum*, 27th ed., 1951, #207). Unfortunately, Vigilius seems to have been normally vague in his pontifical acts, and Cassiodorus was normally vague as a historian.

33   Vriezen, *Outline of Old Testament Theology*, pp. 134, 173.